Software Quality and Productivity

Software Quality and Productivity

Alec Sharp

VNR VAN NOSTRAND REINHOLD
New York

Copyright © 1993 by Van Nostrand Reinhold

Library of Congress Catalog Card Number 92-11908
ISBN 0-442-01218-7

Printed in the United States of America.

Van Nostrand Reinhold
115 Fifth Avenue
New York, New York 10003

Chapman and Hall
2-6 Boundary Row
London, SE1 8HN, England

Thomas Nelson Australia
102 Dodds Street
South Melbourne 3205
Victoria, Australia

Nelson Canada
1120 Birchmount Road
Scarborough, Ontario M1K 5G4, Canada

16 15 14 13 12 11 10 9 8 7 6 5 4 3 2 1

Library of Congress Cataloging-in-Publication Data

Sharp, Alec.
    Software quality and productivity / by Alec Sharp
        p.   cm.
    Includes index
    ISBN 0-442-01218-7
    1. Computer Software—Development.   2. Computer Software—Quality control.
    I. Title.
QA76.76.D47S487   1992   92-11908
                                                    005.1—dc20CIP

Contents

Preface

For about the last three decades there has been a ''crisis in software''—software is too expensive and too unreliable; not only are the initial development schedules longer than we'd like, but the schedules are usually missed. We have software projects that are too big and complex to comprehend entirely, and we struggle to develop products without sacrificing the needs of future maintenance developers at the altar of the schedule gods.

Why do we care? We care because software that is late, of poor quality, or too expensive puts us at a competitive disadvantage. The MIS department that takes too long puts an added expense burden on the whole company. A poor-quality contract project reduces the likelihood of repeat business. A late product misses the window of opportunity, while a low-quality product ensures that potential customers will think hard before buying from us again. Poor quality and low productivity not only hurt us as individual organizations, but they also make American industry just that little bit more uncompetitive in a time of increasing global competition.

What can we do? The trouble with the ''crisis'' approach to the problems of software engineering is that it encourages the search for a quick fix. But there is no Golden Road to quality software, nor is there a single silver bullet that will solve our software problems. Rather, we must advance toward our goals by taking an unending series of small but significant steps. The better approach is thus to look at each area of software engineering and improve each one in a methodical and rational manner, continuously improving anything that can be improved.

Most software today is written by teams of individual developers. As software products and systems have become ever more complex, software projects are rarely done by a single super-talented software engineer; the vast bulk of software projects use the process of "divide and conquer" to divide the work among individuals and groups of people with a more normal distribution of talent. On the individual side, people almost invariably want to do the best they can, but their capabilities depend on their conceptual and technical knowledge. This book is an attempt to help individual developers by increasing both types of knowledge.

While most of the suggestions in this book can and should be done by the individual software engineer, they become even more effective when done by *all* software engineers. The task of project leaders and managers is to ensure that software developers have a good grasp of the concepts of software engineering and a solid knowledge of the tools, techniques, and methodologies available. The secondary audience for whom this book is intended is thus project leaders and development managers who have the responsibility of creating high-quality software in aggressively short times.

But in a sense, I've also written this book for me, and so I've tried to do two particular things. Whenever I read a book, I invariably have questions, many of which are never answered. I've tried to anticipate the questions that someone might ask, pose the question, then give an answer. This explains the question-and-answer format.

Second, the tone and format of many computer books leave me cold. Like most people, I learn better from example than from theory. People generally find it difficult to take a theory or rule and apply it to create a practical instance or example. They usually find it far easier to take a concrete example, modify it to meet new circumstances, and extrapolate general rules from the examples. Unfortunately many computer books work the opposite way—they give lots of theory and leave it to you to struggle with how to implement the ideas.

Because I learn best from example, I've tried to make this a very practical book, filled with examples. You can use the examples exactly as they are, use them as examples, to be modified as needed, or use them to extrapolate general rules that you can apply to your work. The key to progress is to adopt a philosophy of continuous improvement, to learn from all and any sources, and then to apply what you have learned.

Acknowledgments and Apologies

I'd like to mention my parents, Jean and Richard, without whom someone else would be writing this book. I also want to mention my siblings, Candy, Imogen, and James, for no reason other than that they'd probably like to see their names in print.

Many of the people we meet touch our lives in some way or other, and I want to thank all those who, knowingly or unknowingly, taught me something about the profession of software engineering and helped in the creation of this book. In particular I'd like to thank Bruce Hildenbrand for providing many useful suggestions, Daniel Campbell for believing in me, and Jim Willette for help in creating the diagrams in the book.

But most of all, I'd like to thank my wife, Muriel, and my daughter, Nikki, for putting up with my long hours at the computer while I wrote this book.

Now, I need to make an apology. Like most writers faced with the problem of what pronoun to use when describing something done by both men and women, I agonized over whether to use ''he or she,'' ''she or he,'' ''s/he,'' or ''they.'' In the end, like many other writers, i settled for using ''he'' and ''him,'' and so my apologies go to the female readers of this book.

Finally, I want to thank those people who gave me permission to use the following copyrighted material.

IEEE/ANSI standard 830-1984 in Chapter 17, Specifications and Documents, reprinted with permission. Copyright © 1984, The Institute of Electrical and Electronics Engineers.

Information, quotations, and forms in Chapter 28, Technical Reviews, reprinted from *Handbook of Walkthroughs, Inspections, and Technical Reviews, 3rd Edition.* Copyright © 1990 by Daniel P. Freedman and Gerald M. Weinberg, used by permission of Dorset House Publishing, 353 W. 12 Street, New York, NY 10014.

Information and quotations in Chapter 29, Causal Analysis, reprinted with permission from *IBM Systems Journal,* Vol. 29, No. 1. Copyright © 1990, International Business Machines Corporation.

Software Quality and Productivity

PART 1

Quality, Productivity, and Improving the System

1

Quality, Productivity, and Continual Improvement

For many years now there has been a "crisis in software"—software is too expensive and too unreliable; not only does it take too long to produce, but the development schedules are usually missed. What can we do? The trouble with the "crisis" approach to the problems of software engineering is that it encourages the search for a quick fix. However, I don't believe there is a Golden Road to software quality and productivity, or a single silver bullet that will solve all our software problems. I believe rather that we must advance toward our goals by taking an unending series of small but significant steps.

The better approach is thus to look at each area of software engineering and improve each one in a methodical and rational manner. As I'll discuss in greater detail in this chapter and stress throughout the book, I believe that a focus on two things—**reducing rework** and **continually improving the system**—is a sign of an organization that is serious about improving the quality of its software and improving productivity.

Formula One: Reduce Rework

In 1950, W. Edwards Deming proposed a key formula to the Japanese, who were looking for ways to rebuild their economy after the devastation of World War II. That formula was:

Improve Quality → Costs decrease because of less rework, few mistakes, fewer

delays and snags → **Productivity increases** → **Capture the market with better quality and lower costs** → **Stay in business** → **Provide jobs and more jobs**

This formula shows the relationship between quality, productivity, and profitability. I think the Japanese success in automobiles and consumer electronics has shown beyond doubt that this relationship is valid and that a focus on quality really does help business. I prefer to shorten the formula a little:

Improved Quality → **Less Rework** → **Improved Productivity**

Shortened this way, the formula is particularly applicable to software development because of the immediate focus on rework. We've all seen plenty of examples of rework: bugs that must be fixed, algorithms that must be changed because they don't do exactly what we need, or designs that must be redone because we didn't understand what the user wanted.

The relationship between improved quality and less rework is so strong that I prefer to focus on the *Less Rework* part of the equation because it's more concrete and easier to grasp. While less rework doesn't logically imply improved quality, the implication is valid in all but the ridiculous cases such as not fixing bugs or ignoring what the customer wants. I assume that no one would seriously propose such things. Let's look at a diagram of the relationship between quality and productivity.

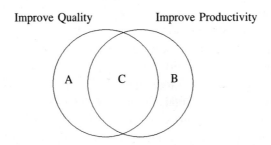

A. *Improved quality without an increase in productivity.* You could get this by increasing the amount of system testing you do once the software is ready.
B. *Improved productivity without an increase in quality.* You could hire developers who can churn out higher amounts of code with the same defect density. Short-term, you could put people under pressure to work long hours (improving monthly productivity, although not hourly productivity).
C. *Improved quality and improved productivity.* By doing things to avoid rework, you improve quality. If these things are cost-effective, you also improve productivity. The focus of this book is on showing cost-effective ways of reducing rework.

How does this apply to the software development environment?

To see how applicable it is, let's take a look at the software development cycle, keeping an eye on what affects quality and rework.

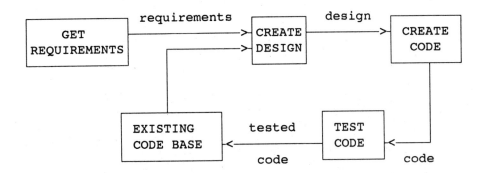

This diagram is simplistic because while thinking about the design we often improve the requirements; while thinking about the code we can improve the design, and so on. There is a certain amount of backward interaction. However, there is a vital and valid lesson in this diagram. The output from each stage provides the input into the next stage. The higher the quality of the output from each stage, the less rework will be required in that stage and subsequent stages.

So we should aim to improve the quality of each stage in the process?

Yes, and this becomes especially true when you remember that we generally go round the process several times before the product is replaced. There's another picture of the process that I'd like to show you.

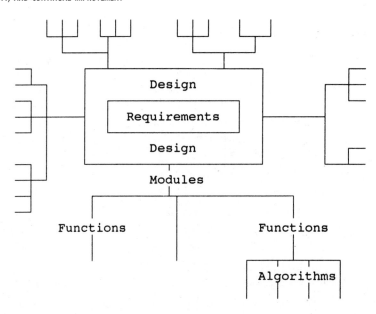

In any software process, you have to get the requirements, create a design, then implement the design. The requirements drive the design, which drives the modules, functions, and algorithms, which drive the actual coding and debugging. Get the algorithm wrong and you'll have to fix the algorithm, then recode and retest it. Get the requirements wrong and you'll have to do a redesign with all the attendant modifications to the modules, functions, and algorithms and all the recoding and retesting.

It sounds like you're saying we should catch errors as soon as possible.

The further an error goes without correction, the greater the cost to fix it. The earlier you can catch errors, the less rework you'll have to do. Our goals should be to prevent errors if possible, and to catch them as soon as possible if we can't prevent them.

Errors aren't free. At a minimum, you pay someone to create the error, you pay someone to find it, and you pay someone to fix it. You may also be paying people to change the documentation, rereview the documentation, and rereview and retest the software changes. An even bigger cost may be the revenues or market share lost by delaying the product shipment.

Give me some more examples of rework.

Rework is anything that has to be done again. Examples of rework include: fixing bugs during development; fixing bugs in the released software; recoding and retesting because of a poor design; redesigning the software because it doesn't meet the requirements; redesigning the software because we got the requirements wrong.

There is also another type of rework—making requested enhancements to the product. It's not caused by anything you did wrong, but it's still reworking an existing product. While this rework is inevitable and appropriate, it's possible to reduce the time and effort involved by making it easier to understand the code, and make and test the changes. Every time a program is difficult to understand, you're paying someone to spend avoidable extra time on the software, and increasing the likelihood of errors in the new work.

Do you have specific suggestions on how to reduce these different types of rework?

Yes, I have a lot of suggestions, which are discussed in depth in later chapters. But first, let's look at the general approach to reducing rework.

Formula Two: Continually Improve the System

I don't believe you can wave a magic wand and everything will be right. Instead, the most we can do is move towards perfection, one step at a time. The key is to be committed to taking those steps rather than being satisfied with where we are. And it's by no means as easy as it sounds. We get satisfied, lazy, or uninterested in improvement. However, in the long run, that's a recipe for failure. There will always be people, companies, and countries that adopt new ideas, techniques, and tools, and put us into uncompetitive positions.

So whether we want our salaries to continue to rise, our products to gain market share, or our countries to remain competitive, we have to continually look for ways to improve.

Improvement is not a matter of figuring out perfection, then implementing it. That never happens. Improvement is a matter of saying at each step in the process, "We could reduce rework a little by doing this."

What is the "system" in the formula?

The system is everything that goes into creating the software product: the people, the tools, the computer availability, the process of getting the requirements, the process of creating a design, the process of implementing the design, the process of testing the implementation, the process of debugging errors, the process of creating maintainable code, the process of scheduling, the process of responding to frustrations over obstacles.

What do you mean by "process" and why is there so much emphasis on it?

A process is the steps involved in doing the thing. Why is it so important? Let's suppose that an individual software engineer wants to improve things. His impact is basically limited to the piece of software on which he is working. He can't ensure that the code he is modifying is of high quality. He can't ensure that the other modules his code interacts with are of high quality. He can't ensure that he has good tools, or even enough computer access. Only by a higher level of focus on the whole system and its processes can all these things be improved.

Let's use a couple of the processes listed above as examples and look at questions we might ask about the process. The next two paragraphs are quite dense with questions, but at this point it's not so much the questions that are important as the idea that there are questions.

Questions we might ask about the process of testing software: What are the best ways we know to test our software? Does everyone know these techniques? Does everyone use these techniques? Are there any tools that would help us test more effectively? Are there any books or magazines devoted to new ideas and techniques for testing? Are we getting better at testing? Is the testing on this product better than the testing we did on the last product? Can the software engineers use a computer whenever necessary? Are the computer resources adequate? Are they better than adequate? Do people have a high-powered debugger available? Do they know how to use it?

Or if we look at the design process, we might ask: What are the best design techniques we know? Does everyone know these techniques? Does everyone use these techniques? How do we review a design for conformance to the requirements? How do we review a design for elegance and quality? What standard techniques do we use for defining modules and their interfaces? What standard techniques do we use for control structures? What standard techniques do we use for commonly occurring features such as sequentially reading a file? What tools are available to help with design? What books and magazines are available with ideas and techniques for improving designs? What other ways to improve our designs are we investigating?

It looks like there's a lot of room for improvement!

Unfortunately, yes. I doubt if any organization is doing all it can to increase quality and reduce rework. Software organizations tend to allow each person to define his or her own processes. Everyone does things differently; some poorly, some adequately, and some very well. To improve quality and reduce rework there are so many things that can be done.

Why the ''continual'' in continual improvement if there's so much to be done?

The world is constantly changing. By the time you've improved everything you can think of, there are new techniques and new tools to look at and perhaps adopt. Once you stop improving or innovating, you get left behind. There's always someone eager to take your place, and they'll use whatever tools or techniques are available to them. But perhaps more importantly, it's a constant reminder that the quest for quality is never done; the system can ALWAYS be improved.

Why not just set quality standards?

If you have a static quality standard you are in one of two basic situations. If you meet the standard, the tendency is to stop trying to improve. If the standard is out of reach, there are no guidelines on how to get there, and the tendency is to give up. On the other hand, improved quality is a simple consequence of the relentless quest for improvements in the system.

Having quality standards puts you in a monitoring situation, and monitoring quality doesn't improve quality. You'll find yourself bogged down in unproductive discussions of the ''does this meet the standard'' kind instead of actually increasing quality.

So the reasons for stressing continual improvement are more human than technical.

Definitely. Absolutes are contrary to the human way of doing things and are paralyzing. How often have you been paralyzed into inaction because the standards expected of you were too high? It's better to do the best you can, ensuring that you can fix the thing if it doesn't work. If you then want to do better next time, you will learn from that experience and from reading, studying, and listening to others, so that next time the quality is higher.

Think of learning to talk, to paint, to play a musical instrument, to play competitive sports. In each case you start by doing the best you can, then, through a process of feedback, self-examination, study, and practice, you slowly improve. Sooner or later most of us stop the process of continual improvement for one reason or another, but it's the only process that allows us to reach increasingly higher levels of performance and quality. It's the human way, and it's also the only way we can achieve increasing quality in software.

How does continual improvement relate to ideas such as quality circles?

In a sense, continual improvement is the parent of all these other ideas. Many of them are great ideas in the right context, but unfortunately, the books that have been popularizing them tend to treat them as things in their own right, whereas they are really fall-outs of continual improvement.

When the popular ideas are considered by themselves, management often assumes that they can go for the quick fix, or keep employees happy by adopting the latest idea. Not only is this deceitful, but it doesn't work. Employees know what is going on, and resent it.

Now, if an organization is serious about continual improvement, it will look at every idea that could help. And of course this means employee involvement as employees are the ones that actually do the job. They have as good an idea as anyone about what is getting in their way and preventing quality from being as high as possible.

When one approaches things from the perspective of management commitment to continual improvement, the ideas become natural. They become simply extensions of the search for improvement.

You mentioned Deming earlier. One of his key ideas is statistical quality control.

Deming was writing about manufacturing, where you can measure the same thing day in and day out. When you can do this, statistical quality control has a lot of meaning. In software, the only truly good measure for statistical quality control would be defect rates from release to release, but employee turnover and the constant attempt to improve the system mean that the numbers become useless for this purpose.

The numbers are extremely useful in helping you determine if processes or changes to processes are having an effect, but are not of any use if you are looking for "common cause" and "special cause" deviations from the statistical mean.

While there's plenty of literature that describes the application of statistical quality control to the car *manufacturing* process, I've seen none that describes its application to the car *design* process, which is a process much more similar to software engineering than is manufacturing. It's important to apply those ideas that can be applied, but not to try and force square ideas into a round reality. To paraphrase Einstein, "Apply as much as possible, but no more."

However, while I don't think statistical quality control has much relevance to the act of creating software, I believe that continual improvement has a great deal to offer.

I assume this book has lots of ideas on how to pursue continual improvement.

Absolutely. As architect Mies van der Rohe said, "God is in the details." Adopting the philosophy of continual improvement means nothing unless you worry about the details of what you will do and how you will go about it. This book contains both general ideas and specific suggestions of ways to improve things. People learn better from examples than from discussions or theory, so I've included lots of examples.

The practical suggestions may not be perfect, and you may be able to find ideas that work better for you or your organization—one of the main purposes of books is to trick the mind into thinking for itself. However, the ideas in this book can generally be used as they are, and you can improve on them as you get more knowledge and experience or learn from other books and people.

The main thing is to slowly but surely try to improve every facet of your software development, which means trying new things and giving new ideas a chance. To insist that existing methods are the best and to refuse to try new ones is the surest path to stagnation.

Since the field is so large, and the situations so different, how can you hope to write a general answer?

I can't possibly cover every small detail so I write suggestions with an underlying philosophy. Use the philosophy to extend the suggestions to your individual circumstances. Indeed, this book is far too small to do justice to any of the areas I discuss. When you decide to really concentrate on improving a particular area of the software engineering process, please read the books that discuss that area in depth.

This book is *not* about doing it perfectly—there are too many obstacles for that to be achieved very often. Different projects have different complexities, and people vary too much in skill sets and personalities to be perfect in everything.

My message is that nothing is good enough. There is no measure of quality that is satisfactory for all time. We must be constantly striving to improve every facet of the system. We don't expect code to be bug free on the first run. We just ask that the software engineer be able to improve it. Why should we ask anything different of the system?

Further Reading

Crosby, Philip. 1979. *Quality Is Free*. New York: Mentor.

Deming, W. Edwards. 1986. *Out of the Crisis*. Massachusetts Institute of Technology.

Summary

There is a strong relationship between quality and productivity. If you avoid errors and rework, quality goes up. If the things you do to avoid errors and rework are cost-effective, productivity also goes up.

If you want to increase the quality of your software and the productivity of your developers, you should be trying to minimize rework by preventing errors when possible and finding and correcting them as quickly as possible if you can't prevent them.

The best way to do this is to constantly look for things that can be improved. Don't set fixed goals, but instead look at every aspect of how you develop software, and ask ''Can we improve the way we do this?'' Never be satisfied with the status quo; constantly try to improve things.

2

Thoughts about Software Development

The Curse of Creativity

Why do you call creativity a curse?

First, programming is, to most people, an esoteric, incomprehensible subject. An idea has grown up that programming is a very creative endeavor, and software engineers use that idea to justify idiosyncratic behavior that does nothing for the software product.

Second, our profession is about solving problems for other people. Writing a tool that already exists, such as a b-tree manager, is not solving a problem; it's a recreational intellectual exercise.

But creativity is something we all admire.

Creativity itself is neither admirable nor contemptible. It's what you do with it that makes it one or the other. There have been plenty of evil geniuses in history. And plenty of brilliant software engineers who simply made wrong decisions. Being creative does not imply being moral, ethical, or always right.

Creativity in software engineering comes from putting together established building blocks to create real solutions to real problems. It doesn't come from idiosyncrasies in naming, from inventing your own sort algorithm, or from writing all your own functions when there are library routines to do the same thing. Put another way, creativity in design is generally a lot more valuable than creativity in implementation.

But it's surely better to be creative than not creative.

If you don't know anything, everything you do will be creative, but it probably won't be much good. The end result will probably take too long and be of low quality. On the other hand, if you have mastered every technique and have immense knowledge, anything creative you do has the potential to advance the state of the art. As Isaac Newton said: "If I have seen further, it is by standing on the shoulders of giants."

Are you saying that developing expertise is more important than being creative?

For most software engineers, yes. There are, of course, some exceptionally gifted software engineers developing new and very creative pieces of software, but for the vast majority of software engineers, being creative is simply inventing something that has already been invented.

What every problem you are working on, there is a high probability that it, or a similar problem, has already been solved. Most software solutions involve putting together common building blocks; the details will vary, but most of the concepts and algorithms have been used many, many times. There are ways to do things and building blocks that you can use. The more programming you have done and the more examples you have studied, the easier it is to know what to do in any situation.

What I hope for in any software engineer is that he learns how to create small building blocks from basic statements, then learns how to create larger building blocks from those smaller ones, and so on. Over a period of time, a software engineer should build up a knowledge base of high quality building blocks so that future problems can be solved more effectively. Those building blocks will consist largely of existing routines, knowledge of algorithms, existing blocks of code that can be cut and pasted, and techniques for doing things.

It sounds a lot like sports.

It's exactly like sports. The more moves you know and the more situations you've been in, the better you perform. That's why people practice. Things are at their easiest when you know how to do something and don't have to think. You just do, and react, in an intuitive way. Similarly in software. The more a person knows, the more quickly he can write good code to solve a problem.

What are these skills and techniques software engineers should know?

There are many techniques that should be known by software engineers: how to do good design, how to modularize, how to use information hiding, when to use what data structures, how to do a sort, how to read and process a sequential file, how to build a state machine, how to do asynchronous communications between processes, how to write code for windows-oriented environments, how to do for-next loops, how to do error reporting, and so on.

And then there are standards that should be known by software engineers: how to name functions, files, and variables, when to use global variables or parameters to functions, and how to use libraries.

How should software engineers get this knowledge?

Through experience, tempered by training and reviews of their work, both of which are the subjects of other chapters.

The NIH Syndrome

What is the NIH syndrome?

NIH stands for Not Invented Here. It is a syndrome that causes people to rewrite or recreate answers to problems for which a satisfactory solution exists. Reusable software gives you one of the greatest boosts to quality and productivity; the NIH syndrome is the antithesis of reusable software.

Why does the NIH syndrome exist?

I'm not a qualified psychologist, so I can't comment on why people fall into it, although there are probably different reasons. However, why it is allowed to exist in an organization is a more useful question. Every technical decision you make is also a business decision. If you decide to recreate something that exists, you are saying that the recreation is the most productive use of the software engineer's time.

Don't people know they're wasting time?

Again, I'm not a qualified psychologist. However, it does seem that people suffering from the NIH syndrome rarely admit it. It's only people on the outside that see it for what it is. People who suffer from the NIH syndrome can give you all sorts of good reasons for recreating something.

Such as?

The performance is unacceptable, it's too unwieldy, it doesn't do exactly what they need it to do, it's too inflexible, it's badly written, it's too flaky, they can't understand it, and so on.

But can't these things be true?

Certainly. And the project manager should have a good idea if that is the case.

When should you use existing software, and when is rewriting okay?

You should use existing software as much as possible. One of the goals of the project manager should be to use reusable software as much as possible because it boosts quality and productivity. So I think I'd phrase the answer as follows: Use existing software every time unless you have a very good reason not to.

What are good reasons not to?

All the reasons people use for recreating software! The project manager must decide if the reasons are valid. To do that, he must understand the reusable software fairly well—not down to the algorithmic level, but in terms of performance, flexibility, purpose, etc. Then he must put on his business hat and understand the relative costs of doing it one way or the other.

Programming as Communication

Programmers communicate with the computer. The programmer writes a program that tells the computer what to do. The computer will give some response, such as compiler errors or perhaps an access violation when the program is running. But the computer will make no attempt to try and understand what the programmer really meant. Communicating accurately is the task of the programmer.

However, programmers are also communicating with other programmers. Sooner or later someone will have to pick up the original program to fix a bug or make an enhancement. At that point the new programmer will be trying to understand what the program does, and what the original programmer intended. Everything the original programmer did—program organization, naming of variables, documentation—is part of the way he or she communicates with the future programmer.

Unfortunately most programmers don't make much attempt to communicate well with subsequent programmers. They can get away with it because they know that, unlike a computer, the subsequent programmer will make an effort to understand what is going on.

Sounds like the way most people approach speaking a foreign language!

Writing computer programs is very much like speaking a foreign language. If you both speak a different language, you may eventually get your message across, but it's likely to be time-consuming, laborious, and prone to error. On the other hand, if you both speak the same language, communication becomes easier and more accurate.

So it is with programming. If there are no standards on how to write programs it becomes a major task to pick up a program written by someone else, understand it, modify it, and debug it. If there is no documentation on what the programmer was trying to achieve, or what tasks functions perform and what they expect, it again makes the programmer's task more difficult. But if everyone uses the same conventions and the same documentation style, it becomes considerably easier to pick up someone else's code to modify.

Adopting standards for programming and documentation makes programs easier to understand and modify. Quality, productivity, and customer satisfaction go up. Costs and programmer frustration go down.

So why don't programmers make more effort to communicate with future programmers?

For a variety of reasons: it didn't occur to them, laziness, lack of care for what the future programmer will have to suffer through, expediency, time pressures. All in all, though, it's because of a lack of well-defined expectations on the part of the project manager that software engineers will conform to certain ''communication standards.''

But remember—the future programmer who needs this help might be you. It often happens that the person who originally wrote a piece of software will be called in to fix a problem or make an enhancement. It gets hard to remember why you made each decision, especially the more obscure ones. Certainly in the future you will appreciate the current effort you made to communicate clearly.

Standards

Why have standards?

Standards improve software quality and productivity. There are two types of standards: communication aids and building blocks. Standards that affect communication help because a program is like a foreign language, and the more similar the language each programmer speaks, the easier it is to understand another's programs. The easier a program is to understand, the easier it is to get changes right.

Naming standards can help every programmer by providing immediate information on the type of a variable. This is especially useful when using lower-level languages that don't do type checking on function calls or on assignments. Stylistic standards make it easier to understand the code and understand what it's doing, as do documentation standards.

Research has shown that it's easier to understand code that is clearly written and well commented. It's also shown that poorly written and poorly commented code not only contributes to errors, but also feeds the desires of the current programmer to rewrite or redesign the code, with the attendant risks of more errors and delays.

This is all fine when you're in maintenance mode, but what about when you're doing new development?

Standards that affect building blocks help because people come with a variety of skill levels and experience. The larger the organization, the greater the chance that the average developer is, well, average. Standard ways of doing things make it easier to create software with fewer errors. Building block standards might include well-defined library routines, skeleton programs with well-defined sections to fill in, standard ways of reading through a file, and standard ways to do interprocess communication.

But from a wider perspective, even when doing new development, people resign, get transferred, change careers, and become ill. The larger the project, the greater the chance that more than one person will work on any given piece of code. Sticking to standards makes it easier.

And from a wider perspective still, the typical software project spends more time in maintenance mode than in development mode, so you probably don't want to ignore the maintenance considerations even if you are in the new development phase.

A lot of people object to following standards.

That's unfortunately true. They tend to have an attitude of "this won't help me," which of course may be true, especially if the developers will be moving onto completely new software once this project is over or plan on leaving the company. So it depends whether you want to look at standards from the project viewpoint, or just that of a single developer.

Doesn't enforcing standards stifle creativity?

That's like saying that the use of sentences and grammar stifles the creativity of writers. Creativity in writing comes from what we have to say, from the new insights and the relationships we describe, and from the beauty of the combinations we make out of established building blocks.

Creativity in software engineering comes from recognizing new classes of problems that can be solved by computers and by putting together building blocks to create new and elegant solutions. Creativity is not manifested by a refusal to follow standards.

The most passionate arguments tend to be in the area of stylistic concerns such as indentation and bracketing conventions. But even there, I defy anyone to present a convincing argument that it's a good business decision to allow a lot of diversity in such areas. In fact, even when there may be justifications for exceptions to a standard, the business reasons for conformity to the standard will usually outweigh them. And most of us work for organizations that are driven by the search for profit.

Further Reading

Straker, David. 1992. *C Style, Standards, and Guidelines.* Englewood Cliffs, NJ: Prentice-Hall.

Summary

- Much of the creativity in programming exists simply because people don't know the basic building blocks of computer software. We would write better software if we spent less time reinventing the wheel, and more time being creative where it really counted.

- Software developers could be a lot more productive if they used standard building blocks that have already been written, rather than rewriting those blocks themselves.

- Software developers communicate with the computer, dictating what it should do. They also communicate with future developers who will be modifying the programs. A lot of time and effort could be saved if developers focused more on the needs of those future programmers.

- Standard ways of doing things make it easier to communicate with future and present developers. They also make it a little less likely that the developer will make errors.

3

Training

The things we can think about are dependent on the concepts and symbols we have available in our language and experience. Similarly, the solutions we find to problems are dependent on the tools, concepts, and experience we have available to us. If we expect our software engineers to develop high-quality solutions, whether they be at the analysis, design, algorithm, or debugging level, we must ensure that their store of concepts, knowledge, and experience is as rich as we can make it.

People learn in two ways: from things done right and from things done wrong. Either way, if we rely solely on our experience and thinking, we can never be sure that we have found the optimal solutions. The best mixture is to take our experience, add in some thought, and temper it with ideas and feedback from others.

In software, one of the best ways to learn from our mistakes is through the review process, which is the subject of another chapter. One of the best ways to learn without making mistakes is through training followed by experience.

It seems that a lot of training that goes on is not particularly relevant.

That's the complaint of a lot of people. I know people who have had classes in C^{++} but who have never had to work on a C^{++} project, and people who have had CASE training, but never used a CASE tool since. There's certainly something to be said for having a background knowledge of different areas of software engineering, but it's not a very efficient use of company time or money to train people in an area they won't use. Training is often one of the first things to be cut in cost-cutting measures, partly, I suspect, because a lot of it has limited value. So try to understand the true needs of the development organization and give people useful, relevant training that they can use on the job immediately.

One of the problems facing organizations is how to keep up-to-date with advances in technology.

Absolutely correct. Over the years we've learned a lot about creating better software, but that knowledge hasn't been disseminated very well. There are isolated pockets that know the latest advances in a given area, but, by and large, the majority of software engineers neither use nor know them. One goal of training must therefore be to keep the organization up-to-date on advances in software engineering.

The problem is deeper than it sounds though. From the perspective of employers, there are two reasons to train employees. First, in the future there will be more competition for employees because of the decline in the numbers of young adults entering the work force. Rather than compete for young people with the latest skills, there is some logic to training the people you have. Second, the economy is becoming increasingly global. If employers don't train their employees, they leave themselves open to losing business to companies whose employees have better skills.

From the perspective of employees, the mergers and layoffs of the eighties should provide ample cause for concern. If you are an employee, ponder two things. One, does your company simply use you up, leaving you further and further behind leading-edge technology? Two, the computer industry isn't old enough for there to be significant data, but what happens to 55-year-old software developers who get laid off? Education, training, and keeping up with new ideas, tools, and techniques can hardly hurt. The best job security is to be better tomorrow than you are today. If your company isn't helping, you have to do it yourself. You might ask yourself a few questions:

- In what ways have you improved since you started in this job?
- How did you improve?
- Why did you improve?
- In what ways are you better than your peers?
- In what ways are you less good than your peers?

Incidentally, if you discover you are good in a particular area, consider doing a training seminar for others on that topic.

It seems there's rarely time for training. Most organizations hire new software engineers when the need is critical and there are tight deadlines to be met.

Most organizations are trying to run fairly lean and mean, so hiring happens when the backlog gets too big, or when someone leaves the project. The new software engineer gets thrown in and is expected to survive and be productive. But people come in all shapes and sizes, and however good your hiring process you will end up with some self-starters and some non-self-starters. Given that not everyone is a self-starter, you have two choices if you want the best possible people: get rid of the ones that aren't self-starters, or train them. Part of the responsibility of management is to ensure that software engineers are trained and are performing effectively.

If you are strong enough to resist the pressure to skip training, and committed enough to quality, you can set up formal training programs for new software engineers. If the pressure is too strong, there are many less-formal methods of training. But training doesn't stop with new employees; training and education should be a constant fact in an organization that wants to improve continually. In some organizations, managers are required to send people on at least two weeks of formal training a year.

Give me some examples of training programs.

Some of the examples that follow are things that must be done at work; some of them can be done by software engineers at home.

- Give each new software engineer a mentor to work with—someone who will be responsible for the education of the trainee. Pick someone who is respected by both you and the other software engineers for his dedication to quality and standards.

- Have seminars or classes on various subjects. Make attendance mandatory if you are serious about training people. If participation is voluntary, classes tend to fall apart before too long. Require each person to give at least one seminar, to involve everyone. People will learn a heck of a lot about the subject of their seminar, and they will be interested in seeing how others do when presenting their seminars.

- Ask people to organize into groups of three to five people, and have each group research and make a presentation on a subject that will be of practical use to other developers. The presentation should also be in written form for inclusion in a developer notebook.

- When developers go to conferences or external seminars, require that they give presentations when they get back. Doing this will force them to consolidate and learn the information they were exposed to, and will give everyone else some of the benefit.

- ◦ Require everyone to describe a real software situation or problem and show how they solved it. Then have a general discussion of alternative and possibly better ways to have solved the problem. Each session should deal with only one problem.

- ◦ A good time to do seminars is at lunchtime, especially if the company buys pizzas. Evenings tend to work less well because people often have family responsibilities. A specific time and day of the week should be allocated for these seminars so that people can ensure in advance that there are no conflicts. A seminar every two weeks seems to work well.

- ◦ Videotape all seminars. You can always reuse the tape if the seminar went badly, but a tape of a good seminar can be used for training new people and for people to refresh their knowledge. A videotape makes a good training tool for people to bring home and watch during the evening. It's something that you can require even of new employees.

- ◦ There are classes you may need to do in small groups, such as showing how to use a debugger. Certain training is much more effective if done with a computer rather than by standing up and talking. Videotape these classes. You might also consider giving separate Basic and Advanced training sessions.

- ◦ Most organizations have one or two people who love to delve into the intricacies of languages and tools. Use these people in a conscious manner. Why have everyone wade through incomprehensible, poorly written computer manuals when you already have someone who loves doing this? Make being the "tool master" part of their job and require them to give training to others. Videotape the training.

- ◦ Start a "tools club." Get software tools and encourage people to learn them, play with them, and meet to discuss them. Start using the good tools on projects, especially before it becomes necessary to do so.

- ◦ Train people in the skills of developing systems. These days, after many years of talk about structured programming, modularization, and so on, any decent programmer should be able to write good programs. The important skills for the future lie in building systems.

- ◦ When a project is complete, have software engineers give seminars on key elements of the project to all people who might need to know. In particular, support and marketing people may find the information useful.

- Organize a "Best Practices" day where managers and senior technical people present their best practices. Topics for best practices might be quality, productivity, and scheduling.

- Provide documentation and examples of all standards that you want projects to conform to.

- Have a recommended reading list with copies of the books that software engineers can borrow. Buy copies of the most important books for the software engineers. Write up a small synopsis and review of all the books to get people's interest. Consider books on subjects such as programming languages, advanced programming, common pitfalls, testing, quality software, analysis, design, algorithms.

- Start a magazine library and circulate articles that you think will be useful or of interest.

- Have a high-level person responsible for staying up with advances and new thinking in software engineering. Give this person responsibility for doing projects with a group of four to seven people, using new techniques. This will train people in the new techniques and also help you evaluate the techniques and tools that work well.

- Involve people in technical reviews and causal analysis. They are great ways to learn new techniques and get insights from other people.

- At the start of each stage in the development cycle (requirements, design, coding, test, etc.), have a kick-off meeting with the teams or people involved, and go through the procedures that apply in this stage. Go through checklists of errors that are commonly found during this phase and mistakes that are commonly made.

- Develop, maintain, and distribute useful documentation. Examples include:
  - Processes, procedures, and methodologies
  - Checklists for inspections, software builds, QA submissions, software prereleases, etc.
  - Coding standards or guidelines
  - Naming conventions
  - Project management guidelines
  - Common error lists
  - New hire education and training
  - New hire workstation setup
  - Templates for requirements and design specs
  - Documentation on tools developed in-house

- Whenever you come across needed information that should be easily available but isn't, consider organizing that information into a notebook. Once you have a reasonable amount of information in the notebook, you have the start of something that might be stored on line and distributed to other people.

What topics would you do training on?

You are limited only by your imagination because there are always more things to learn. You could analyze the weaknesses of your organization and start with those weaknesses. Or you could create a list of topics and pick from the list. A list might include the following topics:

- The operating system

- The file system

- Inter-process communication

- Shell/script programming

- The programming editor. If the editor is customizable, I would start with a rich and powerful set of customizations so that people will spend as little time as possible customizing their own versions differently.

- Compiling and linking

- lint (if you're programming in C)

- Source code libraries and revision control

- Module management (''make'')

- Debugging

- Testing

- Error handling

- Other tools, such as test managers, performance analyzers. Define standard setups to avoid having people spend too long customizing settings, and make videotapes of how to use the tools. Give plenty of examples of how to achieve certain results.

- Analysis techniques

- Design techniques

- Diagramming techniques

- A comparison of analysis and design methodologies

- Modularization

- Designing for change. Have someone from the maintenance group describe what helps and hinders the maintenance group, and discuss the most common poor practices they see.

- Designing for testability. Have someone from the test group describe what helps and hinders the test group, and discuss the most common poor practices they see.

- Computer-aided software engineering (CASE)

- Graphical user interfaces (Macintosh, Microsoft Windows, Presentation Manager, X-Windows in its various flavors, etc.)

- Advanced programming tips

- Third-party libraries such as windowing libraries, database libraries, etc.

- New languages (C^{++}, object-oriented programming, etc.)

- Parser programming—lex and yacc

- Object-oriented design for procedural (function-oriented) languages

- Using "callbacks" in function-oriented programming

- Standards and naming conventions

- Esoteric topics for only the better software engineers

There are so many things to do that it's overwhelming.

On the contrary. There are so many things you can do that you can pick any of them to start with. This is "continual improvement," so pick a training scheme that has the best combination of effectiveness and ease of implementation. Once that scheme is going, choose another.

If it's that easy, why don't more organizations do it?

Because there's no immediate, obvious payback. It sometimes seems hard to justify the cost when you can't see the benefits in an immediate, obvious way. So there's an act of faith here—you have to believe that education helps people perform better and that people performing better help the organization.

Summary

The number-one factor affecting productivity and software quality is the experience and abilities of the software developers. So much of what we can do is dependent on what we know about, so if we want to help our developers create better software, we need to expand their knowledge and experience.

There is not much in the typical day that consciously helps developers enhance their skills. We learn from our mistakes, but we also learn by training followed by practical experience. There are many formal and informal ways to conduct training and learning, and many topics to give training on.

4

Metrics: Measuring for Improvement

How do metrics help you improve your software?

Metrics (or measurements) help in two ways. First, they help individual developers understand what they are doing and provide insight into areas that they might improve. For example, measurements of code complexity give information about which code is over-complex and might be improved by additional modularization. Measurements of numbers and types of bugs give information on what errors a developer is prone to make, and thus what he should be watching out for.

Second, metrics give an organization information about where it is and about the effect of things it is trying. Measure to find a starting baseline value. Implement the ideas that you think will help improve that aspect of the work or the process. Measure again to see if there's any improvement.

Measurement is the best way to tell you if what you are doing has value—without measurements, you are relying on faith or opinion, and everybody has a different one.

What if the measurements show that something doesn't have value?

Then you may be wasting time on something that you shouldn't be doing. Find something else that you think will improve the process, or if you are set on the current thing, figure out why it's not working, and how you can improve it. But the point is that you need hard, definitive facts before you can make justifiable decisions.

There seems to be a lot of disagreement about the value of metrics.

A lot of the disagreement comes from people who have seen metrics held up as the True Way, or who have seen metrics used to evaluate people. Metrics are simply a tool, and like a tool, they can be used well or used poorly. There's nothing magical about metrics—they don't guarantee good software. And if they are used to rate people, people will adopt whatever practices show them in the best light, regardless of whether those practices produce good software.

It's certainly true that some metrics are of dubious value, but trying to use this to discredit metrics in general is throwing out the baby with the bath water. If you are using or plan to use metrics that software developers disagree with, let them come up with metrics that they believe in. And make sure that people understand the problem that metrics are intended to help solve, otherwise you may end up with metrics that have nothing to do with the original problem.

Metrics tend to have support from managers and intellectuals, but not from software developers. How can you get software developers to support metrics?

One of the problems is that metrics are typically seen as a management tool rather than a developer tool, and developers often see management practices as getting in the way rather than helping. Developers also see that the result of metrics-gathering is that they will be told they have to change the way they do things. Then on top of that, there's the fear that metrics will be used to evaluate them. There are several things you can do to alleviate those fears.

- ◦ A useful model, developed by Victor Basili, goes something like this:

  Set your goals. To know if you are meeting those goals, you have to ask certain questions. To answer those questions, you need information, some of which can only come from measurements.

  So, create well-defined goals that are well-understood and well-accepted by developers, then measure only those things that answer the questions that must be answered.

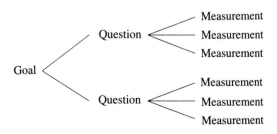

○ Set goals about things that developers have direct control over so that the metrics have meaning for them.

○ Have the developers set their own goals and ask for metrics that will help them see how they are doing.

○ Get metrics about quality rather than about productivity, about the process rather than about the product.

○ Have a person responsible for gathering, analyzing, and distributing metrics information. This person should be outside the management chain, and should be forbidden to ever reveal individual names to management.

○ Only provide information about large groups. This ensures that individual data will be lost in a larger set of data.

○ Gather information automatically. Developers tend to resist having to provide information unless there's pressure to do so. If there's pressure, are you sure you can trust the information?

○ Terms such as ''metrics'' seem alien and intellectual. Give what you are doing a comfortable name such as: taking the pulse, seeing how we are doing, doing a sanity check.

We don't have any tools to gather metrics automatically. Should we wait until we have some?

That depends on what you are trying to do. If you personally want some numbers and are willing to put in the work yourself, go for it. But if you want to use metrics on a larger scale, ones that involve getting information from other people, you'll need some way of gathering data automatically so there's no burden on people. If you rely on other people, you'll either get no information or you won't know whether you can trust the information you get. Basic tools that can help you gather information include:

○ A source code library that can count things such as lines of code, lines of non-commented code, numbers of functions, and numbers of modules.

○ A bug tracking system that also tracks fixes, categories of problems, and time taken to fix bugs.

If you need other tools, you've got a chicken-egg situation. You're unlikely to get the funding before you prove the data they give you will be useful, but it will be hard to get the data without the tool. I'd try to adapt existing tools or software to provide the measurements you need.

Some things are impossible to measure.

Things may be difficult to measure, but there is always a measurement you can do that is more useful than not measuring at all. There's always a way to get *some* information that is more useful than *no* information, although it may mean spending some time thinking about it (one of the main reasons we find things difficult is that we are not prepared to spend enough time on them).

Some things are so difficult to measure that no one will bother.

Code complexity is an example. No one in his right mind will go through and count all the comparison tests and all the variables. However, there are plenty of tools available to do such measurements for you. If you want to measure something related to the software, look for a tool.

But in the more general sense, if you are not going to measure, there probably needs to be general agreement about the thing you are not going to measure. To me, it's intuitive that naming conventions make code easier to understand and modify correctly and that the extra typing time is insignificant. Taking measurements to prove this would be difficult and not worth the effort to me. But there may be other people who feel that naming conventions are something whose worth must be proven.

What can you measure?

What can't you measure? Let's go through a few things that might be useful to measure and list ways of getting that information.

Effectiveness of reviews. Like many of the techniques for improving quality, reviews take time. The time taken is obvious and measurable. The time saved is far less obvious, but it's important to know it if you want to justify having reviews.

Software developers often resist measurements because of a fear that measurements will be used to evaluate them. Rather than counting the number of errors that are removed during reviews, count the number of errors that are found *after* the product is reviewed. Until reviews are accepted, focus on the positive—the reduction in the number of errors remaining. In a sense, it's only an error if it gets past the review. Once reviews are accepted, you can start tracking errors found.

- Time taken to test and debug something with no reviews
- Time taken to test and debug something comparable, using reviews and adding in the amount of reviewer time
- Percentage of products accepted at the first review
- Percentage of products accepted at the second review
- Percentage of products accepted at or after third review

- ○ Percentage of products needing to be redone
- ○ Percentage of products needing major revisions
- ○ Percentage of products needing minor revisions
- ○ Time spent in reviews
- ○ Time spent preparing for reviews
- ○ Number of issues or errors missed but caught in the next phase
- ○ Number of errors of different severity found during reviews
- ○ Cost of reviews
- ○ Cost of preparation
- ○ Cost of review process
- ○ Average cost of finding errors in reviews
- ○ Average cost of fixing error found in test phase
- ○ Savings due to inspections

Note that after a while, the average cost of finding an error in reviews may go up. Fewer errors will be found because people start thinking more, discussing more, and doing things in a way that will get the product accepted. Which of course, is exactly what you want.

Code complexity.   Complex code is usually a sign of poor code. It often means that the code is poorly modularized because it's trying to do too much or too many different things. It's more difficult to understand and thus to modify correctly. It's difficult to test because there are so many possible paths through the code. And it's more error prone than simple code. Various studies have shown a strong correlation between defect density and code complexity.

There are various ways to measure code complexity, and they usually involve counting the number of variables, the number of operators, or the number of comparisons, and applying a formula to some or all of these. The two main measures are the McCabe Cyclomatic Complexity and the Halstead (or Software Science) Effort metric. The McCabe number indicates the number of paths through a module and is obtained by counting the branching statements. The general consensus seems to be that a cyclomatic complexity of greater than 10 significantly increases the chances of errors (except in programs that have a large number of case statements—these increase the cyclomatic complexity without having much effect on errors).

The Halstead number is based on the number of unique variables and operators and the total number of variables and operators. It assumes that the more variables and operators a program has, the more difficult it is to understand. And that the more times a variable is used, the harder it is to remember the state of that variable.

However, if it was left to the software engineer to compute, these metrics would be without value since no one would go to that amount of effort. Fortunately, there are software tools, such as PC Metric, that do the tedious work for you. Better still are tools that show the complexity visually because they give information that has more meaning than a single number.

Information on module complexity can help you decide where to focus test attention, which modules to do code reviews on, which modules need extra documentation, and which modules to rewrite.

Some organizations require software developers to justify any module with a complexity greater than a specified number before checking in the code. Some require code of greater than a certain complexity to be reviewed. Some require that complex code be investigated to see if a review would be useful. Others take the modules considered best, whether from the best developer or assessed that way by a committee, then calculate the mean and standard deviation complexity. Code may be checked in only if the complexity lies no more than one standard deviation above the mean.

Number of bugs against a module. If there were a lot of bugs in a module in the past, there are likely to be bugs in the future. Modules with a large number of bugs previously reported against them are candidates for code reviews, extra testing, and rewrites.

Uninterrupted time. Software developers are more productive during long periods of uninterrupted time. How often have you seen developers working at night or going off to empty conference rooms because that's the only way they can get things done? Measure the number of uninterrupted hours of work and calculate as a percentage of hours at work. If the percentage is low, help people do something about it—redirect phones, close office doors with a ''Do Not Disturb'' sign, have ''visiting hours'' for developers. Measure uninterrupted hours by having the developers, for a week, record:

- Time they started work
- Time they left work
- Time they went to lunch
- Time they started work after lunch
- Time of each interruption
- Time they went back to work after interruption

For additional information, they might track whether the interruption was a phone call, a mail message, someone coming by, etc. That information will help determine the solution most likely to be effective—for example, stopping phone calls is a less effective solution if most interruptions are caused by people stopping by.

Information about errors. Your QA organization should be able to tell you in a monthly report about the numbers of errors found and fixed, categorized in various ways, and with the following information (some of the information may have to come from the developers).

- ◦ Severity of error
- ◦ Product
- ◦ Phase where introduced: requirements, architecture, high-level design, low-level design, coding
- ◦ When located: review, unit test, integration test, system test, field test, customer
- ◦ Module
- ◦ Complexity of module
- ◦ Test coverage percent of module
- ◦ Whether this part of the product was reviewed in the appropriate phase
- ◦ Time spent to fix the error (if you can show how much time is spent on rework, you may come up with a compelling argument for adopting defect prevention techniques)
- ◦ If the error was introduced in the coding phase:
  - • Were source code tools such as lint run?
  - • If not, would they have found the error?

Errors that you make.   Track the numbers and types of errors that you make. An analysis of these will give insight into the areas that you need to pay more attention to.

Number of global variables used.   External scope global variables mean linkages between modules. They make it more difficult to modify code and test code. Knowing the number of globals used lets you make informed decisions about whether to restructure the software or add parameters to functions.

Estimated number of bugs in a module.   There is a formula that predicts the likely number of errors in a program, based on various counts of operators and operands. Again, metrics tools can provide that number. The predicted number of errors can help you decide where to focus test attention, which modules to do code reviews on, or which modules to rewrite.

Individuals.   No, I'm not contradicting what I said earlier! Work with people (or yourself) to identify where people want to improve. Ask them what to measure to track the improvement.

Further Reading

Arthur, Jay. 1985. *Measuring Programmer Productivity and Software Quality.* New York: Wiley.

Card, David, with Robert Glass. 1990. *Measuring Software Design Quality*. Englewood Cliffs, NJ: Prentice-Hall.

Conte, Samuel, Dunsmore, and Shen. 1986. *Software Engineering Metrics and Models*. Redwood City, CA: Benjamin-Cummings.

Ejiogu, Lem. 1991. *Software Engineering with Software Metrics*. Wellesley, MA: QED Information Sciences.

Fenton, N.E. (editor). 1991. *Software Metrics: A Rigorous Approach*. New York: Van Nostrand Reinhold.

Grady, Robert, and Debra Caswell. 1987. *Software Metrics: Establishing a Company-Wide Program*. Englewood Cliffs, NJ: Prentice-Hall.

Jones, Capers. 1991. *Applied Software Measurement. Assuring Productivity and Quality*. New York: McGraw-Hill.

Shepperd, M. 1991. *Software Engineering Metrics*. New York: McGraw-Hill.

Zuse, Horst. 1990. *Software Complexity: Measures and Methods*. Hawthorne, NY: de Gruyter.

Summary

Metrics are a tool, and like other tools, they can be used or abused. The value of metrics, or measurements, lies in their ability to help you determine if what you are doing has value. Without measurements, you are relying on prejudices and opinions. The most effective model is:

Set your goals. To know if you are meeting those goals, you have to ask certain questions. To answer those questions, you need information, some of which can only come from measurements.

The negative side of metrics is that they can be used to evaluate people, and this causes many developers to react badly to metrics programs.

If you want to implement a metrics program, you must make sure that the developers believe the measurements will help them develop better software, and will not be used to evaluate them personally.

5

Change

It's easy to become satisfied, complacent, or lazy, but in the long run, that's a recipe for failure. There will always be other people, companies, or countries, that adopt new ideas, techniques, and tools, and put us into uncompetitive positions. Change is required if we want to stay competitive. However, change is also difficult. Everyone wants to improve, but nobody wants to change. People won't resist improvement initiatives, but they will resist the changes the initiatives bring to their lives.

Software developers have been left largely to themselves over the years. For some reason they haven't been subject to the normal rules of organization and business—perhaps because programming has been such an arcane art for so long. This means that change is often a harder sell. But the one unchanging thing in life is that things change. The only question of importance is: do you want to control the change or to have the change control you and the organization?

Fortunately, new ideas are two a penny. Unfortunately, implementing a new idea is difficult. People resist change, so ideas for change need someone with energy and enthusiasm, a champion who will persevere, overcoming all obstacles. If you want change, there are three fundamental ways to go about it.

- ○ You can have sufficient authority to dictate the changes, in which case you may have to accept some breakage. (If you are after a major cultural change, you may *want* some breakage. For example, the first action of some turnaround experts is to fire the old management team, to make the point that things will now be different.)

- ○ Another option is to lead by example and hope people follow.

○ The third choice is to try and sell change, which requires tact, diplomacy, an understanding of people's needs, and an ability to sell.

This sounds tough.

It's the same throughout life. If you want to just do your job, fine. But if you want to have influence and to change the way things are done, you need an ability to listen to people, to understand their needs, and to persuade them that your ideas will help them meet their needs—you need *selling skills*.

Software engineering is a very human-intensive activity, so any change in the way things are done is mainly a human-oriented change, an organizational change. Technical problems, in the end, are people problems. To effect a change, you must understand the human side of the organization—what type of organization it is, how it reacts to change, what is the best way to effect change, and what is the best way to ensure the organization doesn't slip back to the old ways of doing things. As Sir John Harvey-Jones, a former chairman of ICI Chemicals, said, "Everything I've learned teaches me that it is only when you work with, rather than against, people, that achievement and lasting success is possible."

If you want to control change, develop your selling skills and learn to involve people.

How do I do that?

There is a fundamental rule to understand. As Gerald Weinberg's Buffalo Bridle rule states: "You can make buffalo go anywhere, just so long as they want to go there. You can keep buffalo out of anywhere, just so long as they don't want to go there." Or, as Dale Carnegie puts it, "The only way on earth to influence the other fellow is to talk about what he wants and show him how to get it."

How do you respond to change? If you're like most people, you want to know why change is happening. How will it make things better? What problem will it solve? How will you benefit? If you want to sell change, focus on the benefit of the change. How will the change help the people it will affect? If you're like most people, you also want to be involved: to be consulted about the change and to feel that you are contributing to the solution of the problem.

Who should I be trying to involve in change?

Larry Constantine identifies four groups of people who are involved in changing things.

○ **Starters** initiate the change, but by themselves they are unlikely to be successful.

○ **Sponsors** are people who have the power and authority to make things happen.

○ **Advocates** support the change but don't have the power to do anything.

○ **Agents** are people with special influence, such as consultants or star developers in other groups, who have no power to do things, but whose suggestions may carry additional weight.

Besides the four groups who can effect change, there are two other groups involved in change.

○ Those people who will be affected by the change.

○ Those people who will resist the change.

If you are reading this and hoping to change things, you are almost certainly a starter or possibly a sponsor. If you don't have the powers of the sponsor, find sponsors—the more the better; and turn the people who will be affected by the change into advocates or agents. Don't let them become resisters.

Tell me about sponsors.

Sponsors are the most important of the groups because it's hard to accomplish anything without the support of the people who have the power and authority to effect change. So you want as many sponsors as possible, starting with your boss. Good sponsors will be obsessed with new results and will reinforce this with a strong dissatisfaction with the status quo.

Consider the interests of potential sponsors. For example, quality is probably the biggest benefit for life-critical and mission-critical software, so stress quality in this type of software project. However, most software is neither life- nor mission-critical. Increasingly, time to market is the key factor in software development—a lot of people have difficulty looking at software development from the quality perspective because cultures still tend to be focused on schedules. Generally the most important benefit for most software projects is a shortened delivery time, with cost savings following close behind.

Changes that reduce rework will improve quality and productivity, and help you shorten the schedules. But when trying to sell change, focus on how the change will help you deliver the product sooner and reduce the costs.

The easiest way to get sponsors is to find a solution to an obvious problem: everyone has a finite amount of political capital, and few people will squander it on something unimportant. There are two downsides to sponsorship. First, in a highly political organization, potential sponsors may be unwilling to get involved in something that they see as politically dangerous. Second, change causes resistance, and some people may resist the change so much that they end up resigning. Some changes will put sponsors in the position of having to accept the loss of key people.

So, it's often going to be more difficult if you are trying to improve something which is already pretty good, unless the change is non-threatening.

What if I can't get my manager's support?

It depends on the situation. If you are a sponsor, you can often implement the change anyway, unless your manager has forbidden you to. If you are not a sponsor, you can often change the way *you* do things, or persuade others to adopt the change. You can persuade people over time by showing that things work better after the change. Persevere. Show enthusiasm for what you are trying to do. And be repetitive—eventually what you are saying becomes part of people's subconscious. Repetition breaks down the barriers.

What about advocates and agents?

The more advocates you can get, the better, whether in your organization or other organizations. The more an idea permeates the culture, the greater its chance of success. But the most important advocates and agents are the people the change will affect. The last thing you need is for those people to become resisters. The approach you take will depend on whether you are the manager of the group, or just another group member.

Suppose I am the manager.

There are several things to consider:

- ○ Set the goals and let the developers figure out what to change.
- ○ Involve the key opinion leaders and get them on your side.
- ○ Involve everyone who will be affected by the change.
- ○ Pay attention to what is important to you.
- ○ What gets measured, gets done.
- ○ Use everyday words rather than intellectual words.

Set the goals and let the developers figure out what to change.   Set goals that people agree with, find a way of determining whether people are meeting the goals, then move out of the way and let the developers decide what changes are necessary. There's no point in change unless it achieves something, so you are obviously trying to achieve something. You should also be able to tell if you are achieving it, otherwise why bother? Once you have the goals, make the problem of meeting the goals the developers' problem, and get involved in the details only if they request it. People would much rather decide on the change than have change forced on them.

Involve the key opinion leaders and get them on your side.   People take their cues from a few key opinion leaders. Software developers tend to respect those with the best technical skills, the people who know the answers to technical problems and who can write good code quickly. These people are usually the opinion leaders. They are the people to get on your side, because most of the other developers will come along with them.

Change in a software development organization is best driven by a combination of managers and technical people—managers because management support is usually essential, and good technical people because theirs are usually the opinions that software developers value.

Ideally, you will have opinion leaders who share the same philosophies with you about how to do software development. However, most managers inherit groups, and so don't have much choice, but when you hire senior-level people, you can consider each person's approach to software development as well as his other skills.

If the change can be implemented gradually, rather than all at once, find a key opinion leader, and ask that person to try doing the new thing. Wait for the program to develop before formalizing it. You'd like it to live past either you or the individual who started it, and once it's established and working no one will have a problem with formalizing it. Enlist champions.

Involve everyone who will be affected by the change.   You achieve success when you set goals after discussion with the people who will be affected, then involve people in planning what to do and how to do it. Once you have agreement from the key opinion leaders that a change is useful, involve everyone in deciding exactly what the change entails. If people agree to implement naming standards, involve them in deciding what the naming standards should be. If they agree that better documentation is important, let them decide on documentation standards. Let them discuss design methodologies and decide which ones best fit their needs and situation. They need to buy in and own the change. If you think there are alternative ways that may be more efficient, mention them, but don't force the issue. If you still feel that the solution is inadequate, revisit the problem later. Go for incremental, continual improvement.

Pay attention to what is important to you.   Actions speak louder than words, and the things you pay attention to tend to be the things people will focus on. Stop by people's offices to find out how things are going in the area of interest to you. Make heroes out of those whose behavior you'd like emulated. Every developer will be watching you to see if you are serious about the change you are proposing, or if it's simply the new idea of the day.

If your group is large enough, you might find a technical person specifically to help with change, which will show people how important this is. One way to do this is to hire a software developer as a Development Methodologies Specialist—this person must be someone who is experienced, talented, and able to work well with others and get their respect. A possible job description would be:

- ○ Help set up and become involved in:
  - • Formal reviews
  - • Testing
  - • Software reuse system
  - • Document templates and notations
  - • Defect prevention through causal analysis
- ○ Create tools to assist in development procedures

If you are going to make changes, be prepared to train people. After all, if you aren't prepared to train people, they will legitimately wonder how important this really is to you. You can't insist that people adopt some practice if they don't know how to. Agreement to use Entity-Relationship diagrams is meaningless if people don't know how to use them.

What gets measured, gets done.   That's one reason schedules have so much power—they are often the only thing that is measured in a software organization. Measuring does two things: it gives people direct knowledge of how they are doing, and it shows what is important to you. When people know how they are doing, and know that you know, it makes them more likely to do whatever gives the most positive measurements. If you find it difficult to figure out what to measure, brainstorm with someone who is interested in the same change.

Use the Goals/Questions/Measurements model. What are the goals? What measurements do you need if you are to know whether you are meeting the goals? Make the measurements. As a manager, you can take the goals and measurements and make them part of people's performance reviews.

A word of caution though—if you measure something, you will probably get it. So make sure that what you are measuring is really what you want.

Use everyday words rather than intellectual words.   Developers often resist things that are called model, process, metric—words that sound intellectual rather than practical. Use words and phrases that are comfortable: how we do things around here, taking the pulse, checking how things are going, etc.

What if there are still individuals who won't participate?

Why are they resisting? Do they see this as change for change's sake, without a well-defined goal? Or as a change that will help reach an accepted goal? Do they feel the change is being pushed down their throats? Did you involve them? Sometimes you have to involve the people most likely to resist if you are to succeed.

Can you use peer pressure to make them participate? Can you make participation a part of their performance evaluations? Can you ask them to come up with a better solution to whatever problem this change is addressing? Is this change essential? Is it worth preserving your political capital for a more important change?

What are the consequences of resisting the change? In most organizations there is no consequence. Deadlines may be missed, quality may be poor, but so what? Seldom do the software engineers feel repercussions, so why should they welcome the change? One way to implement change is to make the current way of doing things sufficiently unpleasant that the change will be welcomed.

How valuable is the developer? Reassigning him, or "inviting" him to work on another project, might send a powerful message to everyone else. (No person is indispensable. What would happen if the person left the project or the company?) Can you do a partial implementation of this change, and require the reasonable people to follow the procedures, while letting the resisters do their own thing?

What do I do if I am just a group member?

You can lead by example, and you can be persuasive. Be enthusiastic about the change. Keep at it, smiling all the time. Show people how it will help them reach their goals. If it's something you can start by yourself, start it. Keep measurements and show how the change saves money or time. If it's an "all or nothing" change—one you can't do as an individual—read the literature, and research other organizations that have done what you are proposing. What were their results? Can they demonstrate that it saved time or money? In these harsh economic times, when everyone seems to be downsizing, money saved is important. In this tough, competitive environment, speed to market is vital.

Involve people, get sponsors and advocates. Talk to people one-on-one rather than in groups; in a group you have to worry about the group dynamics—who's supporting whom, who's trying to impress whom, who's waiting for someone else to commit (however, if you're hoping to let peer pressure do some of the work, talking in a group might be the right approach). Of course, it also helps if you have people's respect, which generally means you must be very good at your job.

What about implementing the changes in other groups?

If you were unable to implement change in your group, but can persuade another group to implement it, its success may eventually persuade your manager to implement the change in his group. Patience, perseverance, and a willingness to approach problems from all angles are virtues!

You mentioned documentation standards earlier. We have standards that were created by the developers, but no one follows them.

That's one of the interesting facets of software development—people agree to standards and procedures, then don't follow them. If you look at the possible consequences of following the standards and procedures, you can often see why. Let's look at the consequences of doing documentation.

- ○ Have to write documentation.
- ○ Spend less time programming.
- ○ Schedules may slip if we do all the documentation.
- ○ Documentation will be better for future developers.
- ○ Managers will be happy.

There are three aspects to the consequences of doing things: will the consequences be positive (P) or negative (N); will they be immediate (I) or future (F); will they be certain (C) or uncertain (U)? People will tend to do things that provide plenty of P, and avoid things that provide N. They will especially do things that result in PIC consequences and avoid things that result in NIC consequences. Let's analyze these consequences.

NIC	Have to write documentation.
NIC	Spend less time programming.
NFU	Schedules may slip if we do all the documentation.
?FC	Documentation will be better for future developers.
PFU	Managers will be happy.

(I put ?FC for better future documentation because this may not affect the developer at all. Someone else may end up maintaining the software he writes.)

Looking at the consequences, they are stacked in favor of *not* following the documentation standards.

If you want to get people to change, or do a particular thing, look at the consequences, and try and structure things so that you provide NICs for undesired behavior, and PICs for desired behavior.

It's better to motivate people by providing PIC consequences for doing some desired thing than NIC consequences for not doing it. However, that's easy to say and often difficult to achieve. Sometimes the only thing that makes sense is to apply more NICs to the undesired behavior than exist for the desired. Or to change the structure of things. Keeping documentation current has more negative consequences than positive, and it's difficult to change that, so a possible structural change would be to hire a person and give him the job description of assisting developers with documentation (there's more about this in the chapter on Specifications and Documents).

I've heard of the SEI and the five levels of software organization. How does that fit in with change?

The Software Engineering Institute (SEI) at Carnegie Mellon University defines five levels of maturity and describes a plan of action to move from one level to another. The SEI has a Software Capability Evaluation Questionnaire that you can use to determine the maturity level of your organization. Eighty percent of companies are at judged to be at level one, the lowest level.

To help move to a higher maturity level, the SEI recommends setting up a process group and a management steering committee, describing the process you currently use, defining the process you'd like, figuring out how to get from what you have to what you'd like, then setting up working groups to work out the details.

It's a very formal approach, whose intention is to involve people in the change. It's a slow process and can be very frustrating as you try to get a group of people to agree. Watts Humphrey, the former head of the SEI, is from IBM, and I suspect that the SEI way of doing things is geared towards large, bureaucratic companies where you have to get a lot of people involved to accomplish change. Small companies can often get by with far less formality.

One aspect of the SEI approach is that you have to understand where you are today and where you want to be tomorrow. There's nothing wrong with this, but I don't believe it's required. Most software development organizations have so much room for improvement that I believe there are plenty of things you can do to help, without spending the time understanding and formalizing where you are today and where you want to be tomorrow. This book is filled with things that you can use to do things better, without having an all-encompassing vision of where you want to be.

For more information about the SEI approach, you can write to the Software Engineering Institute at Carnegie Mellon University, Pittsburgh, Pennsylvania, 15213, and ask for a copy of the *Software Engineering Process Group Guide*.

If I want to initiate change, what should I start with?

Start with the change most likely to succeed. Nothing succeeds like success. Don't worry about doing everything at once—it's probably too much and you'll end up frustrated. Pick something and implement it, consolidate the change, then go on to the next change. Pick the changes that people will be most likely to agree to. Get people involved and on your side. If you can't influence other people, do what you can as an individual—lead by example. Start with the improvement you feel most strongly about.

In terms of the most bang for the buck, start with requirements reviews and design reviews. If you're starting a new project, you might decide on naming and documentation standards because that will affect everyone who comes after.

But above all do something. This is continual improvement, and even if you don't start with the best improvement, it's better to start somewhere than nowhere. Don't get into the analysis paralysis trap. Some people may argue that it's not worth worrying about the little things when there are big things to do, but this is simply not valid—you can score from singles as well as home runs, and you can score more easily and more often. Improve everything that can be improved.

People will react differently to different changes. If you are telling people *how* to do their jobs, they will resist. On the other hand, if you let them do the job as they want to, but also tell them the product will be reviewed, you'll get a different kind of resistance. This time it will be from the people who are too insecure to willingly accept other people's scrutiny of their work (interestingly, people tend to react more negatively to code reviews than to requirements or design reviews— code seems to be more an extension of the person than is design—which is unfortunate, considering that design is the more critical aspect of software). People have been known to quit rather than have their work criticized.

On the other hand, implementing reviews can lead more naturally to other changes. Peer pressure for consistent formats, use of document templates, standards for documentation, use of tools before reviews to save time, and so on, can often do more to effect change than any argument you can make.

Suppose the change doesn't work?

Be willing to admit defeat and change the change. Try to understand why it didn't work, then do something different. It may mean refining the change, it may mean doing something completely new, or it may mean going back to the old way.

How often should I do new things?

Don't flit around from change to change, letting things work back to the old way of doing things. Consolidate changes before trying to do the next one. Once a change is consolidated, go on to the next one. Make continual improvement an expectation. The fact of change should be so predictable that people expect more change.

Further Reading

Bouldin, Barbara. 1989. *Agents of Change: Managing the Introduction of Automated Tools.* Englewood Cliffs, NJ: Yourdon Press.

Buckley, Fletcher. 1989. *Implementing Software Engineering.* New York: Wiley.

Carnegie, Dale. 1983. *How to Win Friends and Influence People.* New York: Simon and Schuster.

Humphrey, Watts. 1990. *Managing the Software Process.* Reading, MA: Addison-Wesley.

Pressman, Roger. 1988. *Making Software Engineering Happen. A Guide for Instituting the Technology.* Englewood Cliffs, NJ: Prentice-Hall.

Weinberg, Gerald. 1985. *The Secrets of Consulting: A Guide to Giving and Getting Advice Successfully.* New York: Dorset House.

Summary

Change is difficult. While people don't resist improvement initiatives, they do resist the changes those initiatives bring to their lives. However, improving the way we do things is required if we want to remain competitive. So, change is necessary. When trying to change things, consider the following:

- Work with, rather than against, people.
- Show how the change can help people succeed.
- Involve people in the change.
- Get sponsors for the change.
- Get the key developers on your side.
- Lead by example.
- Consider the consequences of things to people—are they PIC or NIC?
- Start with the change most likely to succeed or with the one for which you have the greatest enthusiasm.

6

Software Tools

Tools let us do three things: leverage our abilities, do things previously impossible, and alter our framework for thinking and problem solving. A person wielding a chainsaw can cut down more trees than a person with a handsaw. Someone driving a backhoe can dig ditches a lot faster than someone with a spade. A calculator makes long division easier for some, and possible for others.

At the other extreme, without tools we would never see cells, do CAT scans, create printed circuits, or go to the moon. Increasingly sophisticated tools let us see ever smaller things, cram ever more circuits on computer chips.

The third aspect of tools is less obvious, but consider language. It's certainly a tool for communication, but without it, the things we could think about would be radically different, as would our approach to problem solving. Research-oriented organizations, such as IBM and Xerox, are developing ways to use computers to enhance collaboration between individuals, tools that could radically alter the way we work and solve problems.

Tools unique to our organization give us competitive advantages in two ways: First, they help us leverage our people by letting less skilled people do tasks previously the domain of the more skilled, and letting the skilled people do things more quickly and more effectively. Second, they give us the ability to do things we previously couldn't do. Tools for creating denser computer chips let us sell chips no one else has.

By the same token, if our competitors use tools unavailable to us, we put ourselves at a potential competitive disadvantage.

(As an aside, consider yourself in the job market. Job security comes from being better tomorrow than you are today and from being better than other employees or potential employees. Are there any tools that can help you leverage your abilities more effectively? Are you ignoring tools that other people are using to their advantage?)

Give me some examples of leverage in software development.

Compilers let us write code much more rapidly than if we wrote in machine code. Fourth-generation languages let users develop their own reports, freeing up developers for the tougher problems. Prototype tools let us create models so that we can truly collaborate with users in the design. CASE tools leverage our abilities to create and modify diagrams by letting us print new diagrams with a keystroke, rather than redrawing them manually.

There is certainly an upper limit to the size and complexity of a project that can be completed by five people in three months. Future tools will help us exceed the limits manyfold.

How do you decide which tools to use?

If the tool helps you leverage skills, you ask: Does the tool leverage our skills more than what we are using now? Is the additional leverage cost-justified? If the tool lets you do things previously impossible, you ask: Will this tool help us increase market share or reduce our costs?

What about the intangible aspects, such as a particular tool being more fun to work with?

Intangibles are part of the cost justification. If people are frustrated, they produce less. If people enjoy what they are doing, they produce more. However, there's the learning curve cost to consider, and the length of time over which the tool will be used.

Can you overemphasize tools?

If you can't cost-justify the additional leverage, you're overemphasizing the particular tool. For example, a language such as Modula-2 may be better than C, but how easy is it to find software engineers who know the language well? C may be more glamorous than COBOL, but will you be able to find experts in C who want to work on business applications? A new editor may be marginally better than an old editor, but are the additional benefits worth the learning cost?

Sometimes we know a tool would be useful in the long term, but we can't justify the cost or the ramp-up time.

It happens! There are several things you can do, especially in the PC world where things don't cost very much. Get software on a trial basis where possible. Assign one person to learn the tool and teach it to others. If necessary, pay that person overtime to learn it in the evenings or on the weekends. Use the tool on one small project at first, then over time increase the number of people who use it. Ask vendors for videotape instructions for the tool. Sometimes you can buy videotape courses from third parties.

Is there anything extra you can do in the PC world?

Buy everyone PCs for home use. When you get new tools, ask people to play with the tool on their PCs at home. Organize a PC tool club that meets once a month at someone's house and goes over what the tool can do, the leverage it provides people, and the benefits it can bring to the organization. Start a Tool of the Month club—get a new tool every month and encourage people to take it home to try it out and evaluate it.

How can you understand the leverage of a tool without having used it over time?

Talk to other people who have used it—ask about their experiences. Look for reviews of the product in magazines. Call up the publications, asking if they have reviewed products or product categories of interest. Call or fax the vendor of the package you are interested in and ask for literature. Ask the vendor for any reviews of the product that have been published—these are usually a lot more informative than product literature (but don't expect the vendor to furnish negative reviews). Ask for demonstration software—many vendors provide software with an expiration date. If the vendor you talk with doesn't have demo software, suggest that they make an evaluation copy available and explain that you aren't allowed to buy software without evaluating it first.

How do you discover what products are available for the platform you use?

Read the magazines for your platform—they will have advertisements and sometimes reviews. Most vendors of minicomputers and mainframes have a list of software packages available for their particular machines; ask for the list.

There are many more products available for PCs than for minicomputers and mainframes. A good source of information is The Programmer's Shop. Call them at 1-800-421-8006 and ask for their catalog. They can also fax you reviews of many of the products they carry. Some of the products they carry also work in non-PC environments.

Software Quality Engineering, at 3000-2 Hartley Road, Jacksonville, FL 32257 (1-800-423-8378) publishes a catalog of tools that are useful for analyzing and testing code: *Testing Tools Reference Guide: The Catalog of Software Quality Support Tools*. This catalog describes a variety of tools, the platforms that they run on, their cost, etc. It currently costs $145, with annual updates for $45.

Another company that offers a catalog of commercially available software tools is Applied Computer Research (ACR), at P.O. Box 82266, Phoenix, AZ 85071-2266 (1-800-234-2ACR). The *Guide to Software Productivity Aids* costs $150 for a single version, or $225 for an annual subscription of two issues.

Which reminds me, tools can be so expensive.

They tend to be priced according to the number of copies they will sell. PC tools have the largest market, so the prices are cheaper. On the other hand, you aren't going to sell mainframe tools to that many customers, so prices will be higher to recover the development costs and make a profit.

However, I don't understand the marketing strategies of some of the larger hardware vendors. If the tools really do improve productivity and quality, as I believe that most of them do, why isn't there a marketing manager there saying:

> Hey guys, let's give these tools away. The market is becoming more competitive, and one of the things that will sell our hardware is well-priced, high-quality software. Let's help our value-added resellers (VARs) to improve their software and help them produce it quicker. Let's not only give away the tools, but also train their people how to use them. We'll offer free training for anyone who signs up to use the tools, and then we'll go back three months later for advanced training and to hear their feedback. We'll help our VARs develop their software, and we'll benefit because more people will buy our hardware to run our VARs' software.

However, there are things you can do even if you can't afford expensive tools for the larger platforms. Most things that don't deal with the compiled code or real data can be done on a PC. If you are designing a Motif windowing scheme, prototype it first in Windows on a PC. If you want to use CASE for analysis and design, do it on a PC. Use PC project-management software. If you can transfer source code easily between a PC and your platform, use PC editors, code formatters, and so on.

What type of tools are worth looking at?

All types of tools are worth looking at! Tools are justified if they leverage people's talents in cost-justified ways, or let you do new, useful things. In this chapter we'll look at:

- Code analyzers
- Code formatters
- Code generators
- Code translators
- Compilers
- Debuggers
- Documenters
- Editors
- Integrated development environments
- lint
- make
- Performance analyzers
- Prototyping tools
- Source code libraries
- Test tools

There's overlap between some of these topics, so I'll just go through them in alphabetic order, and treat them as topics in their own rights.

What about CASE tools?

I've devoted a section at the end of this chapter to CASE.

Tell me about code analyzers.

There are two basic types of code analyzer. One looks at all the source code files and builds relationships between them. It will give you information such as:

- Tree diagrams showing function call hierarchy
- Cross-reference of functions and files
- Use of global variables: read, write, define
- Use of functions: called, defined

An integrated code analyzer of this type will let you browse or edit the source file where a particular variable or function is used or defined. The UNIX ctags is an example of this type of code analyzer. The other type of code analyzer examines individual source files to give information such as:

- Code complexity. While not definitive, code complexity is a good indicator of how easy a piece of code will be to maintain. A good, well-priced complexity analyzer is PC-Metric from SET Laboratories. More expensive complexity analyzers will show the complexity in graphic form, which tends to be a lot more striking and useful than a number.
- Portability problems between platforms.
- Compliance to corporate coding standards. CodeCheck from Abraxas Software does this and also gives information about possible portability issues, plus complexity and maintainability information.

Tell me about code formatters.

Studies have shown that reformatting source code is one of the best ways to make it more understandable. Reformats that make the code more obvious include:

- Indentation levels for blocks controlled by if, for, while, do, etc.
- One statement per line
- Blank lines between logical blocks

Formatters generally allow you to define templates, which they use to reformat the source code to your requirements. Examples of code formatters include C Beautifier and C-Clearly for DOS, and indent on UNIX. Code formatters also take care of some of the disagreements over style by allowing you to define a ''standard'' style, then letting people reformat the code into the style they prefer when working on it. You'd then reformat the code back to the standard style before storing it in the library again.

Tell me about code generators.

Apart from CASE tools, there are several types of code generators available:

- Form generators, which allow you to draw the form on the screen.
- Graphical user interface generators, which usually let you enter information about the user interface into a graphical user interface, then generate the GUI code from your data. These tools will typically let you animate the interface once it is designed but before it is integrated with your code, allowing sliders to slide, buttons to click, etc., to give you a feel for the interface.
- Report generators, which usually work with a data dictionary. They allow you to create formatted queries then generate the code to extract the data and format the report.
- Fourth-generation languages (4GLs) which allow you to create screens and reports using a very high level language. Some 4GLs also allow you to do general update processing. 4GLs are typically non-procedural, which

means that you specify *what* you want, but not *how* to do it—you leave the implementation details up to the code generator.

Tell me about code translators.

Source code translators do one or more of these three things:

- ○ Translate unstructured code into more structured code.
- ○ Translate code into a newer, more structured, version of the language.
- ○ Translate code from one language to another.

This is beginning to get repetitious, but tell me about compilers.

Compilers allow you to write software in high-level languages. There are certainly times when it's more appropriate to write in assembler, but as a general rule it's more effective to write in a high-level language, let the compiler optimize the code, then rewrite the bottlenecks in assembler. You can usually solve speed problems by replacing between one and five percent of the debugged code with assembler.

This is both a technical decision—most modern compilers have excellent optimizers that generate better code than the average developer can produce in assembler—and a business decision—in most places it's harder to hire good assembler programmers than good high-level language programmers, and the average programmer is a lot more productive in a high-level language than in assembler.

A brief note about C. This is the "hot" language these days (C^{++} may be even hotter), which is in some ways unfortunate. C is a language that allows you to do anything, including all sorts of inappropriate things. About the only two things that can actually help you to do things right are prototype functions and lint. However, most compilers don't enforce the prototype function rules rigorously, and most don't include lint as a preprocessor option!

Fortunately, some compiler vendors allow different environments for testing and production. Products such as Saber-C and Instant-C provide additional functionality such as:

- ○ Ability to run the program in "interpreted" mode rather than compiled mode, allowing you to change, add, and delete lines while in the debugger.
- ○ Run-time checking for uninitialized pointers and uninitialized variables.
- ○ Run-time checking for improper function arguments.
- ○ Run-time checking for array indexes out of bounds.
- ○ Run-time checking for overwritten return addresses.
- ○ Incremental compiling, where only the changes are recompiled.

Tell me about debuggers.

Get a symbolic debugger that allows you to step through the source code and examine and change the values of variables by name. One of the best ways to check your software is to step through it in the source code debugger when you first run it. Doing this often makes you notice things you did wrong, or situations you didn't consider. Without a source code debugger, it's tough. The debugger should allow you to:

- Examine and change the value of variables by name
- Evaluate expressions
- Do things in octal, hex, decimal, etc.
- Set breakpoints on functions or source code line numbers
- Set conditional breakpoints
- Break when the value of a specified variable changes
- Break only after a specified number of times past a breakpoint
- Automatically execute specified procedures at breakpoints
- Trace the values of specified variables as they change
- Show the call stack with arguments
- Single step through the code
- Step into functions, over functions, or to the end of functions
- Step backwards from a point where you know an error has occurred
- Start execution from a particular line number or function
- Debug child and detached processes
- Work with screen-oriented programs without destroying the screen
- Use a graphical interface to do things
- Use macros or data files to automate repetitious tasks

Tell me about documenters.

These tools help you document your code. In particular, you can get tools that document functions, showing:

- Functions that call this function
- Functions called by this one
- Parameters
- Global variables used

What about editors?

At a minimum an editor should be screen-oriented; line-oriented editors should by now be a thing of the past. It should have all sorts of useful capabilities such as:

- Insert/overstrike mode

- ∘ Delete characters, words, lines, and blocks
- ∘ Search
- ∘ Search and replace
- ∘ Cut and paste
- ∘ Keystroke macros
- ∘ Multi-level undo
- ∘ Split screen/multiple windows
- ∘ Edit multiple files
- ∘ Matching parentheses/brackets/braces
- ∘ Automatic indent for structured programming

Additional features might include:

- ∘ Language-specific templates
- ∘ Macro programming language for repetitive tasks
- ∘ Support for popular compilers, with tracking of lines in error
- ∘ Support for popular debuggers, and other tools
- ∘ Context-sensitive help
- ∘ Column cut and paste
- ∘ Bookmarks—jump to bookmark
- ∘ Mouse support
- ∘ Graphical user interface
- ∘ Easy to tailor
- ∘ Binary file editing

A good general-purpose programming editor is Emacs, but there may be better ones for your specific environment. On the PC, Brief and MultiEdit are among the most popular.

As a final point, I would try to get everyone to use the same editor. If it's tailorable, get the best tailoring you can, and make that the standard editor. It's a lot easier to train people, and it makes it easier for programmers to help each other if everyone starts from the same powerful base—most people will probably never extend it.

What about integrated development environments?

At the most basic level, integrated development environments (IDEs) give you an editor from which you can compile, link, run, and debug the software. When you compile the code, any errors are marked in the code, and it's usually easy to go from error to error. When stepping through the code in the debugger, you can usually go from a particular line in the debugger to the same line in the editor to make changes.

Some IDEs also integrate a source code library, allowing you to reserve code while in the editor. Some integrate source code analyzers, allowing you to do things such as finding all references to a particular function call, or finding where a particular variable or function is declared.

What is lint?

"lint" is a program that looks at a C program and detects things that the compiler allowed, but which either are bugs or might be bugs. For example, lint will typically detect errors such as:

- ○ Variables that are used before being initialized
- ○ Incorrect function parameters
- ○ Incorrect variables in a printf statement
- ○ Order of evaluation problems

A typical lint will pick up suspicious things such as:

- ○ Strange indentation levels.
- ○ Statements such as *if (a=b)*—did you mean *if (a==b)*?
- ○ Statements such as *while ((i_stat=if_get_rec(ca_buff)) !=0);*—did you really want a semicolon at the end?
- ○ Nested comments, which often happen because you forgot to terminate a comment.

It will also provide information such as:

- ○ Variables that aren't used
- ○ Include files that aren't used

A good lint that I like comes from Gimpel Software—it comes as PC-Lint for the PC, and FlexeLint for UNIX, VAX/VMS, IBM VM/MVS, and various other operating systems.

Other lint-like tools include CodeCheck, an expert system that checks C or C++ for conformance with a set of user-defined rules. Thus you might extend lint functionality to include certain organization-defined standards such as indentation rules, bracketing rules, etc.

What is make?

"make" allows you to set up lists of dependencies, which it will use to rebuild your executables, compiling only the files that need to be recompiled. This is particularly important if a structure changes, and every file that references that structure needs to be recompiled. For example, if dc_data_capture.exe is created from the three files: dc_capture_data.obj, dc_process_data.obj, and dc_store_data.obj, we would indicate that dependency as:

```
dc_data_capture.exe:      dc_capture_data.obj \
                          dc_process_data.obj \
                          dc_store_data.obj
```

Implicit rules in make tell it to recompile the object files if the corresponding source files have changed since the object was last created. You can go a step further and put in specific dependencies. For example, in C, the source files include files (suffixed with .h).

```
dc_capture_data.obj:      sys_project.h \
                          sys_error.h \
                          dc_capture.h

dc_process_data.obj:      sys_project.h \
                          sys_error.h \
                          dc_capture.h \
                          dc_i_process.h

dc_store_data.obj:        sys_project.h \
                          sys_error.h \
                          dc_capture.h \
                          dc_i_database.h
```

Suppose a key structure defined in dc_capture.h changes. Errors are likely if the process is such that a software engineer has to find all the programs using that structure, and recompile them individually. On the other hand, make automatically says: "The following objects are dependent on dc_capture.h. Let's compare the date and time dc_capture.h was modified with the date and time those objects were created. If dc_capture.h is newer, we'll rebuild the objects." So we can let make take care of all the details.

Most organizations without make have experienced *version skews* at one time or another—situations where incompatible objects are linked together because one object changed, and no one realized that another object needed to be rebuilt.

Many makes will work with a source code or version control library. Besides comparing the object timestamp with the timestamps of the file it's dependent on (such as the source file and include files), it will also look at the timestamps of the library versions of those dependency files. If the source file in the library is more recent than the one in the local directory, it will extract the file from the library, and compile it.

Tell me about performance analyzers.

Performance analyzers help you improve software performance by pointing out the bottlenecks. By using a performance analyzer, you can do the bulk of your development in high-level languages for quicker development, then optimize the bottle-necks in assembler. Performance analyzers give the following types of information:

○ Information about where the program is spending time, based on the process CPU time. This gives you information about where the algorithm and function bottlenecks are. Typically, the value of the Program Counter is sampled periodically.

○ Information about where the program is spending time, based on the system or wall time. This gives you information about where the program is waiting for I/O, and where page faults are happening. Typically, the value of the Program Counter is sampled periodically.

○ Page fault information. This typically shows where the program was executing when the page fault occurred, and the memory reference that caused the page fault. Page faults occur in a virtual memory system when you need either data or program instructions that have been paged out to disc. This information is useful for analyzing your data clustering and your program structure.

○ System services or kernel calls. Performance analyzers can often show which system services calls your program makes, how often it calls them, and which parts of the program do the calls.

○ Input/Output information such as the number of opens, closes, reads, writes, flushes, renames, deletes, rewinds, and read and write byte counts.

○ Timing analysis, showing how long the program spends on source lines, functions, etc.

○ Count analysis, showing how many times source lines, functions, etc., are executed.

○ Test coverage information, showing which parts of the program are executed and which parts are not.

○ Stack usage.

A typical performance analyzer will also let you:

○ Show information in graphical, tabular, or numerical form
○ Specify only certain modules or routines to cover
○ Analyze the data by routine or by line
○ Filter data
○ Combine data from different runs

Tell me about prototyping tools.

Prototyping tools, by this definition, are tools that let you create, or at least modify, prototypes in real time—while you are sitting down with a user, designing something in collaboration.

These tools are typically fourth-generation languages that let you generate screens and reports, or user interface tools that allow you to create screens and menus and link them together. A good user interface prototyper, whether GUI or text-based, should let you animate the menu system, moving from menu to menu to screen to screen, getting a feel for the appearance, ease, consistency, and intuitiveness of the user interface.

How do source code libraries fit in?

The purpose of a source code, or revision control, library is to:

- Provide a central repository for all source code.
- Ensure that everyone can find the most up-to-date version of the code.
- Ensure that two people aren't making changes to the same piece of code at the same time, except in very controlled circumstances.
- Track the revision history and changes to each piece of source code.
- Provide the ability to go back to any previous version of the code.

A source code library will typically:

- Store all the source code modules (most libraries will store and track both text and binary files).
- Allow you to check out software modules, provided no one else has the module checked out.
- Allow you to check back in a software module after changing it.
- Keep track of all the changes between different versions of the module.
- Show you the differences between different versions of a module.
- Give you a listing showing the version in which each line was added or modified.
- Keep track of the revision history of each module.
- Allow you to group software modules so that a number of related modules can be checked out or checked in under a single group name.
- Mark all checked-in modules as requiring review.
- Allow you to define a release and include specified versions of specified modules in the release.
- Allow you to build an executable file from any specified release in the library.

○   Allow you to start new variants of a module. The standard version number sequence might be 1, 2, 3, etc., and a new variant sequence might be 1, 2, 2a1, 2a2, etc. This allows you to track custom changes.

○   Have an override that will allow several people to check out the same module. The library remembers that there were multiple check-outs of the module, and either requires that all but one be checked in as variants, or flags the software in such a way that a merge of the changes is done either on check-in or on the next check-out.

What about test tools?

Test tools do the following sorts of things:

○   Analyze the test coverage.
○   Capture and replay keystrokes and mousestrokes.
○   Compare screens and output files from different tests, allowing you to mask things such as timestamps to prevent comparison of things that are bound to be different.
○   Allow you to group individual tests into test suites, and play entire test suites through.

Test tools are useful for creating regression tests that can be run after software modifications to ensure that nothing was broken. Regression testing is not done particularly well by people sitting at keyboards. It's better to set up test suites that can be run time after time in the same ways. Every time an error is found and fixed, add a test for that symptom. If you yourself don't plan to integrate testing capabilities into your software, you should definitely investigate test managers.

What is CASE?

CASE is computer-aided software engineering. Despite the relative newness of the acronym CASE, computer-aided software engineering has been around for a long time. Let's take a look at a brief history.

When computers were first invented, people wrote software at the machine level. The next big step was the invention of assembler, which allowed people to write things like MOVL A B—move longword at symbolic location A to symbolic location B. A software program took care of translating programs dealing with symbolic locations into instructions the machine could understand.

Next came higher-level languages, where programmers could do in one instruction something that had taken several assembler instructions. The corresponding tools were the compiler and interpreter. And along with assemblers, compilers, and interpreters came debuggers—another computer tool to help with the software engineering process. Then came 4GLs, fourth-generation languages, which would do in a single statement what previously took several using languages such as Cobol and C. Often the 4GLs were non-procedural, allowing people to specify *what* they wanted done, without having to specify *how* it should be done.

All these computer tools were applicable at the individual program level, making it easier to write better programs more quickly. However, programmers could still write unstructured code to solve the wrong problem. They could still write large systems that had incompatible interfaces and huge holes in the solution.

So computer-aided software engineering had to provide tools to help with these problems. And now we are getting into the area that most people think of when they talk about CASE. As of today, most CASE tools do a specific task: analysis, design, screen creation, etc., although some do several related tasks, such as analysis and design. None can generate code from general requirements, although some will generate code in well-defined problem domains such as database access or window/menu systems. There is a lot of work going on to provide full development environments where you can use your CASE tool of choice for each component of the process, and the output from one CASE tool will provide the input into the next component, but the promise still lies in the future.

What are the advantages of using CASE?

- ◦ CASE tools will generate code for well-understood applications such as database access and user interface systems. You never have to modify any code: just modify the design and regenerate the code.

- ◦ CASE allows you to do analysis and design on a computer instead of on paper. Software engineers tend to feel they are not working unless they are sitting at a keyboard. Computerized analysis and design tools make it rather more likely that there will be some analysis and design. (Remember the idea of getting things as right as possible up front to reduce rework?)

- ◦ CASE forces a rigorous approach to analysis and design. Few people know how to do analysis and design well, and even fewer actually do it. To implement CASE involves first implementing some methodologies, and then implementing the computer tools. If you take seriously the idea of reducing rework and constantly look for ways to help, you soon and inevitably run up against doing analysis and design better. Using CASE forces you to pay more attention to analysis and design methodologies.

- ◦ CASE tools make it easy to create documents that can be distributed and reviewed. They give you the opportunity to communicate among people.

- ◦ CASE tools make it easy to reprint diagrams when changes are made, rather than having to go through a tedious redrawing process. They make it more likely that designs will be up-to-date.

      ○ CASE tools can check the consistency of your design, ensuring that inter-
faces match.

What are the disadvantages of using CASE?

I have some serious reservations about the use of CASE tools in software development. Certainly the control they give you over revisions to designs and solutions is
worth having, as is the code generation that a few tools provide. But I believe that
until CASE tools in general can create code from the requirements there are some
major problems with the use of integrated CASE tools. One problem is inherent in
the software development process using CASE, and the other is psychological.

    The problem inherent in the process is that the CASE environment doesn't
make it easy to test the requirements and test solutions. CASE channels you
towards creating the requirements, then creating a solution, then creating an architecture and design, all sequentially and all on the computer. There is an implicit
assumption that customers know what they want, which is rarely the case (excuse
the pun). Thus CASE tools tend to force you to develop in a manner ineffective for
creating solutions to tough problems where a lot of feedback is needed.

    The psychological problem is that people have a tendency to focus on the
CASE process rather than on the end product. There grows a fascination with the
boxes and arrows on the computer screen and the focus becomes the data structures
and processes represented in the diagrams. There is a feeling of control over the
intellectual product. Meanwhile, the customer is ignored because reality is messy
and gets in the way of the elegant solution.

    CASE implementations have a mixed success rate, largely because of these
problems. CASE succeeds best where the problem is well-defined and well-understood, and fails most where the problem is ill-defined and poorly understood. Of
course, if the software you write is solving well-defined problems, integrated CASE
tools may prove very useful.

What are the limitations of CASE?

The biggest limitation of CASE today is the inability to generate code from the
requirements, except in well-understood applications. This means you still have a
fairly lengthy process of creating a design, then creating and testing code, all to
meet a set of requirements that are probably flawed.

    I believe that CASE tools in the future will be able to generate code for ever
more sophisticated applications, but the leading edge software will always be a step
ahead of the capabilities of CASE. Fortunately, most software development is not
leading edge, so CASE will be able to automate an increasing percentage of applications as time goes by, leaving people to focus on getting the requirements right.

Doesn't the idea of CASE go against what Tom Peters preaches?

Yes and no. In books like *A Passion for Excellence*, Tom Peters describes how small, highly motivated groups of people let loose can far outperform large groups that follow so-called good techniques. I think Peters is right—*if* you can create a group of highly motivated, highly talented people, people who are willing to put in tremendous work and effort. But that's hard to do. Many people have a family life they're not prepared to sacrifice, and half the people have below average talent. You need to find the right people, you need to find a catalyst around whom the group can form, you need management capable of supporting it properly, and you need to be prepared to either burn the people out or reward them in extraordinary ways.

The IBM-New York Times project done by Harlan Mills and Terry Baker is always quoted as an example of such success. But why is it always quoted? Because it's one of the few great successes. Most of the time, in most organizations, you have to make do with the people you have, who on the average have average talents. In this environment, big projects need lots of people. Lots of people doing software in traditional ways means lots of communication to go wrong and lots of misunderstanding. Modern CASE tools help with communication and understanding.

Why don't more organizations use CASE tools?

Quite a few organizations do use CASE. Military contractors are the most obvious group, largely because many CASE tools automatically generate the documents required to conform to the DOD-STD-2167A standard. Software houses creating software for sale or doing contract work seem to be the most resistant to using CASE, partly because of the expense and partly because of the mindset that you need total freedom to be creative. Ironically, software developers have been automating the rest of the world, but resisting automation themselves. So vendors of CASE have two problems—how to solve the technical problems, and how to persuade software developers that CASE really works.

There seem to be several reasons for organizations not using CASE, but ultimately it comes down to the fact that people don't think it will do much for them. The bottom line is that everyone knows they need an assembler, interpreter, or compiler. Most people know they need a debugger. But who knows that they need CASE? ''We've always done it this way and it's worked for us.'' But it hasn't really worked—there has just never been a choice.

By and large the natural domain of CASE is the huge project, which, by its nature, is most likely to be based on platforms other than the PC. The more expensive the platform, the more expensive the CASE tools, and who wants to pay tens of thousands of dollars for something they don't even know they need. At the PC level where the tools are cheapest, they are least likely to be integrated, and people are likely to have the greatest concerns about their effectiveness. There's also the concern about the quality and performance of generated code, especially at the PC level where products in fiercely competitive areas, like word processing, have to be *fast*.

Even if the CASE tool is cheap, there's a cost to trying it. It can be a significant investment in time, people, and money. Most software groups are late with their current products. How are they going to invest people and money in experiments? Users have found that it can take several months before people are even productive using CASE tools, and up to a year before people are more productive than before.

After all these negatives, why should you use CASE?

Because the industry *does* change over time. Tools to help software development do get created and do help. Assemblers found acceptance, as did compilers, as did debuggers. Why should tool development stop with them? Even today, CASE tools can help in some situations, and unless you investigate them and are prepared to experiment a little, you'll never be able to take advantage of them.

One thing you can be sure about—if CASE tools do provide competitive advantages, someone will eventually be using them while competing with you. Whether it's another company, or another country taking that next step, such as Japan doing with software what it did with manufacturing, it's guaranteed to happen.

How should one go about justifying and using CASE?

Using CASE is just another business decision. You put money in now in the hope of getting more back in the long term. There are ways of staggering its implementation so that not everyone becomes unproductive immediately. A good way would be to implement CASE on a single project, with people who want to try it. If that works, expand the scope to other projects as they start. Another method would be to get some of the better software engineers involved first so they can figure it out, and then have them teach the others.

Ask vendors for trial versions of their software. Ask for a videotape demonstration of a CASE product to save you time and expense in learning it. Ask for self-paced training materials.

Further Reading

Darwin, Ian. 1991. *Checking C Programs with lint.* Sebastopol, CA: O'Reilly & Associates.

Fisher, Alan. 1988. *CASE: Using Software Development Tools.* New York: Wiley.

Kernighan, Brian, and P.J. Plaugher. 1976. *Software Tools.* Reading, MA: Addison-Wesley.

Lewis, T.G. 1991. *CASE: Computer Aided Software Engineering.* New York: Van Nostrand Reinhold.

McClure, Carma. 1989. *CASE is Software Automation.* Englewood Cliffs, NJ: Prentice-Hall.

Schindler, Max. 1990. *Computer Aided Software Design.* New York: Wiley.

Talbott, Steve. 1991. *Managing Projects with make.* Sebastapol, CA: O'Reilly & Associates

Summary

Tools make software development easier because they let us do three things: leverage our abilities, do things previously impossible, and alter our framework for thinking and problem solving. Poor or non-existent tools can make development very frustrating; correspondingly, good tools can make development more fun and thus more productive. This chapter discussed various software development tools.

PART 2

The Software Life-Cycle

7

Requirements through Coding

What is the relationship between requirements, analysis, design, functional specs, and so on?

If you've ever tried to fully understand the relationship between requirements, analysis, design, functional specifications, and so on, you've probably come to the conclusion that it's all very complicated. There are several reasons for this. First, people mean different things when they refer to the different documents and phases. Second, each software project is different. Third, there isn't a clear-cut switchover point between phases.

Give me examples of people meaning different things.

Okay, let's go through the different phases and documents that cause the most problems: analysis, requirements, and functional specification.

Analysis. Also called requirements analysis, problem analysis. Some authors consider the analysis simply the analysis of the problem, with the appropriate diagrams. Others consider it to include the proposed functional solution. This phase may include analysis of the different options and feasibility studies. The waters get really muddied here because to do an options analysis means to look at different designs and their implications. So design is now happening before requirements, although you must of course have an idea of what you want before starting the options analysis!

Requirements.   Sometimes called requirements document, marketing requirements document (MRD), requirements specification, software requirements specification, functional requirements, functional specification, or functional description. The goal of the requirements document is to describe *what* the software will do, and the constraints that will be imposed on it in that effort. *How* the software will do its stuff is described in the Preliminary Design phase. There is little agreement on whether the Functional Specification is included in the requirements, mainly because of disagreement over what the Functional Specification is. Similarly, some people consider the user interface to be part of the requirements, while to some it's part of the design, to some it's the main part of the functional spec, and to others it has its own phase. The requirements document is often created by the marketing department and given to the development organization.

Functional Specification.   Sometimes called functional requirements specification or functional requirements document. It shows the user's view of the system, listing the functionality and features required. Different people mean different things by the functional spec—to some it is simply a listing of the required functionality, without showing how the system will operate. To others, the functional spec shows the user interface, and shows the various processes, with a description of the input, output, and data transformations in the process. To the former set of people, the functional specification is part of the requirements document, while to the latter, the functional spec is tightly bound with the design—it's part of the solution.

The lack of agreement on names and phases is compounded by the type of problem posed by reports. Is a particular report layout a requirement, or just one possible solution to a particular requirement? If report layouts appear in the Functional Spec, does that make the Functional Spec part of the requirements or part of the solution? It's fairly common for organizations that are technically driven rather than marketing-driven to start with the functional specification rather than with a requirements document. However, this makes it more likely that the real requirements aren't fully met.

How does each project being different affect the phases?

When writers describe software models, they have specific examples in mind, and few of them are exactly like your project. Let's consider various facets of a project.

Maintenance or new systems.   Most software projects are simply improvements to what is already there. Little analysis needs to be done. We start with some functional requirements, then move on to the design.

Computerizing what exists or using the computerization to improve what exists.   When we are doing analysis with a view to computerizing a manual business system, we may be trying to understand the manual process so that we can replicate it. On the other hand, we are sometimes not too concerned about how an existing system works, but are more interested in what people want out of the system and with giving them what they want.

The size of project.   If the project can be done by a single person, the documentation produced will be geared more at the review cycle, to help get things right. If the project needs large numbers of people, the documentation must also describe the interfaces between components for other people.

The type of software system.   Business systems, for example, often have predictable, known solutions. The important part of the development process is modeling the existing system to understand the requirements, then inventing a new system to perhaps improve the business system. Engineering software, on the other hand, often has a well-understood problem but no known solution, so research, feasibility studies, and prototyping technical solutions are a large part of the development process.

With some new systems, the problem is often vague and ill-defined. It's not until a solution has been created that we have a better understanding of the problem we're trying to solve. Problems like these have been called "wicked problems." Imagine trying to create the first desktop publishing program for example.

And some problems require no analysis. It's well-understood what has to be done, and so it's just a matter of describing the interface and designing the modules. Creating a linked list manager is an example.

Who will be using the software.   If the software has human users, you will need to create a user's guide at some time. If the software is simply called by other software, no user's guide will usually be created, but you'll need an Interface Specification.

Department of Defense-related or not.   If the project is DOD related, you'll probably have to use the process defined in DOD-STD-2167A.

Abilities of developers.   The better the developers, the more they can do and the more they can keep in their minds at the same time—the greater the overall picture they can maintain. Thus prototyping becomes more of an alternative. The less able the developers, the more they will need documents to work from.

The way individual developers work.   Some developers are more effective if they can design as they code, working in a prototype manner. It's as quick for them to type the code in as it is to write pseudocode on paper, and in doing so, they discover better designs, using cut and paste to modify the design.

You mentioned that there isn't a clear-cut line between the phases.

There are several reasons, the first being that it's very hard, perhaps impossible, to get a phase completely right first time. Doing the design will often show you things that you missed or got wrong in the requirements. You'll learn more of what you missed when you've finished the implementation (remember that users often don't understand what they want until they see it, they are unused to specifying every detail, and they overlook things). Doing the coding will point out errors in the design.

What you do in the next phase will often show you errors or omissions in this phase or a previous phase. The software process is iterative—you do the best you can in any phase, then you learn more in the next phase and go back and improve things in a previous phase.

Second, much as you might like to separate out the *what* from the *how*, life isn't like that. As you decide what you will do, you also think about how you will do it. People can't stay strictly in one phase—our minds don't work that way. While analyzing, we're also thinking of solutions. While doing a high-level design, we're also thinking of the design details. While doing a low-level design, we're also thinking of coding issues.

The phases we're describing are not discrete, sequential events. Each phase is iterative within itself and iterative with respect to the stages around it. For example, the design will be continually refined, with design reviews providing feedback and ideas on how to improve it—it's iterative within itself. While doing the design, it may become apparent that we are missing functionality, requiring a change in the functional specification. While writing the user guide, it may become apparent that something is too clumsy to use, or that it's impossible to do something the user will want to do, which may require changes to the design. So the diagram we looked at in Chapter 1 really looks something like this:

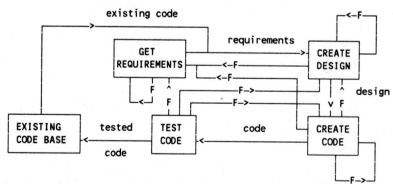

F = feedback loop

Let me give you a real-life example. I worked for a company that developed software on workstations, but it was English-language only. We wanted to internationalize the software so that it could put up menus and messages in other languages, and so that people could enter text in their own language. The company has distributors around the world—Canada, South America, Europe, and Asia.

What were the requirements? Simply to provide a way to translate menus, etc., into the language of the country where the software would be sold? When the design was investigated, it turned out that it would be relatively easy to implement a scheme that used one byte per character, just like the current English version. However, a single-byte scheme wouldn't cover all languages, nor would a single character set. ISO-Latin would cover the western European nations, but would not allow some of the accented characters of eastern Europe, let alone Cyrillic. To do Asian languages such as Kanji would require a multi-byte-per-character scheme, which would be quite a bit more costly to implement. However, if the user interface could be replaced with something like Motif, the multi-byte capability would come for free, but the software would have to be totally restructured to take advantage of Motif's capabilities.

So what were the requirements? Perhaps it depended on the cost and timeframe for implementation, and that should have been specified up front. Not so easy. Perhaps the company could afford 10 person years for a scheme that would cover all languages, but only 3 person years for a West European solution. How do you specify that without knowing the options? And perhaps the company might specify no more than 10 person years for an all-language solution, but if it turned out the solution would take 11, they'd agree, but they'd have preferred the 3 person year West European solution if they'd known about it.

To do the options analysis means looking into possible designs up to the point where you understand the implications about feasibility, cost, and timeframe. Then you can make a decision about which option you want, and create the requirements from the option you've selected. The process now looks like: *Have a rough idea of what you want; look into the options by looking at the different designs; choose an option; create the requirements; do the design, etc.* Even if you wanted to do things in a strict sequential fashion, reality has a way of getting in the way and forcing you to do things out of sequence and in circles.

If there's not a clear distinction between phases and it's difficult to get them right, why do we go for the "Do it all then deliver it" approach?

Otherwise known as the Big Bang or Waterfall approach. People use this approach because it's required, it's what they are most familiar with, or it's what they're most comfortable with. The idea that software development consists of distinct, clearly defined steps gives people a feeling of much greater control than does a recognition that software development is a messy, iterative process, where things change after they are done. The Waterfall approach would work perfectly if people had perfect foresight, but omniscient developers are hard to find.

There are other approaches, such as prototyping and evolutionary delivery, that produce better results because they recognize the essential, iterative nature of software development. However, the phases and documents we've talked about have their place in any system of delivery. It's just that you have to understand that process is iterative and that the Big Bang approach is not necessarily the best.

If the development is as poorly defined as this, what can I do?

Let's start from first principles. Up to the point of coding, the process will go something like this (bearing in mind that certain phases will be done in conjunction with other phases):

- Analyze and understand the problem.
- Gather and understand any other requirements and constraints.
- Describe the resource constraints.
- Describe the functionality—what it must do, not how.
- Describe the attributes or constraints on the functionality.
- Invent the new system.
- Describe the solution—what it will do, how it fits together, how it will appear to the user.
- Design the software modularization and its interfaces.
- Design the workings of each software module.

Tell me more about each part of this.

Analyze and understand the problem.   The analysis phase is an attempt to understand and describe the problem, prior to creating the requirements for the solution. It's important to remember that the analysis is not the goal—the analysis is only useful if it helps you come up with a good solution. Also the analysis stage may or may not be significant.

Let's look at three things you could be doing:

- Enhancing existing software. You probably have a good understanding of the problem, and the main difficulty will be modifying the existing design to accommodate your new needs.

- Automating an existing process. You will be analyzing the inter-relationships of the data, looking at the events and the actions they cause.

- Creating something totally new. You will be analyzing the problems that you might be able to solve, trying to get a feel for what you can do and what you think people will want.

In the analysis document, you should concentrate on describing the problem, and avoid coming up with a solution. To understand the exact problem you want to solve may involve doing an options analysis, i.e., looking at the various options and getting a feel for the implications (time, cost, etc.) for each one. This may involve doing some preliminary design on each one. The analysis phase may also do a feasibility study to determine if the thing you want to do is even possible, or what it will involve.

Gather and understand any other requirements and constraints.   There are bound to be other requirements and constraints. You have to understand the cost, manpower, hardware, and timeframe goals. You have to get a feel for rates of data flow, for required response times, for ease of use requirements, for ease of modification requirements. And so on. The most difficult part of this phase is to understand the additional requirements and constraints in measurable terms. If you have no measurement to aim for, you can't tell if you satisfied those requirements and constraints.

Describe the resource constraints.   This is the first part of what we'll call the requirements specification. You specify how long the project should take, how much money it should cost, how many people you have to work on it. Of course, once the design is better understood, you may find that the resource constraints are at odds with the functionality and attribute requirements, in which case you'll have to change something.

Describe the functionality—what it must do, not how.   This is the second part of what we'll call the requirements specification. In it we describe the functionality we need. We do not mention how things will work, only what will be provided. Thus the user interface is not described here. Note that if you use Data Flow Diagrams at this point, you may be showing an implementation. On the other hand, State Transition Diagrams show what will happen if we are in state A, and get input B.

Describe the attributes or constraints on the functionality.   By themselves, statements of functionality are not enough—you need to describe their attributes. Response time, rate of transaction processing, rate of data flow, and time to do things are all attributes of the functionality, and if you don't describe them, the system isn't likely to satisfy them. Attributes of the system, such as quality, maintainability, etc., should all be specified in measurable terms. If you can't measure it, you can't design for it and you can't test for it. What does quality mean? Mean time between failures? Number of crashes a month? Number of user complaints? What does maintainability mean? Number of person months required to add specified functionality? Number of global variables used? You need to specify each attribute in clearly measurable terms; otherwise you won't get what you think you want.

Invent the new system.   Once you understand the problem and have specified the functional requirements, their attributes, and the resource constraints, you can invent the new system. In reality, you will probably be inventing parts, if not all, of the system as you are gathering and documenting the requirements and their attributes. In fact, sometimes you think of certain requirements only when you've thought of solutions. Since the user interface affects how users perceive the system, try to invent this in conjunction with users. Prototype the user interface if possible.

Describe the solution—what it will do, how it fits together, how it will appear to the user.   At the risk of muddying the waters, let's call this the Functional Specification. In it you'll describe what the software will do, how things fit together, and how the system will appear to the user. The designers will use this document to design the software. The test organization will use it to make sure the software does what it's supposed to do.

Design the software modularization and its interfaces.   In this phase, you modularize the software in a way that gives a structure that is efficient, flexible, and maintainable. You design the file access, the data structures, and the error handling, and specify all the interfaces. With modern windowing schemes using User Interface Languages (UIL), you can create the user interface relatively independently of the software design. So it's possible for user interface experts to refine the user interface independently of the software designers.

Design the workings of each software module.   You take each module in the high-level design and describe all the interfaces, return values, algorithms, error handling, etc. You may describe the module logic in structured English or pseudocode.

How do these all relate to the normal documents we hear about?

Let's go through the list again, putting it into sections.

- ○ Analysis
  - • Analyze and understand the problem.
  - • Possibly do an options analysis or a feasibility study.
  - • Possibly create an *Analysis document* with data flow diagrams, etc.
- ○ Requirements
  - • Gather and understand any other requirements and constraints.
  - • Describe the resource constraints.
  - • Describe the functionality—what it must do, not how.
  - • Describe the attributes or constraints on the functionality.

- Create a *Requirements document*, with sections for:
    - General requirements such as timeframe, cost, resource, quality, etc., all described in measurable terms.
    - Functional requirements, in terms of what, not how.
    - Attributes of the functional requirements (speed, rates, flows, etc.). (Very often, especially with maintenance-type development, the requirements document will end up consisting of the last two parts: functional requirements and attributes, and will be simply called a Functional Specification.)
  - Solution
    - Prototype the user interface if possible.
    - Describe the solution in the *Functional Specification*:
        - What the software will do.
        - How it fits together.
        - How it will appear to the user.
    - Create a *User Guide*, showing how the user will do things that he or she wants to do. This is an extremely effective tool for helping understand whether the requirements are correct and the design will work. It should be filled with examples of how to do particular tasks, because examples are how people learn best. The act of writing the user guide often provides insights into where the design is flawed or the requirements are incomplete. It's often the case that the functional spec and the design look good in a vacuum, and the flaws show only when you try to describe how to use the software.
    - Design the software modularization and its interfaces.
    - Create a *Preliminary*, or *high-level Software Design document*.
    - Design the workings of each software module, usually in pseudocode or some other language for describing programming or algorithmic details.
    - Create a *Detailed*, or *low-level Software Design document*.

Show me a diagram of all this.

Here's a diagram that shows the approximate times of the different components in the normal software cycle. But remember, the process is iterative, not cleanly defined as it appears in the diagram.

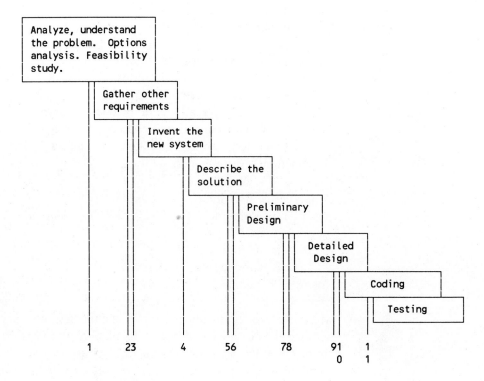

1. Possible analysis document

2. Requirements Document, including:
    • General requirements
    • Functional requirements
    • Attribute requirements

3. Review Requirements Document

4. User Interface prototype

5. Functional Specification

6. Review Functional Specification

7. User Guide
    Preliminary, or high-level, Design Document
    Test Plans

8. Review User Guide
    Review preliminary, or high-level, Design Document
    Review test plans

9. Detailed Design Document

10. Review Detailed Design Document

11. Code review

How do you decide when to review the documents?

There's a separate chapter on Reviews, Chapter 27.

How do you keep the documents up-to-date in an iterative development cycle?

Each document should have an identified audience, most of whom are "customers" for the document: marketing, support organization, QA organization, documentation group, future developers, other development groups, etc. Each customer has a real need for an accurate, high-quality document. So if a developer learns something that will require a change to the document, someone should update the document and distribute the new information to the document customers.

If the changes are major, you should probably distribute the whole document with some form of change bars to show the changes. If the changes are minor and the document large, distribute a document showing just the changes. Of course people should be able to get copies of the main, updated document if they need it. If any of the customers feel that the changes should be reviewed, you should schedule a new review.

People are so busy. How do you make sure they read the changes?

The easiest way is to require their signature to show that they agree with the changes. With the modifications, include a sign-off sheet that you collect from the customers.

```
Document:      _____

Revision:      _____

Date:          _____


Name:          _____

Signature:     _____


Accept as is:          _____

Accept with changes:   _____

Needs review:          _____


Changes:
```

Further Reading

DeGrace, Peter, and Leslie Hulet Stahl. 1990. *Wicked Problems, Righteous Solutions.* Englewood Cliffs, NJ: Yourdon Press.

Summary

This chapter discussed the different phases of software development and the documents associated with them. We showed that there is neither a clear agreement on what each phase is, nor a clear boundary between phases.

We then tried to describe in practical terms the different things that usually have to be done in a software development project, and the different documents that are produced.

8

Maintenance

Despite the importance of new product development, the costs of new products are largely just the tip of the iceberg—most software costs occur while maintaining the software between the initial release and when it becomes obsolete. Various studies have shown that up to 80 percent of software life-cycle costs are devoted to software maintenance.

Why do we need to maintain software?

There are several reasons:

- To fix errors, whether oversights or bugs
- New functionality is requested
- The environment is changing, e.g., the software must:
  - Port to another operating system
  - Provide full international support
  - Work with a new graphical user interface scheme
  - Support a new type of terminal or workstation
  - Support a new type of printer
  - Support more users

In fact, studies have shown that about 20 percent of maintenance work goes toward fixing errors, 25 percent to adapting the software to changes in the environment, 42 percent toward meeting new user requests, and the remaining 13 percent toward improving efficiency, documentation, etc.

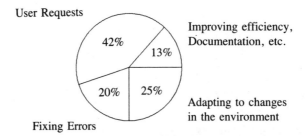

Why is maintaining software so expensive?

Let's start by looking at the software development cycle picture again.

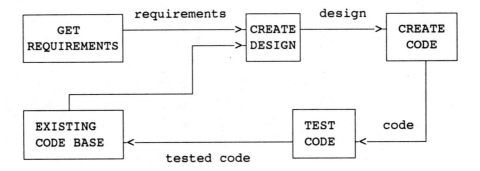

The development process goes round and round until the product becomes obsolete. Each time it goes round, the quality of the existing code base partly determines the quality of the next code base. There are two main reasons that the quality of the code base suffers:

○ There is so much emphasis on getting the product out that the costs and issues of future maintenance are often overlooked. When the product is developed:
  • Not enough thought is given to what users may want next.
  • Not enough thought is given to possible operating system ports, new printers, new terminals, etc.
  • Not enough thought is given to designing for change—good modularization, structured techniques, hiding of implementation details, etc.
  • Too many shortcuts are taken to meet schedules.
○ It's not easy to change the code correctly.
  • Introducing a change often has hidden side effects. Studies have shown that fixing an error has a 20 to 50 percent chance of introducing another error.

- Studies have shown that if a modification requires less than 10 program instructions, there's a 50 percent chance of getting it right the first time. If the number of instructions goes up to 50, the chance of getting it right the first time goes down to 20 percent.
- The person modifying the code is often not the person who originally created it. The creator usually has the whole concept in his mind, plus all the details, and he understands the interrelationships. The maintenance person is less likely to have all this knowledge.
- Maintenance is often done by a separate group of less-experienced software engineers. The maintenance group is often where new developers are first placed.
- There's a stigma attached to maintenance programming—it's not as challenging as new development, and you don't get to learn new techniques and new tools; thus motivation suffers.
- A fix made in crisis mode is often done as a quick fix, rather than as a well-thought-out change that may require restructuring of the software.
- Problems are often solved by introducing new global variables.
- After a while you often end up with patches on patches. The code soon becomes awful and more and more time is spent maintaining it.
- The product has gone through too many iterations without being rewritten.

So what can we do?

Prevention is better than cure, so to get a maintainable system, our first choice is that we don't have to change it. Failing that, we should design it for change. Our goals for a maintainable system should thus be:

- ○ Not to have to change the software.
- ○ Design the system for change, keeping in mind that the software should be:
  - Easy to understand
  - Easy to modify correctly
  - Easy to test

Let's go through each goal in turn.

How can we avoid having to change the software?

We can rarely avoid changes completely, but we can minimize them by:

- ○ Getting the requirements as correct as possible up front: through prototyping, better requirements and analysis techniques, and reviews of the requirements and analyses.
- ○ Thinking about future hardware and operating system requirements.

- Designing software with no hardware/operating system dependencies.
- Allocating memory dynamically when you know how much you need, rather than allocating fixed amounts before you know how much you need.
- Determining sizes of things by calculation if possible. If this is not possible, determine the sizes by reading a file or looking at an environment variable. Hard code as little as possible.
- Using a database that supports fourth-generation languages (4GLs) so users can create their own reports.
- Implementing designs with fewer people and thus fewer interfaces between people leads to fewer bugs.
- Hiring better people for software development.
- Storing data in third normal form (there's more information about third normal form in the design section of Chapter 13, ''The Solution'').
- Using defensive programming techniques to avoid having to fix bugs:
  - Check passed parameters for valid data (make sure pointers aren't null, etc.).
  - Check input data for validity.
  - Check that pointer arithmetic doesn't lead to invalid pointers.
  - Check that division by zero can't happen.
  - Check that array indexes are in bounds.
- Using standard library routines where possible to avoid having to make bug fixes.
- Having a chargeback scheme so users won't ask for unjustifiable changes.
- Including an experienced maintenance person in the design reviews for new products.
- Never relying on how a particular compiler or computer implements things—if it's not part of the standard language specification, do things explicitly. For example, on one platform, variables may be initialized to zero, but on another platform, they are not. On the other hand, global variables in ANSI C are, by language definition, initialized to zero.
- Never relying on side effects of function calls. If the effect isn't documented, it may change.
- Having the software report on conditions it can't handle, but not crash. The software should be able to continue if at all possible.
- For databases, when possible creating additional unused storage in each record so that when new fields are added, you don't have to recreate everyone's database. Ensure that additional data is initialized to zero. If the database requires individual fields, integers are probably the most useful. Otherwise just reserve a string of the appropriate size.

How do we make the software easy to understand?

- Consistent style.

- No clever/trick/obscure code (if trick code is absolutely necessary to get required performance, document it extremely well).
- Standard language features.
- Minimize complex data structures.
- Define structures, etc., in a few obvious places, so people can find them easily.
- Simplicity.
- Standardized documentation for functions.
- Good documentation for blocks of code; show "what" and "why."
- Distinguishing between quick fixes and well-thought-out, well-tested changes in comments.
- Good modularization.
- Good program structure and layout.
  - White space between logical blocks aids comprehension.
  - Good indentation has been found to have a dramatic effect on comprehension.
- Tools such as documenters, diagrammers, and formatters to make the code visually appealing and to provide additional visual information.
- Choosing a language that aids comprehension by long variable names and control structures, such as while, case, for.
- Naming conventions.
- Meaningful names.
- Tools to check the code for conformance to organization rules.

How do we make the software easy to modify correctly?

- Make the software easy to understand.
- Use good modularization (see Chapter 14, "Modularization").
- Use good program structure.
- Generalize the software to make it flexible (not to the point that simplicity is lost).
- Use table-driven techniques to control flow, rather than multiple tests.
- If there are hardware/operating system dependencies, use generalized calls for these functions, then hide the hardware/OS dependencies in machine/OS-specific modules.
- Don't let the main software know about I/O or about specific devices; hide the details of the following in separate layers:
  - File access
  - Screen access
  - Printer access
- Isolate functions that are likely to change in separate modules.
- Design function interfaces for expected or likely changes.
- Provide a precise and complete definition of inter-module interfaces.

- Dissociate the user interface from the processing logic.
- Identify programs/systems on which too much money is spent and rewrite them using better techniques.
- Do not use global variables.
- Use variables for one thing only.
- Use a database management system.
- Use fourth-generation languages (4GLs).
- Don't use hard-coded values.
- Keep all #defines, etc., in one place.
- Keep all structure definitions in one place.

How do we make the software easy to test?

- Have a built-in testing capability to do regression testing and save and play back test cases.
- Have the ability to do tracking and to show on request:
  - All function parameters
  - All other input
  - Program flow and intermediate values
- Have the ability to restart from specified points.
- Have good error reporting.
- Have good modularization.
- Use reusable software (library functions).
- Use test managers.

You've concentrated on the technical side of maintenance—what about the non-technical side?

Let's look at the following aspects from the non-technical side:

- Make new products more maintainable.
- Make maintenance easier.
- Reduce the stigma of maintenance.
- Improve the quality of software changes.

Remember again that we must help the individual software developers by improving the systems in which they work. Change the system to make it easy for individuals to do things well.

How do you make new products more maintainable?

- Hire better people for software development.
- Adopt the conventions and techniques described throughout this book.

- Start people in maintenance and require that they periodically write down what they have learned:
  - What went badly; what difficulties did we encounter?
  - How can we avoid those things in the next project?
  - What activities improved the way things were done?
  - How can we make those things permanent?
    Require that they put into practice what they have learned and documented both while they are doing maintenance and when they move into new development.
- Train people to look at everything from the perspective that it will be changed, expanded, or modified.
- Make sure one of the people in technical reviews is looking at the product from the perspective of maintainability and ease of change.
- Make maintainability an obvious, visible priority. Studies have shown that people achieve their top priority. In an experiment, two comparable programmers were asked to write a program to perform a particular task, but were given different objectives: one was given efficiency as his priority, and the other was given simplicity. The efficient program contained 10 times as many errors as the simple program.
- Have the maintenance group document what they consider poor practices in the software and what would make life easier for them. Managers of the maintenance group should consolidate all the suggestions into a single document and discuss the list with managers of the new development department. At a minimum, changes should be based on a cost-benefit analysis, but ideally all changes that improve the process should be implemented.
- Have a "maintenance acceptance test." Have an independent party insert at least ten bugs, at random and one at a time, into the software. The maintenance group accepts the software if assigned and trained maintenance programmers can find at least 90 percent of the bugs within 30 minutes (this doesn't include fixing and testing the fix). Because the development group wants the maintenance programmers to find the bugs easily, they now have a strong incentive to follow standards, to document well, and to modularize well.
- Document which developers consistently have poor practices. Train these people.
- Rotate people between maintenance and new development. They should take the lessons with them.

How do you make maintenance easier?

- Hire good people for doing maintenance.
- Give maintenance people tools that help, tools for formatting, documenting, cross-referencing, restructuring, etc.

- ○ Make maintenance people responsible for modules; expect them to give talks on the code once they have learned it.
- ○ Make maintenance people document all the functions that they are responsible for. The documentation should include:
  - Function overview
  - Caller obligations
  - Function obligations
  - Parameters
  - Acceptable/unacceptable values
  - Global variables used
  - Return values
  - Error reporting done (displayed, added to linked list, etc.)
  - Danger points—potential problems
  - Limitations
  - Assumptions
  - Dependencies
  - Impact of changes on other modules
  - Where the function is called from (non-library functions only)
  - Functions called
- ○ Make sure maintainers document their changes well. The revision history should contain:
  - The revision number. This should also appear in comments at each change.
  - The reason for the change—what the programmer is trying to accomplish.
  - Details of the change.
- ○ Rewrite poor modules either on a worst-first basis, or when the next change has to be made to the module. The 80/20 rule says that the majority of the changes will be made to a small number of programs. The ''poorness'' of the module may be determined in a variety of ways:
  - Greater than a certain size.
  - Greater than a certain age.
  - Greater than a certain complexity (defined as you think necessary: too many different things being done, too many levels of indentation, too many gotos, too high a cyclomatic complexity value, etc.)
  - Has had more than a certain number of changes already made to it.
  - Has had more than a certain number of errors reported against it.
  - Has had more than a certain cost associated with changes or bug fixes to it (lifetime, per year, per month, etc.).
- ○ Rewrite the modules that change the most often to be more generalized, to be table-driven rather than to handle specific instances (generalization should aid simplicity, not get in its way).

- ○ Redo modules to pass lint or similar code-checking tools.
- ○ Keep a record of accumulated wisdom for future maintainers.

How do you reduce the stigma of maintenance?

- ○ Pay maintenance people better than new development people.
- ○ Rotate people between maintenance and new development.
- ○ Pay people a ''maintenance differential'' while they are working in the maintenance group.
- ○ If you can't reduce the stigma, consider hiring long-term contractors for the maintenance work.

How do you improve the quality of software changes?

- ○ Adopt all the good software engineering practices described elsewhere in this book.
- ○ Require that all bug fixes be reviewed before the fix is implemented. The reviewer should review both the design of the fix and the implementation details.
- ○ Document quick fixes with some unique and searchable symbol; e.g., @@@ or #$#. When things are a bit calmer, revisit these quick fixes and do them properly.
- ○ Require that the programmer have a test plan. Review the test plan.
- ○ Add your own documentation to code that you've struggled to understand.
- ○ Don't share temporary variables. Add your own when you need them.
- ○ Keep a detailed record of your changes so that you can refer to things that you did.

Further Reading

Higgins, David. 1986. *Data Structured Software Maintenance: The Warnier/Orr Approach.* New York: Dorset House.

Martin, James, and Carma McClure. 1983. *Software Maintenance: The Problem and Its Solution.* Englewood Cliffs, NJ: Prentice-Hall.

McClure, Carma. 1981. *Managing Software Development and Maintenance.* New York: Van Nostrand Reinhold.

Parikh, Girish (editor). 1988. *Techniques of Program and System Maintenance (2nd Edition).* Wellesley, MA: QED Information Science.

Parikh, Girish, and Nicholas Zvegintov. 1983. *Tutorial on Software Maintenance.* Washington, DC: IEEE Computer Society Press.

Summary

This chapter showed why it's so expensive to maintain software, and suggested various ways on the technical side to:

- Avoid having to change the software
- Make the software easy to understand
- Make the software easy to modify correctly
- Make the software easy to test

It also gave various suggestions on the non-technical side to:

- Make new products more maintainable
- Make maintenance easier
- Reduce the stigma of maintenance
- Improve the quality of software changes

9

Delivering Software

Evolutionary Delivery

What is evolutionary delivery?

Evolutionary delivery means delivering the product in an evolutionary manner. Rather than delivering just the final product, you figure out how you can deliver the product in stages, starting with something the customer can use productively, then gradually building on it and delivering more, in useful incremental stages, until the full product has been delivered.

What's the value of doing it this way?

The great value is that you rarely get the requirements completely right until the users see the product. This way you give them something useful as quickly as you can. While they are using it, they realize how they'd prefer it, so you use the feedback to reengineer what they have so far, while adding the next phase. By the time they get the final product, they've already been using and refining it, so they get something they want, rather than something that's less-than-satisfactory. This approach is also more motivating for software developers because they are able to complete and ship products quickly.

It sounds like prototyping.

Some people call this approach prototyping, but a prototype is really a quick and dirty product, created specifically to test things out and get feedback quickly. A prototype should be thrown away because it's not well-structured or well-written, and it doesn't do error checking. It's hard to retrofit quality into a prototype.

In evolutionary delivery, you go through the requirements, design, coding, testing, and delivery phases, but you do it in smaller chunks. So the quality is there at each delivery of the product, unlike a real prototype. The purpose is to get working software out to the customers so they have something they can really use, but it's small enough that you get quick feedback and can modify the system based on the feedback.

Why is this better than prototyping the user interface?

When you prototype the user interface, you get feedback on the user interface. While this is a major factor in determining customer acceptance of the software, it's not the full story. A user interface prototype usually doesn't contain much real functionality, and what functionality it contains is not robust enough to be used in production work. So the first delivery will give you feedback on how well the product works in use. Both types of feedback—user interface and production use—are important.

How is evolutionary delivery different from the phased approach?

There's a key difference. In most phased approaches, the project managers acknowledge that it will take too long to deliver the full product, so they choose a smaller timeframe and ask ''how much can we deliver in six months?'' They choose some constraint—time, cost, etc.—and see how much can be delivered within that constraint.

The evolutionary delivery approach looks at the problem differently and asks ''how little resource can we spend and still deliver something useful in the direction of our ultimate goal?'' The focus is always on providing the most usefulness with the least effort.

How do you decide how to split the product into deliverable steps?

That depends on the product of course. Some products are easier to split into steps. The key is to analyze possible steps in terms of usefulness to the customer, and cost or time to do. As a general rule, choose the step that provides the greatest usefulness/cost ratio. You should always be thinking ''what is the smallest amount of work you can do and still provide great value to the customer.''

Now, this approach is product-dependent. If you are doing contract work, evolutionary delivery is perfect. If you are creating commodity products for the PC market, the cost of multiple small releases is probably too high. If you are somewhere between, where you have a number of customers who pay maintenance fees and get software updates, you don't have to ship to everyone—just to key customers. The purpose is to get things right as soon as possible, so giving key customers (ones who provide good feedback) the software will help you. Because the software is production software, rather than a prototype, you can also deliver the software to anyone else who needs it or who will pay for it. It's just a matter of judgement.

The approach is also situation-dependent. If you are trying to be the first vendor into a product niche, quick evolutionary steps will get you there first. Competitors may later deliver more functionality, but there are great advantages of being first in a niche and getting that mental association in the customer's mind.

I imagine a flexible design is vital for evolutionary delivery.

Absolutely. I'd say that design flexibility is the most important attribute of a good design in the evolutionary delivery approach. You have to be able to go back after each delivery and redesign the software based on the feedback. Of course, even with the Big Bang approach of delivering only the final product, the product doesn't remain static. There will probably be many enhancements to it (most software development consists of enhancing existing software), so flexible design is pretty important to all software. Since flexible design is so important, you need to ensure that your designers can design flexible systems. This may mean training them, reviewing all designs, or having only a few people do designs.

How does this relate to the normal requirements-design-code-documents cycle?

It's independent of it. Evolutionary delivery is simply an approach that gets useful product out quickly. How each step is created is another matter. You still have the choice between the traditional process of creating and reviewing documents, and using prototyping to understand requirements and investigate designs. Whatever approach you take in your software development, it will work with evolutionary delivery.

Doesn't it cost more to go through the design-code-test-release cycle many times?

If the software architecture is flexible, it should be cheaper. You get your product to the user quicker, software he can use and comment on. Based on the feedback, the next iteration of the product better meets his needs. The product evolves to what he wants before it's complete. If the product is flexible and well-designed, it should be unnecessary to retest every little thing, because changes should be isolated. Even if you do have to retest each part of the software, it's cheaper to deliver in steps than to deliver a Big-Bang product, discover that it's not what the user wants, and redo it and retest it to give him what he wants.

Management usually prefers the evolutionary approach because it gives reassurance that things are happening—it reduces the risk. It's a lot more reassuring to see a product delivered every few weeks or months than to wait three years hoping that the product will be on time and will be what people want. Evolutionary delivery reduces the risk in other ways too: with a long release cycle, software developers often leave, lose their focus, or treat the project as resume-enhancing work.

Growing Software

What does "growing software" mean?

It's a form of top-down development, where you start with nothing much more than a set of stubbed function calls, then gradually expand the functionality to do more and more, so you always have a system that runs. Initially, the software doesn't do much, but over time, as you fill in the stubbed functions, it grows in visible functionality.

What is the value of this approach?

People like to see things happening. To work on software for a year without seeing anything running can easily put you in a "this is my eight-to-five job" mentality. To get something running quickly is inspiring and makes people enthusiastic to get more functionality working
   . The top-down, software-growing approach also lets you make design changes more easily, since you haven't written all the low-level routines that do the real work. As you add more functionality and show it to people, it soon becomes apparent if the software doesn't meet their needs. Because there still may be much unwritten software, it's easy to go back and change the design.

Are there any dangers?

The danger with this type of software-growing approach is that you can do it with no design in mind. It's easy for people to simply start coding, and grow the software at the same time they grow the design. This *can* work, but it takes someone with high maturity, a strong desire to create a maintainable product, and lots of discipline. Ninety-five percent of the time you end up with a hacked-together, unmaintainable mess.

What does it take to make it work if you don't have a design?

You must be talented, understand what it takes to make a maintainable software product, want to create maintainable software, and have a lot of discipline, because as you get feedback you'll need to restructure the software as the design changes. You must be able to keep all the software in your mind, and see and remember the relationships between the various components. As you get feedback, you'll have to resist the temptation to change the functionality by adding global variables or making functions do too much. You'll need the discipline to restructure the software, cutting and pasting, and changing interfaces, so that at each step you have a high-quality design.

If this sounds harsh, it is. I've seen too many hacked-together solutions because people have grown software without a design and without any discipline. Sure, you can do it, but you end up with crummy software.

So you need a design to grow software effectively.

At all stages in the growing process, you should be implementing a design that has been thought about, discussed, and reviewed. You must think the solution through and have as much of a design as you need. You need to have the architecture showing the components and their relationships. You need to understand the main data structures and the interfaces between components. You need to understand what components will be doing later, even if you haven't thought through their implementation completely.

As you grow the software, you'll find that users don't like some of the functionality you have, and that you can't implement some functionality as you planned. You'll have to go back and redesign the software, changing the way things work and are connected. So for software growing to work, you must recognize that requirements will change, and that you'll have to redesign the software. This means you must have a mechanism for discussing and reviewing changed designs as well as new designs.

It sounds like a cultural thing.

You must have a culture that says design is necessary and that designs can change. But that's true of all software development, not just software growing. The software will change, and the process must be able to handle that. Software growing is simply a very effective way of developing software that generates enthusiasm, is conducive to showing people incremental functionality quickly, and is conducive to making changes as you understand needs better. It's a strategy for implementing a design.

Further Reading

Gilb, Tom. 1988. *Principles of Software Engineering Management*. Reading, MA: Addison-Wesley.

Summary

In this chapter we discussed evolutionary delivery and growing software, both ways of developing software iteratively. In evolutionary delivery, you go through the normal software development phases, but you try to deliver the software in small chunks, looking for a high usefulness/cost ratio for each chunk. In doing so, you get usable software to the customer quickly, then get feedback on the functionality that can be incorporated into the next release.

Growing software is a form of top-down development, where you always have a system that runs, but doesn't do much. Over time you fill out the previously stubbed functions and add functionality to the system. The value of doing development this way is that people like to see things happening. It's psychologically better to have software that runs and does things, than a set of modules that won't do anything visible until they are all tied together in six months' time.

10

Project Teams

In my experience, the best way to run projects is to form teams rather than to give work to individuals. There are several reasons this works well:

- ○ Most people enjoy working with other people.
- ○ Most ideas can be improved by discussing them with others.
- ○ People work hard to meet the expectations of their team peers.
- ○ Teams help people focus on the common goals.
- ○ Communication is better in a team.
- ○ Difficulties are discussed and taken care of more quickly.

How do you form the teams?

There are two basic ways. One way is to match the abilities of people to the work that has to be done and create a team for each task. The other way, which I prefer, is to define the tasks and let people organize themselves into teams which then bid on the tasks. The second way has the advantage of letting people work with others with whom they enjoy working.

If you let people choose their teams, how do you form teams for the boring tasks?

Not all tasks are interesting and challenging, but for many people, who they work with is more important than the interest and challenge of the particular task.

How do you make sure there's enough talent to get the job done?

If people are organizing together to form their own teams, they will know the level of ability and expertise needed for the task, and will organize to include that level of talent. Perhaps they will include a technical leader, but perhaps they will share the leadership, each being the leader when the situation is right for it. The developers probably know better than the manager the expertise needed for the job, and will probably do a better job of rounding it up than would the manager.

On the other hand, if the teams are being organized from above, it's beneficial to have a technical leader for the team, someone who will be responsible for the work of the team, and who can make technical decisions and help people when they get stuck.

How many people should a technical leader lead?

It depends on how good the technical leader is, where his interests lie, and whether he will be coding. As a rule I'd try for teams of about four or five—one technical leader and three or four other developers.

How do you make sure everything fits together properly between teams?

By having a system architect who is responsible for the overall architecture. This person would make the final decision on interfaces between components done by different teams.

What sort of people should be on a team?

My preference is to have a small number of software developers, a test expert, and a documentation expert. Everyone gets involved in everything. The documentation person sees things from a user perspective and adds insight to the solution. He also points out things that are difficult to describe and therefore likely to be poorly designed. Since the user guide is being written while development is going on, this increases the chance that the requirements will be understood. The test expert is involved in the design because he wants to make sure the implementation can be easily and effectively tested. He makes sure the solution lends itself to test harnesses and regression testing. As there is someone focusing on testing, the software developers give more thought to their test cases and test plans.

Should everyone be part of a team?

In my experience it's always been worth having some of the better developers available to rove about, helping where needed and being a resource for others. There again, you might form a team of such people, a team who's job it is to firefight, to get involved where necessary.

What about people who don't want to be part of a team?

Let them work as individuals. Not everyone wants to be part of a team, and there are always things that can be done by individuals. More important is what that person does to the general atmosphere. Get rid of individuals who poison the atmosphere (easier to say than do).

Are there any particular teams you recommend?

In one company where I worked, we created a team called Team Q (Team Quality). It was headed by one of the senior developers, and it had two charters. The first was to ensure quality in the product. Primarily, this meant responding to bug reports from the field, evaluating them, and fixing them. Its second role was to be the training ground for new hires. New developers spent about six months in Team Q, working under the guidance of the team leader. During this time they got a good overview of the product and learned the sorts of errors that can happen. Each then joined one of the other teams, bringing along a broad knowledge of the product and a feel for how to avoid creating bugs.

Tell me more about the common goals you mentioned earlier.

Before starting a project, it's important to understand the goals of the project. If you don't know the goals, it's hard to achieve them, and you can't tell if you are succeeding or failing. Communicate the goals to the members of the project team, clearly and concisely; if people don't understand the goals, or if there is disagreement over them, you'll end up with people problems.

There are two types of goals: the general goals such as efficiency, maintainability, portability, simplicity, and meeting the schedule on time; and the specific goals that relate to what the project is trying to achieve.

General Goals.   You can't have everything as a general goal—you have to be focused. In an experiment mentioned in Chapter 8, two comparable programmers were asked to write a program to perform a particular task, but were given different objectives: one was given efficiency as his priority, and the other simplicity. The efficient program contained 10 times as many errors as the simple program. People achieve their top priorities, so make sure the priority is what you pay attention to. The amount of time you spend on things tells people what you consider important—it's what you do that counts, not what you say. If you are a manager or a technical leader, constantly pay visible attention to the general goals. Spend time on them and make clear to everyone what is important.

Specific Goals. The best way for people to understand the specific goals is for the system architect to give an overview of the project. It's worth doing when the design is complete, then again a few months into the project. The first time gives people an idea of what's going on, and the second time gives them a deeper understanding because they've been working on the project for a while now. It also reflects experience gained and changes made. Videotape the presentations so people can review them, and new people can get the same knowledge. The overview should cover:

- What is the problem?
- What are we trying to achieve?
- What alternative solutions were discussed?
- What were the trade-offs?
- Why was this solution chosen?
- What are the key points of this design?
- How does everything fit together?
- What are the unknowns?
- What are the dependencies?

How does a manager do performance evaluations for team members?

It's difficult to do the normal performance evaluation because you usually let the team organize how they do things. Most of the time you'll have no idea who is doing what, nor should you care if the team is performing well. Individual evaluations tend to be negative experiences, demotivators rather than motivators. Deming has the following words to say about the performance evaluation:

> It nourishes short-term performance, annihilates long-term planning, builds fear, demolishes teamwork, nourishes rivalry and politics. It leaves people bitter, crushed, bruised, battered, desolate, despondent, dejected, feeling inferior, some even depressed, unfit for work for weeks after receipt of rating, unable to comprehend why they are inferior. It is unfair, as it ascribes to the people in a group differences that may be caused totally by the system that they work in.

One of the jobs of a manager is to help people grow and develop. Individual ratings don't contribute to that process. People also want pay raises, but there's no requirement to tie raises to individual performance ratings. There are many alternative approaches, but they are beyond the scope of this book.

Further Reading

DeGrace, Peter, and Leslie Hulet Stahl. 1990. *Wicked Problems, Righteous Solutions.* Englewood Cliffs, NJ: Yourdon Press.

DeMarco, Tom, and Timothy Lister. 1987. *Peopleware: Productive Projects and Teams*. New York: Dorset House.

Deming, W. Edwards. 1986. *Out of the Crisis*. Massachusetts Institute of Technology.

Schrage, Michael. 1990. *Shared Minds: The New Technologies of Collaboration*. Random House.

Summary

This chapter advocates the use of teams when creating software. Teams can be formed in two ways: from above, in which case the team should have a technical leader; and by people organizing themselves into teams.

PART 3

Requirements and Design

11

Prototyping

What is prototyping?

A prototype is a quick and dirty version of the software, created to give you quick feedback. It gives you a chance to evaluate possible solutions or user interfaces before you have to commit to one that might be inadequate. A prototype will usually not be able to handle all the unexpected cases, special cases, or exceptional conditions, probably doesn't do much error detection or error reporting, probably doesn't have too much documentation in the code, and is probably structured very differently than it will be in the end product.

But isn't this a poor quality product?

In any project, sooner or later you have to show it to the customers, and they are likely to want changes. In many cases the requirements were poorly thought out and perhaps even unnecessary. You can improve them by using the techniques described in Chapter 12, ''Requirements,'' but until there is something to see, there will always be a gap between the requirements and what people really want. Only when something tangible exists do people really clarify their thinking.

Few people read specifications, especially those written by programmers; fewer still will get a feel for the product and its implications from the specs. And the reality is, most people don't really know what they want until they see it. People rarely think about the problem in the detail necessary for a requirements specification.

What should you prototype?

Let's use an analogy. If you are building a house or a bridge, one of the first things you do is make sure the buyer likes the look of it. You may create sketches, you may create a cardboard model, or you may build a detailed scale model. The point is that you realize the buyer won't get a good feel for what he's buying from the architectural drawings. The software equivalent is the user interface. No amount of writing and pictures of screens will convey the feel of the user interface the same way as seeing it and moving around it on the screen. No number of pictures of reports conveys the same information as holding a computer generated report.

Such a prototype involves the end user, and lets the developer design *with* the user rather than *for* the user. The prototype becomes a stimulus to conversation and new ideas; it enlarges the vocabulary with which you can communicate, and provides a shared framework within which to communicate. It helps give the user ownership of the design.

How can you give a user a feel for the software if all you prototype is the user interface?

Sometimes the user interface alone will be sufficient, and sometimes it will be meaningless without some underlying functionality. In the second case, you'll need to add enough functionality, in a quick and dirty way, to give the user a feel for what the software will do.

Can you prototype a design?

Certainly. On a large technical project such as a bridge, before spending millions building it, you build prototypes to test out the technical aspects. How will the various parts react to the stresses to be placed on them? Sometimes you'll build a small-scale physical model, although increasingly you'll build a prototype on a computer and model the stresses.

The software equivalent is to explore various possible technical solutions for their performance, code size, etc. If a design requires that the code be able to handle 50 messages a second between processes, with an average message size of 500 bytes, prototype that communication before doing anything else. Try different ways of passing the information—will writing multiple disk files work? Writing to a circular disk file? Using the operating system message facility? Writing a message facility of your own? Allocating and using shared memory? Using a circular shared memory buffer? Prototyping allows you to investigate the technical unknowns before committing to a design that may not work.

What are all the reasons to prototype?

Prototype to:

- ○ Get the requirements right.
- ○ Involve the end user and help him develop ownership of the design.
- ○ Demonstrate an existence proof.
- ○ Learn the pitfalls quickly.
- ○ Explore technical questions before committing to a design.

It sounds like a prototype is a throw-away product.

Exactly. When you build a prototype, plan to throw it away. Its main purpose is so you can learn what to do and how to do it right. If you decide to prototype, you must be prepared to throw what you have away and do it again. Use the lessons and salvage what you can, but be prepared to rewrite.

I've heard the term "prototyping" used to describe the process of building a product in an iterative way.

Some people give the name prototyping to the process of creating a rough product, showing it to a customer, getting feedback, enhancing the product, and so on. At each iteration the customer gets something that fits his needs a little better. But here, we are just playing with terminology. I don't consider this to be prototyping—a prototype is a quick and dirty creation for the express purpose of getting feedback that can then be used to help *design* the product. There's more on iterative development in Chapter 9, "Delivering Software."

How long should a prototype take?

It depends what you are prototyping. A user interface should be available within days if not hours, while changes should happen within minutes. Exploring technical problems might take a few days. Even the largest prototype of a full system should be available within 90 days. Any longer and you're taking too long over it—it's more than a prototype. You might need several successive prototypes as you learn better what is needed, but none should take long.

In general, set time limits on prototypes and push people. Push people because it's a prototype, not a full product. Set time limits because people develop ownership of their work (which is one reason that prototyping can be done so fast and successfully), but ownership can blind people to reality. "Just two more days" drags out to three or four or a week.

Use prototyping tools for maximum speed. Use 4GLs, databases with 4GLs, or user interface tools such as Dan Bricklin's DEMO III and some of the CASE tools. Read the advertisements in the technical magazines to find what's available for your hardware platform.

Can anyone prototype?

Of course, but people have different abilities. Effective prototypes are ones done quickly by someone excited to put in the necessary effort. Give prototyping tasks to people who are good, who know the function libraries well, and who can do things fast. Another requirement for prototyping well is the ability to see and remember relationships between things. The larger the project, the better the person needed. Better prototyping tools can help because they can reduce the amount you need to remember and the length of time you need to remember it.

Do you have an example of the effects of prototyping?

I used to work at a company that developed word processing and office automation software. We were planning to introduce software to track multiple revisions to a document (this is known as redlining). Our software was innovative because it would track thousands of revisions of the document, and keep all the revisions in the same document, so that you could simply copy the document to another person or another system and all the changes would go with it.

Unfortunately, in all the excitement, neither Marketing nor Development realized that the software wouldn't do one of the basic necessities. While it would print out the document showing *all* the changes or all the changes up to a particular revision level, it would not print the document showing the differences between two specified revisions. Of course, the thing our customers wanted to do 99 percent of the time was to print the document showing the differences between the latest revision and the one just before it.

Of course, we discovered this the first time we demonstrated the software to prospective customers. Naturally, the programmer who had worked on the changes to the printing software had been reassigned to a new project, the software and test departments were tightly scheduled on other projects, and it was too late to make the changes to this release of the product. The software that customers wanted came out about a year later.

The goal should therefore be to get something in front of the customer as soon as possible. Get the real requirements out in the open as quickly as possible.

But won't this alert your competitors to what you are doing?

Possibly. But, except in extremely rare cases, it doesn't matter. Rarely is what you're doing so unique that no one else had thought of it. Even if a competitor does learn what you are doing and decides to copy you, they still have to figure out how to do it, get it approved by management, get it scheduled and staffed, and get it built. You have quite a margin there.

Further Reading

Martin, James. 1991. *Rapid Application Development*. New York: Macmillan.

Smith, M.F. 1991. *Software Prototyping*. New York: McGraw-Hill.

Summary

A prototype is a quick-and-dirty version of the software, created to give you quick feedback. There are two main types of prototype, the first being a requirements prototype, created to get feedback on what the users *really* want. Customers usually need to see software on the screen before they can tell if it's what they want—reviewing requirements on paper is rarely adequate.

The second type is the design prototype, created to explore the technical feasibility or performance of a particular design.

A prototype should be fast to create; it should be built in the best possible language for prototyping, and will rarely be robust enough for production use. You should be prepared to throw it away after you've learned the lessons that will go into the real product.

12

Requirements

The biggest cause of software project failure is that developers don't spend enough time understanding what people will be doing with their software. Sometimes there is simply a lack of understanding of what the users want; sometimes there are gaps in what gets specified and developers make assumptions to fill the gaps. Some people estimate that 90 percent of all software projects are either cancelled or fail to satisfy the users fully.

Understanding the requirements is the first critical stage of software development. Get the requirements wrong, and it doesn't matter how good the design is—the wrong product is built. Getting the requirements wrong is the most costly place to make a mistake. You pay developers to create and implement a solution, test and debug the implementation, then you ship the product. By the time you realize you've built the wrong product, you've wasted both time and money. Millions of dollars are lost by companies building the wrong product, building for the wrong platform, or missing the window of opportunity by building in the wrong timeframe.

What it usually boils down to is that writing code is easy, fun, and gives instant gratification, while figuring out the requirements is difficult and less fun. So people find it easy to skimp on the requirements phase. Unfortunately, this fact is often hidden because errors in coding are obvious, while errors in requirements are often masked by calling the changes ''user requested changes.'' Many of these ''user requested changes'' happen simply because the software engineer didn't do a good enough job of understanding the requirements.

But there are successful projects that don't have requirements.

I could win a lot of money betting on the toss of a coin, but it would be pure luck. There are enough software projects going on that simple probability allows some to be successful by chance. If you want to try your luck, go ahead. But if you want to increase your odds of success, try to understand what people want the software to do.

In fact, many of the successful projects that don't seem to have requirements tend to be smaller projects in which one person is doing most of the work, and for which a common understanding is not important. This person may have a good grasp of the requirements, but they are in his head, not on paper. There are some big assumptions if you choose to do things this way: that the developer really does understand the requirements, as there's no way to easily review them; that the requirements are right, as again, there's no easy way to review them; that the developer won't leave in the middle of the project; that there's either only one developer or that everyone has the same understanding of the requirements.

But projects that try to specify everything precisely and exactly up front are often the projects that fail.

Let's refine that statement. Projects often fail if they try to specify everything precisely and exactly up front, and then refuse to modify their plans when reality intrudes. Reality has a habit of getting in the way of our best-laid plans, but having a plan that can be modified is better than not having a plan. If you try to get the requirements right, perhaps 5 percent will change later, whereas if you don't try, perhaps 50 percent of the requirements will change. Trying to understand the requirements helps minimize the changes.

Okay, you've made your point. How do we get the requirements right?

There are three components to a statement of requirements: functional requirements, resource limitations, and quality objectives. We must describe all three in clear and measurable terms. Before talking about each component, I want to mention a few general points.

- If a goal is fuzzy, you won't know if you've met it.
- People tend to give higher priority to goals that are clear and measurable. That's why there's often so much focus on meeting a schedule to the detriment of quality objectives. The schedule date is clear, whereas the quality objectives are fuzzy.
- If you want to improve something, you should state, numerically, the current level of performance and the planned level.

○ Provide evidence for every critical fact, estimate, and value. Document the sources so that people can check the information.

○ People work to meet their top priority. Some of these requirements may be contradictory, for example, high performance might conflict with maintainability. You must stress and make obvious the priorities.

Tell me about the functionality requirements.

The functional requirements should simply be a list of the functionality users want. There should be no indication of performance, reliability, or any of the attributes of that functionality. If there are any data transformations that are absolutely required, this is the place to put them. (The danger here is that in describing the data transformation, with its inputs and outputs, you may start describing a solution.)

How do the quality objectives fit in?

All products have requirements that are independent of the actual functionality. We want our word processing software to be blindingly fast. We want our transaction-processing software to be able to handle a high throughput. We want our airline reservation system to respond in no more than a few seconds. We also have more general quality objectives, such as the software should be reliable, flexible, maintainable, and so on.

It is the satisfaction of these quality objectives, perhaps more than the functionality itself, that makes people feel the software is "good." I can put up with some missing functionality in my word processor, but if there's a noticeable time delay in response to my typing, I'll throw it out. My friend can handle his financial market software not calculating the Dow Jones correctly, but if it can't keep up with the day's trades, he'll find some other software.

But how do you specify the quality objectives? There are two contradictory points I'm going to make—part of the skill of software development is to reconcile the points. First, if you can't specify it, you can't measure it; if you can't measure it, you can't tell if you've met it. Second, people have a hard time specifying things exactly. People usually think in terms of "It's a bit slow" or "It's a bit clumsy," rather than in hard, measurable terms.

To reconcile the two, you may need to show people things as soon as possible, then react to the feedback. Prototype if appropriate, and plan on evolutionary delivery of the product.

But you must end up with something measurable. In fact, you generally need two measurable quantities: a usual, or planned, value, and a worse-case value. What is the planned data flow in transactions or bytes per second? What is the worst-case data flow you'll have to deal with. It's important to specify these values; it's vital to specify the values that are considered "critical"—i.e., if these values aren't met, the product is useless. You should also try to show the distribution of values—how often is the maximum value going to occur? Is the average skewed because the maximum is extremely high, but occurs only 0.01 percent of the time?

How do you specify values for maintainability and other "soft" qualities?

These are the most difficult ones to quantify, but if you don't try, you're very likely to end up in the type of situation where someone complains that a design is not maintainable, and someone else says that to make it more maintainable would mean sacrificing some other, measurable requirement. Another problem is that you can't usually test out the maintainability aspect until several months or years after the product is created when you next need to add new functionality.

There are no simple answers, but what does maintainability mean to you? The ability to increase the maximum number of employee records stored? The ability to add a new financial service data feed? The ability to add a new type of modeler to a CAD package? Can you specify a normal and worst-case time allowed to change the software to accommodate these new needs? Perhaps you might choose to agree on the attributes of a maintainable system—all data structures in third normal form, no external scope global variables, no modules with greater than a given complexity, and define your maintainability requirements in these terms.

If I try to give numeric values, a lot of them will be estimates.

Write down the values, even if they are estimates. If you're not sure about them, put down the probable range—these values are estimates and the true value probably lies within plus or minus 30 percent. Write down an uncertainty estimate, and the reason for that uncertainty.

You should also provide evidence for your estimates. Document the source of your evidence: the person, publication, internal document, or whatever. If you don't know the source, you can't check the information, you don't know whether you can change the value when conditions change, and you don't know how important the value really is, should design considerations suggest that it can't easily be met.

What about the resource limitations?

This simply specifies the limitations that are imposed on the solution. Examples are the number of people who can work on it, the timeframe it must be ready in, any computer availability restrictions, design constraints, etc.

The products that I work on don't have all have these requirements.

There's no way all types of product can have the same type of requirements document. Different organizations have different templates (for example, the Department of Defense has DI-MCCR-80025A, NASA has SFW-DID-08, and IEEE has 830-1984). In Chapter 17, "Specifications and Documents," I've shown various requirements document templates. IEEE acknowledges that no format will fit all software projects, and has four versions of the requirements specification in its 830-1984 standard. I'd start with the specs shown in that chapter and use what's in them to create a requirements document template that seems to work for the software you create. As you use it you can refine it to meet your needs more precisely.

A template with headings is a good starting point. Better to have a description under each heading that tells people the sort of thing to put there. Better again to have a real example which is as complete as you can make it—people learn and understand things best from examples. As you think of more or different things that you'd like to see in the requirements document, modify the example template. I've given examples of these in the Specifications and Documents chapter.

How do you get the requirements information you need?

It depends on what you are building. Are you automating an existing manual system? Building a new state-of-the-art missile tracking system? Adding new CAD/CAM functionality to an existing product? Depending on what you are building, you could:

- Talk to the people who will be paying for the software.
  - What problems will the software solve?
  - Why do they want to solve the problem?
  - What problems will the software create?
  - How much time do you have for the project?
  - What is the trade-off between time and functionality?
  - Is there existing software that could be copied?
- Talk to the people who want the software or who will be using the software.
  - What problem will it solve?
  - Why do they want to solve the problem?
  - What must the software do?
  - Is there existing software that could be copied?
- Ask questions:
  - Why do you do it this way?
  - Is it because the existing system (whether manual or computer) forces this way of doing things?
  - Would it be easier if things were done a different way?
  - If you could, how would you change things to make your job easier?
  - Try to ask questions that require thoughtful answers rather than leading questions that can be answered Yes or No.

- Sit with users while they do the tasks your software will be helping with. Watch what they do. Can you create software to achieve the same result more easily?
- Follow people through a day and watch the information flow, then figure out ways to automate it better.
- Think of alternatives and ask people if they would make things easier. (Keep in mind that some people are resistant to change.)

There are several other things to consider:

- Remember that group dynamics change responses and feedback. Work first with individuals, then with groups.
- Use a tape recorder when possible.
- Work in teams of two. Two people can often provide more insight than one. Discussing what you've heard and exploring ideas can often lead to a better analysis.

I have to do an analysis document as part of the requirements.

The analysis should be a description of the problem, and as such is obviously related to the requirements. The requirements may ask you to create a solution for the problem as described in the analysis document. Equally, once the problem is described it may become obvious that this is definitely *not* the problem you want solved.

Let's talk a little about the analysis document. The goal of the analysis phase is to describe the problem, not develop a solution. However, the analysis should be complete enough that it's easy to create the solution. Besides describing the problem, include the reasons why things are the way they are—the reasons for things tend to be constraints on the solution, and constraints are one of the most critical aspects of the design. Because the constraints are so critical to the design, I'd have a separate section in the analysis document where you discuss the constraints, as well as discussing them in the main part of the document.

I'd also have a recommendations, or proposed solutions, section of the document where you describe the ideas you have for the solution. Most people can't resist thinking about solutions while they are thinking about and describing the problem, and this section gives an outlet for the creative urge and makes it easier to focus on the problem description in the rest of the document.

It seems that a lot of requirements are really solutions.

It can be very difficult to get the real requirements because people tend to think in concrete terms rather than in abstractions, so you'll often be told solutions rather than requirements. You have the potential for a better solution if you can abstract from what you've been told because you now have more solution options (including the one you've been told). If you don't abstract, you'll end up with the functionality requirements looking remarkably like the Functional Spec (which is where the proposed solution is described). That's not to say you'll have a bad solution—just that you may not have considered other, better, solutions.

Some of the requirements will probably be solutions masquerading as requirements, so ask "Why do you want this?" If there is a more general reason for this particular requirement, that general reason is the real requirement.

How do you distinguish things the software really must do from things that would be nice if it did?

Ask which functionality is required and which would be nice, but is not essential. To get a better feel, ask what must be there in the first release of the software, what could be put into a second release, and what could be pushed out to a future release.

Should you review the specification?

Definitely. Errors in requirements are the most costly of all errors so it's vital to catch them as soon as you can, and reviews are the quickest ways to catch errors. But while you'll get feedback on the requirements from users, you'll get more feedback when you show a solution—something they can relate to. So you haven't really finished reviewing the requirements until you've reviewed the proposed solution. Do a prototype of the user interface if you can; that's where you get the best and fastest feedback.

Review the requirements both for what is specified and what is not specified. If there are holes, the designers and implementers will happily fill in the holes, but they may fill them in incorrectly. It can be difficult to see what's missing, and again, you may only realize things are missing when you're creating the solution.

And look for solutions masquerading as requirements. Is this particular solution really a requirement, or is there an underlying requirement that can be stated in non-solution terms?

I thought you were supposed to finish one phase before starting the next, and here you are telling me that you won't finish the requirements until you've also finished specifying the solution.

That's right. Reality has this unfortunate way of intruding on the nice clean plans people make. You probably won't fully understand the requirements until you have a solution. But that doesn't mean you shouldn't try. After all, if you can get the requirements mainly right, that's a lot further in the right direction than if you have them mainly wrong. Your goal should be two-fold: get the requirements as right as you can, and get a solution in front of your customers as quickly as you can.

What if you can't get users to review the requirements?

Form a "devil's advocate" group. To prevent "shouting down" or subtle punishment of the devil's advocate group, put in the group your most senior or powerful person who was not involved in the specifications. Given the importance of the requirements, you want a group that can and does discuss the requirements. At a minimum it can point out inconsistencies and holes.

I've heard of group requirements. What is this?

It's an approach that involves getting all the key people into one room and conducting intensive sessions to get out all the requirements. It's often very effective, especially for large systems with large numbers of users. It's success depends on getting the right people involved, setting the expectations, using the right technology, having a skillful facilitator, and getting the requirements out quickly using personal computers, prototyping, CASE, word processing, and photocopying. If you want to try this approach, you need someone who is an expert in prototyping, the methodology you are using, and CASE—someone who can think, organize, and type as people are talking.

We often seem to be developing for a moving target.

Developing to moving targets happens because of two things: the requirements weren't well-thought-out, and you are trying to do too much for the resources you have (in which case, again, the requirements weren't well defined in terms of the trade-off between functionality and timeframe).

Where does the analysis phase fit into all this?

The analysis phase is an attempt to understand the problem prior to creating the requirements for the solution. Very often, the analysis produces pages and pages of data flow diagrams or pictures from some other methodology, and it's easy for the analysis to become a goal in itself. But the analysis is useful only if it helps you come up with a good solution.

You always need to understand the problem you are solving, but that understanding doesn't have to come from a distinguishable analysis phase. If you are enhancing existing software, you probably have a good understanding of the problem, and the main difficulty will be modifying the existing design to accommodate your new needs. You don't need a separate analysis phase to do this. Similarly, if you are creating something completely new, you may not even fully understand the problem you are solving until you've been through several rounds of solutions. Let's look at a sample of tasks for which you might be writing software, and figure out what the analysis phase means:

○ *Automate an order entry, shipping, and billing system.* You need to understand the flow of data. Analyze the existing process and describe it: where data originates and is stored, what gets printed, where and how data is transformed, where and how it flows. The analysts will interview users and collect copies of the various forms and procedures to gain this understanding.

But remember, the analysis is useful only if it helps you come up with a good solution. When I first started in software development I was writing software for small construction firms. One client came to us after commissioning another company to do an analysis of his operation and needs. That analysis produced folders of data flow diagrams and cost more than the software and hardware we sold him. And we didn't even use the data flow diagrams because we realized that he didn't need a replica of his manual system, so once we understood his goals from the system, we invented a new system.

○ *Create a word processor when people only had typewriters.* Analyze the problems facing a typist—can't make corrections easily, can't rearrange things on the page, can't check the spelling, can't send the same letter to multiple people without retyping, and so on. It meant sitting with a typist, asking questions, and coming up with your own ideas on what would make things better.

○ *Create a system to consolidate financial transaction data from all the stock exchanges.* You need to understand all the places data can come from, the size of data transactions, peak numbers of transactions, distribution over time, how quickly the data must be consolidated, when it must be consolidated, what different types of transactions exist and what to do with them, etc.

○ *Create a cruise control system.* Analyze the driving environment, identify all the events that your system should respond to, and identify all the responses.

What is options analysis?

If you have a broad enough problem you want to solve, there are probably many possible solutions. Some of them will be economically feasible, while others won't. Some will lead to an extensible solution, while others will be specific and dead-end. Some will be better solutions, but more expensive. An options analysis gives you a feel for the different options and their implications. Once you have a feel for the options and can make a choice, you can refine your requirements to specify the functional requirements more precisely, or to put in the relevant resource constraints or even design constraints.

To do an options analysis you'll probably have to go down to the preliminary design level if you really want to understand the implications about feasibility, cost, and timeframe. Which is another example of how intensively iterative the software process really is:

> **Have a rough idea of the requirements → Look at several possible designs → Choose an option → Create more refined requirements → Do the design, etc.**

Of course, another way to look at the Options Analysis is to consider it as part of the solution phase. You get the requirements, come up with several solutions, refine the requirements, then narrow the possible solutions down to one. It's all a question of semantics. The key point is to understand how iterative the requirements/solution process is, and to make sure that your software process can handle a high level of iteration.

What is a feasibility study?

A form of options analysis is the feasibility study. You'd do a feasibility study when you don't know if what you are trying to do is even possible. It's an attempt to see if a solution is possible, so usually the main focus of the feasibility study would be a prototype.

Further Reading

Davis, Alan. 1990. *Software Requirements: Analysis and Specification*. Englewood Cliffs, NJ: Prentice-Hall.

DeGrace, Peter, and Leslie Hulet Stahl. 1990. *Wicked Problems, Righteous Solutions*. Englewood Cliffs, NJ: Yourdon Press.

Dorfman, Merlin, and Richard Thayer (editors). 1990. *Standards, Guidelines, and Examples on System and Software Requirements Engineering*. Los Alamitos, CA: IEEE Computer Society Press.

Gause, Donald, and Gerald Weinberg. 1990. *Exploring Requirements: Quality before Design*. New York: Dorset House.

Gilb, Tom. 1988. *Principles of Software Engineering Management*. Reading, MA: Addison-Wesley.

IEEE Guide for Software Requirements Specifications. Institute of Electrical and Electronics Engineers, 1984.

Orr, Ken. 1981. *Structured Requirements Definition*. Ken Orr and Associates.

Thayer, Richard, and Merlin Dorfman (editors). 1990. *System and Software Requirements Engineering*. Los Alamitos, CA: IEEE Computer Society Press.

Summary

The biggest cause of software project failure is that developers don't spend enough time understanding what people will be doing with their software. Getting the requirements wrong is the most costly place to make a mistake, especially if you don't discover it until the product is shipped to the customer.

Unfortunately, it's more fun to write code, so developers often skimp on the requirements gathering. This is often hidden by the tendency to call errors in the requirements "user requested changes."

Requirements should be clear and measurable. They should describe the functionality needed, the resource limitations that may affect the solutions, and the soft requirements, such as performance, reliability, quality, and maintainability. If the soft requirements are not measurable, they will often be ignored as requirements.

13

The Solution

The next logical step after the requirements is the solution, when you invent something that will meet the requirements. The solution consists of two parts: the part that the customer sees—the user interface and functional behavior—and the underlying software design.

User Interface

There are three general requirements for the user interface. It should be:

- Intuitive
- Predictable
- Optimized by frequency of operation

The nice thing about the user interface is that there are quite a few tools available for prototyping it, which makes it easy to work with users and get quick feedback. Getting quick feedback means it's easier to achieve these three goals.

Tell me more about the three goals.

The user interface should be intuitive.   It should be easy to figure out. Most people take the approach "when all else fails, read the instructions." One goal of the user interface should be to make it unnecessary to read the instructions. It should be obvious how to do common and frequently done things. Things that are less common may not be so immediately obvious, but it should be clear how to start looking for them and where they are likely to be. It's immensely frustrating to search around a system and be unable to find how to do something. Context-sensitive help obviously helps, but it's a poor substitute for a good user interface.

Of course, intuitiveness may be in the eye of the beholder. A beginner might be boggled by the power of the system—power that is needed by the experienced user. So it's easy to make a case for having different user interfaces for different levels of experience—the classic beginner/expert mode system.

An example of poor intuitiveness is character-based WordPerfect (the word processor I used to create this book). It's very hard to figure out or remember how to do things—you press F6 for Bold and F8 for Underline—or is it the other way round? And of course Shift-F6 centers the line. A more obvious way would have been to have an Emphasis key, say F6. Pressing this might bring up a line at the bottom of the screen (Bold, Underline, Italic), or perhaps F6 would be Bold, Shift-F6 would be underline, and so on.

The user interface should be predictable.   Once a person knows how to do something, it should be easy to guess how something else is done. Similar things should be done in similar ways. Specific things should always be done in the same way—a particular action always brings up the help information, another action always cancels an operation.

Using WordPerfect again as an example, while the F1 = cancel and F3 = help are used consistently within WordPerfect, they go against the standards adopted by just about every other PC vendor, which are Escape = cancel and F1 = Help, for example.

The user interface should be optimized by frequency of operation.   The goal is obvious—the operations done most frequently should be the easiest to do. This requirement requires interaction with real users—software engineers simply can't predict how people will want to use the software and what the patterns of use will be.

Commonly performed actions should require few keystrokes, or should be at the top of pull-down menus. Less common actions can require more keystrokes, or can be in nested pull-down menus.

How do you figure out the patterns of use?

Well, it depends on whether you are automating manual processes, creating software to replace existing software, or enhancing existing software. But, while the details may vary, the basic idea is the same.

- Sit with users while they do the tasks that your software will be helping with. Watch what they do, the order in which they do things, and how often they do them.

- Ask questions:
  - Why do you do it this way?
  - Is it because the existing system (whether manual or computer) forces this way of doing things?
  - Would it be easier if things were done a different way?
  - If you could, how would you change things to make your job easier?
- Think of alternatives and ask people if they would make things easier. (Keeping in mind that some people are resistant to change, preferring the devil they know to the devil of learning new ways.)
- Prototype the user interface, using tools that allow you to make rapid changes while sitting with the user.
- Remember that group dynamics change responses and feedback. Work first with individuals, then with groups.

Tell me more about the help system.

Even though you have a spectacular, intuitive, predictable user interface, there will be times when people can't figure something out, or want to know more about something. They need a help system to give them information. Help systems come in three flavors: basic help, context-sensitive help, and hypertext help. A basic help system would give the same help information wherever you are. Context-sensitive help gives you different information depending on where you are; it gives information about what you are currently doing and what you might want to do from that point. Hypertext help allows you to expand on a concept mentioned in the help you are looking at, and generally lets you keep expanding outward, following concepts or actions of interest. Probably the best help is one that is context-sensitive with hypertext capability, and that allows users to easily get full hypertext help about the whole system.

The help system should follow the same user-interface rules that we've just described. It should be intuitive, predictable, and the commonly done things should be the easiest to do.

However, having said all this, the help system will not sell more products. It's more of a checklist item. If your competitors have help, you need help. If they have context-sensitive help, you need it. The lack of a help system may prevent the sale, but the presence of it will rarely make the sale.

What about beginner/expert modes?

Some software allows users to select a beginner or expert mode, and the options available to the user are distinctly different. Beginners get a much easier, but less powerful interface. When they are more familiar with the product, they can change to expert mode, where they get the full range of options.

More powerful than simple beginner/expert modes is software where the user can tailor the user interface to meet his needs. No static user interface can be optimized for everyone, but tailorable user interfaces can be optimized for the specific things each user or organization does.

Of course, this can present a support nightmare, so I don't know if I recommend it for commodity (PC) software. If support and maintenance revenues are a significant part of your organization's business plan, you might tailor user interfaces for a price. The main support requirement will be that there is some way to tell at all times what the context is and what action the user is trying to perform. This usually means having a keystroke or mouse action that will show information about the context and callback function bound to the keystroke or menu selection the user wants.

You said in Chapter 12 that many new GUIs allow you to separate user interface from functionality.

Many of the new graphical user interfaces allow the software developer to associate "callbacks" with actions. Thus, the software developer designs the software to be based on callback functions. The callback function performs a particular task. It must know the current context, and it must know what to do given the current context. For example, in word processing software, executing a "cut" function will result in different things depending on whether text has been selected or not. So the software is designed to maintain information about the current context and each callback function makes its decisions based on the context, and if appropriate, sets information about the new context.

The key point is that the function neither knows nor cares how it was invoked. If it can find the appropriate context information, it can do its job. This lets the user interface be separated from the software that actually does things. The user interface expert can draw on his experience with user interfaces and psychology to create an intuitive, predictable, optimized user interface with pull-down menus, dialog boxes, sliders, radio buttons, etc. He can associate actions with either other pull-down menus and radio buttons, or with callbacks that actually do something.

The software designer can forget about user interface questions, and focus simply on the things the software must do, and the context information it must have to do its job. He can then design and modularize the software to do its job independent of the user interface.

Once the user interface is separate from the functionality, it becomes a lot easier to optimize it for specific organizations and industries. The software functionality remains untouched—only the user interface is changed.

Where does the user interface fit in with the normal requirements-design-code process?

The user interface is a funny animal, with traits of both requirements and design. If the requirements simply list functionality needed, it becomes part of the design phase to invent a user interface that makes it easy for users to do the things listed. On the other hand, once users see the user interface, they often realize that the functional requirements are incomplete or wrong.

So while the user interface is part of the design phase (user interface design), it is tightly bound to the requirements. If you want to really nail down the requirements as early as possible, prototype the user interface and show it to the users. Feedback will be quick. In fact, it's rare when users don't want changes. One of the biggest flaws in the Big Bang approach is that the user sees the user interface for the first time when the product is finished (seeing pictures of screens doesn't seem to make it), and when there's little chance for changes. The Evolutionary Delivery and Prototyping approaches both give better solutions.

Design

Great design is like great literature—some people have it and some people don't. It can't be taught. Fortunately, just as there are certain rules to follow if you want to improve your writing, there are things to look for when creating a design. The quality of the design is important because, next to requirements, it's the thing that most affects the quality of the software product. Let's look at some of the attributes of a good design.

- Flexibility/changeability/extendibility
- Performance
- Ability to test the software

Flexibility/changeability/extendibility.   These are all recognition that the software will change. It will change because when customers get the software, they'll tell you what they really wanted it to do. It will change because their needs will change over time. It will change because new customers will get it and have different needs. It will change because the window of opportunity closes and you have to create something different. As needs change and the competitive environment changes, there will always be necessary enhancements. The goal of flexible design should be to make the changes easy. There has to be an acknowledgement that you're not going to get things completely right the first time and that you'll need to make changes. And, because things will change, the design has to be flexible.

○ *Separation of functionality from user interface.* Most modern graphical user interfaces (GUIs) are user-driven rather than menu-driven. In the older menu-driven systems, the software knew exactly where it was, and controlled what the user could do at each point. The new GUIs give the user far more control over what he can do, so the software has to be written differently. Software has to be written so that context information is always available, and routines know what they must or must not do based on the context. How they were invoked is of no interest. So GUI-based software can be written in a way that separates the functionality from the user interface, which makes some types of changes much easier to make.

○ *Information hiding.* One of the goals of good design is to hide information from routines that don't need to know about it. For example, application software doesn't need to know anything about the way data is stored. So a good design would completely hide those details from the application. This means that the data storage could be ASCII files, ISAM files, a relational database, or an object-oriented database, and the application would neither know nor care. The storage scheme could be changed without the application having to change at all—the only thing that would change would be the file access function layer. The value of information hiding is that it can easily change the details in that software layer without affecting anything else.

○ *Good data structures.* The heart of software design lies in the data structures and the things done to the data structures. You want to create data structures such that:
  • Information about an entity is easy to find, rather than being scattered throughout many different data structures.
  • The data structures used are the most appropriate for the actions performed on them. Once you understand the way the data is used and manipulated, you can decide how to represent it. Is it better to use linked lists? Or trees? Or arrays? Do you need direct access? Or is the ability to insert and delete more important?
  • Each data field is used for only one thing.
  • Data structures are in third normal form if possible (there's more about third normal form at the end of the chapter).

○ *Modules do one thing only.* If modules do more than one thing, it's a lot harder to change the software as requirements change. Suppose you have a routine that asks the user for several points in space, uses a particular formula to calculate the curve joining them, then displays the curve on the screen. In the future you may want to display a curve based on points from a data file, or you may also want to give the user a choice of formulas to calculate the curve, or you may want to display two parallel curves separated by a specified distance. Any of these changes will create havoc with your implementation, simply because your design forced a routine to do too much. If there were separate routines to get the user point values, to calculate the curve, and to plot the curve, it would be a relatively simple task to enhance the software to do any or all of these extensions.

o *Modules have well-defined interfaces with minimal sharing of data.* Flexible software requires simple modules with small, well-defined interfaces. It's certainly possible to consider global variables as part of the interface, but it's rare that people take the time to document them as part of the interface. It's also rare for people to use variable-naming conventions that clearly show that a variable is global. So, in practice, using global variables means poorly defined interfaces. Worse still, it's easy to change the interface by adding the use of a global variable, so the module interface changes without anyone knowing it. Global data complicates interfaces and relationships between modules, making it more difficult to modify the software.

o *Restrict the use of value-retaining variables.* The problem with subsystems or routines that retain values is that they can't shift context. A routine or error subsystem that logs error messages to a file might store the handle to the file (file pointer, file descriptor, etc.) in a static variable, setting it once, then remembering it. This may be sufficient, but if you decide you need to log different types of errors in different files, you won't be able to. There are certainly times when value retention is useful, but there's a trade-off with flexibility.

Performance. Most people want their software to have high performance. Unfortunately, some people strive for performance at the expense of flexibility and maintainability of the software. But there are plenty of ways of getting performance without compromising these.

o *Good data structures.* Data structures can have a dramatic effect on performance. They should be designed such that:
  - You don't need to constantly get or store data structures.
  - The data structures are the most appropriate for the actions performed on them (arrays, linked lists, hash tables, etc.).

o *Information hiding.* If you hide the implementation details of things in separate layers, you can optimize a layer without affecting other parts of the system. If file access is slow, you can speed it up. If memory management is slow, redesign it. But the layer must be well modularized, with implementation details hidden (no globals).

Ability to test the software.   While it's important to catch errors before they happen, there's still a need to test the system prior to shipping the software. The system design should be such that you can replay known situations and check for differences in results. You must be able to do good regression testing. We'll get more into this in Chapter 24, "Testing," so the point here is that you must figure out what you want the system to be able to do with respect to automated testing. You also need to design the modules such that they are easy to test in isolation (unit testing).

Is there anything else to consider?

The design aspects I described above are probably the most important, but there are certainly other things to consider. For example:

- Ability to recover from software and user errors
- Ability to cancel out of operations

Ability to recover from software and user errors.   Error handling needs to be considered when designing the system. There are different types of error and the software should be able to handle both types:

- Errors that are returned from function calls.
- Errors that are caused by exception conditions, such as divide by zero or referencing an invalid memory address.

Another way of classifying errors might be:

- Errors that users make that are easy to handle (e.g., user enters the name of an employee who is not on file).
- Errors that prevent operation (e.g., can't initialize the window manager).
- Errors that may or may not be recoverable (e.g., failure on a call to a memory allocation routine such as malloc).
- Errors that are recoverable, but that cause the end result to be wrong (e.g., an error while processing trading transactions for a stock that affects the Dow Jones).
- Errors that are recoverable and that don't affect the overall result, but have a disastrous effect on the current operation (e.g., an error that occurred while doing the payroll, preventing a check being printed for one employee, but printing checks for everyone else).

The different types of errors should be considered, and some ways of handling them defined and designed in. It's much more difficult to retrofit error handling than to design it in.

Ability to cancel out of operations.   Of course, not all software needs this capability, but any software that deals with the user, and does time-consuming things needs an ability to trap user input and stop doing the thing. This should be designed in, rather than added as an afterthought.

How do you go about creating a design for a procedural language such as C, Fortran, and Cobol?

In procedural design, you start at the top with what you want to do, then work your way down, using a process of divide and conquer, splitting up the work into a set of smaller modules, each of which does a particular task. This is called top-down design, or stepwise design. Imagine that the design process is like a system of tree roots. You start with the tree, then divide this into a set of main roots. Each main root splits into smaller and smaller roots. Once you get down to the smallest level, you are at the individual function level.

A good top-down, modular design allows you to have different people working on the project. It also makes it easier to make changes to the code. It protects against system bugs by making it impossible (or at least difficult) for changes in one area to affect another area. The suppression of detail at each level makes flaws in the structure more apparent. And the design can be tested at each of its levels, so testing can start earlier and focus on the proper level of detail at each step.

Should you write down the design?

Yes, for several reasons. Writing the design gives you something to communicate to others and to review. The act of writing forces you to clarify your thinking and shows the gaps in your ideas. You are forced to make decisions about things rather than letting them slide.

What about the use of flowcharts?

They're a waste of time! They were perhaps useful in the early days of computing when each step in the flowchart might have taken several lines of machine code or assembler to code, but with high-level languages, each step can be coded in a single statement. Why bother with a flowchart? Do the stepwise design in pseudo-code and you'll be able to translate the pseudo-code to real code with very little effort. I've never seen anyone use flowcharts; perhaps they're extinct by now.

What is the difference between object-oriented design, and design with procedural languages?

The main difference is in how you view the world. In normal, or procedural, design, you think of the things you need to "do," then figure out how to do them and what data structures you need. In object-oriented design, you figure out what data "objects" you need, then figure out what can happen to the objects.

For example, let's look at something that everyone can relate to—a payroll check. If you think of the process in procedural terms, it goes something like: find the employee file, look up his pay rate, do some calculations, look up the tax tables, do some more calculations, print out a check, and store the data in the employee payroll record. If you think in objects, the check is an object that can have actions performed on it. You can create it, destroy it, save it, or print it.

This is a very simplistic example, but it does illustrate one important aspect of object-oriented software development. In procedural design, you modularize the software until you end up with a set of small modules, each of which does a particular task. When they are all combined and executed in the proper order, you end up with the desired result. However, there's nothing obvious about what data structures you want, there's no obvious way to decompose the modules so that you end up with reusable software modules, there's no obvious way to keep information hidden, and there's no obvious way to ensure that you have a design that's easily modifiable.

Thinking in objects overcomes all these objections, at least in theory. Objects are data structures with actions that can be performed on them. So start by thinking in terms of data structures. Since you are creating objects, potentially all of which could be reused, you are more likely to gain the benefits of reusable software. The encapsulation property of objects ensures that other software doesn't know about the internal data structures of the object. And, since your software consists largely of discrete objects that have messages sent to them, it's potentially easier to modify as new needs arise.

(Object-oriented languages add other features, such as inheritance, that overcome other shortcomings of procedural languages. Inheritance allows objects to inherit routines that act on them (also known as methods), and also to define new methods, or override or enhance the inherited methods. In a procedural language, you need routines with fixed interfaces, but having a fixed interface limits the future enhancements you can make to the routine. Objects that can inherit what they need and add other methods, give the equivalent of a routine with an interface that is both fixed and modifiable.)

However, much of object-oriented development can be done with procedural languages. You can still think in terms of objects, and still create your data structures and routines that act on the objects.

Who should do the design?

Ideally the person best at it. The higher the quality of design, the less will be the problems and rework later on. However, you have to give software engineers a chance to develop their own skills, so there is a trade off. However, the less experienced the designer, the greater the need to review the design, both to ensure the design is good and to help the designer learn better techniques and ideas. It's also important to keep a consistency, or integrity, across the product. There should be one person, or a small group of top designers, who ensure that the overall architecture is consistent across the product.

How does one cope with the rapid change that leads to constantly moving targets?

Moving targets are a problem in fast-moving areas, such as PC software. If you have a new word processing program but a competitor comes out with a new and better product before you can get to market, you have some serious thinking to do. But not all seemingly moving targets are really moving targets. It may be a problem of your own making because you didn't understand the requirements well enough. Much of the time the second is true.

But let's say you are in a market with valid moving targets. Moving targets tend to happen because of one of several things: either the customer (perhaps the marketing department) didn't understand the needs correctly, you overdesigned and overbuilt the product they wanted, or you are not organized to do things in a fast enough way.

When figuring out what to build, it's important to differentiate between new concepts products and mature products. If the product is like no other on the market, it's better to fill the niche quickly, get the name recognition associated with the niche, then improve the product. If it's a mature product, you need an unquestionably superior product. So software development and marketing jointly must figure out which is the correct approach, and commit themselves to that approach. And, because software development tends to not be very fast, you need to work very closely with marketing to fully agree on the market niche and the exact requirements. Remember, bells and whistles are nice if you can sell your product because of them, but are very expensive otherwise.

If you just can't do things fast enough, you need to look at the way you are doing things. Did you design for change? Is testing designed into the product to avoid a lengthy test pass at the end? Do you have a system architect who has the overall system well established in his mind? If the design is going to change, you need to ensure that the best designers will do the appropriate redesign and other people will implement the redesign. Many organizations leave the individual redesign to the programmer, which is expensive if you have moving targets to hit.

You will probably go through cycles where you want to give people the opportunity to do their own design, and where you want to do things fast. You need to be structured in such a way that you can respond fast and that you can redesign fast. So you must have an attitude that allows programmers to be told to implement another person's design.

Tell me more about third normal form data structures.

Empirical evidence suggests that if data is organized and stored in "third normal form," change is easier, i.e., the design is more flexible. There are other books that describe first, second, and third normal forms, but here is a brief illustration of third normal form organization. In fact, the examples show records that are *not* in third normal form because this gives a better understanding of what third normal form is. I've chosen an example from data processing because it's an example that everyone can relate to.

- There should be *no* repeated data or repeated groups of data.

Employee #	Name	Salary	Skill 1 Code | Level	Skill 2 Code | Level	Skill 3 Code | Level

The problem with grouped data is that you have to reserve the maximum number of groups in advance, but there may still come a time when you need to expand the number. To avoid these problems, you would split up this data record so that the skill data is stored in records with a combination key (employee number + skill code).

- In records with a composite primary key, there should be *no* data that is dependent on only part of the key. All data should be dependent on the entire primary key.

Employee #	Project #	Employee Name	Hours

The problem with this example is that Employee Name is related only to Employee #—it has no relationship with Project #. Employee Name should be in another type of record, with Employee # as the key. The Hours field is okay, because it's the number of hours worked by a given employee on a given project—it's associated with the whole key.

- *No* non-key data element should be dependent on any other non-key data element.

Employee #	Name	Salary	Department #	Department Name	Hire date

The problem with this example is that Department Name is dependent on Department #. There should be another type of record for departments, with Department # as the key, and each record containing information about the particular department.

There are always trade-offs, and sometimes there may be advantages to storing the data in a non-third normal form structure. However, it's good practice to *always* design initially in third normal form, and then to deviate if there are valid reasons for doing so.

Further Reading

Booch, Grady. 1991. *Object Oriented Design with Applications.* Benjamin-Cummings.

Page-Jones, Meilir. 1988. *The Practical Guide to Structured System Design (2nd Edition).* Englewood Cliffs, NJ: Yourdon Press.

Shneiderman, Ben. 1987. *Designing the User Interface: Strategies for Effective Human-Computer Interaction.* Reading, MA: Addison-Wesley.

Summary

The solution to the problem usually consists of two parts—the user interface, and the underlying software design. The user interface is the part that users see, and it's generally worth prototyping this to get something that users like. The *user interface* should be:

- Intuitive
- Predictable
- Optimized by frequency of operation

Other things to consider when creating the user interface are:

- Help systems
- Beginner/expert modes
- Separation of user interface from the functionality

The *software design* is the other key aspect of the solution, and there are various things to consider when creating the design:

- Flexibility/changeability/extendibility
  - Separation of functionality and user interface
  - Information hiding
  - Good data structures
  - Modules do one thing only
  - Well-defined module interfaces

- • Minimal use of global or value-retaining variables
- • Minimal use of hard-coded array sizes
- ○ Performance
  - • Good data structures
  - • Information hiding
- ○ Ability to test the software

14

Modularization

Why modularize software?

The main reason for modularizing software is that it allows you to break down large problems into small parts and solve each small problem in isolation. By the process of "divide and conquer," it allows you to develop systems of far greater complexity than if you didn't modularize.

In 1972, B.H. Liskov pointed out that modularization was often ineffective in reducing software complexity for three reasons:

1. Modules are made to do too many related but different functions, obscuring their logic.
2. Common functions are not identified in the design, resulting in their distribution (and varied implementation) among many different modules.
3. Modules interact on shared or common data in unexpected ways.

Twenty years later, these problems are still with us! Since Liskov made these points, much has been written about design and modularization, and module attributes have been analyzed and categorized. If you read any of the books describing modules, you are likely to run across the following phrases: common coupling, content coupling, control coupling, data coupling, external coupling, stamp coupling, classical cohesion, coincidental cohesion, communicational cohesion, functional cohesion, informational cohesion, logical cohesion, procedural cohesion, sequential cohesion, and temporal cohesion.

Getting into this level of detail is both informative and confusing. Informative because there are many, many things to consider when modularizing a software solution. Confusing because if you are like me you find it hard to remember all these names and what they mean.

What do you do then?

We approach the problem from a bottom-up perspective. Given that we modularize, what do we want to see in a "good" module? The answer depends on who "we" are. Which part of the software engineering process are we involved with? Facets of the process we might consider are: design, coding, testing, finding bugs, fixing bugs, enhancements and maintenance, redoing data structures and access methods, bringing in new people, code reusability, portability, and optimization. While most of what follows is relevant to any stage in the modularization process, some of it is specifically oriented towards the function module.

Design and coding.   It's the job of the design phase to "divide and conquer" the problem. How we design and then code the modularized system will affect all the subsequent phases.

Testing.   The fundamental requirement of the testing process is that we are able to easily test a module. This implies the following:

- The data that govern the module's actions are easily controlled. Parameter lists give the greatest control over the data. Global variables hide data that can govern a module's actions and make it harder to figure out what test cases to use. Global variables, both external and module scope, can also retain values, making the action of a module differ from invocation to invocation. Globals thus introduce additional complexities to the test process.

- There aren't too many pieces of data that can affect the module's actions. Thus parameter lists shouldn't be too long. The longer the list, the harder it is to cover all the test cases.

- The module does only one "logical" thing. If a module does several unrelated things, it becomes more difficult to test it thoroughly.

- No module is too large to test effectively.

Finding bugs.   The main requirement in the bug finding phase is that we are able to find bugs easily. This implies:

- Knowledge of something is isolated in as few modules as possible. We can then generally identify at most a few modules where the problem is likely to be found.

    ◦ Low use of global variables. When data is obtained from global variables, it is much more difficult to determine where the values originated than when they are passed through parameter lists. If an error occurs because of data passed through a parameter, it's easier to track down than if it occurred through a global variable.

Fixing bugs.   The requirements in the bug fixing phase are that we are able to fix bugs in such a way that the fixes are easy to test, there is a high probability the fix actually fixed the error, and there is a low probability that the fix broke something else. These requirements imply:

    ◦ The module has the attributes already discussed for testing.

    ◦ Knowledge of data structures and access methods is restricted to as few modules as possible, so that we can restrict any changes to a minimum number of modules.

    ◦ What is done in one module has no effect on other modules, except through well-defined and well-controlled interfaces, i.e., that global variables are not used. Thus we can be more certain that our changes won't break other code.

Maintaining the software and making enhancements.   The requirements in the enhancements/maintenance phase are that we can add or modify functionality easily, test the changes easily, and have the minimum chance of breaking the existing software. These requirements imply:

    ◦ The module has the attributes already discussed for testing.

    ◦ The code is easy to understand. Thus, rather than cramming many lines of unrelated code together, the code is broken out into functions that perform specific actions, and the code consists of well-named function calls that show the code flow in an obvious way.

    ◦ Knowledge of things such as data structures and access methods is restricted to as few modules as possible, so that we can restrict any changes to a minimum number of modules.

    ◦ A given action is done in only one module, otherwise we have the potential problem of finding, changing, and testing many different pieces of code. If several modules need to perform the same action, that action should be put in a separate module.

    ◦ Modules do only one logical action. When we change the code in a module, we have to retest the module. If a module performs several unrelated actions, we will have to test code that is unrelated to our changes. Better to

have modules that perform one action so that we don't have to retest unrelated functionality.

- ○ What is done in one module has no effect on other modules, except
  through well-defined and well-controlled interfaces, i.e., that global variables are not used. Thus we can be more certain that our changes won't
  break other code.

- ○ The use of global variables is restricted. A fundamental problem with
  globals is that over time people may give the same name to two different
  global variables in a large system, with very unpredictable results. Strict
  naming standards generally solve this problem, but these are often not
  enforced.

- ○ It should be easy to understand the input and output of a module. No one
  should have to read the code to understand this. Unless the documentation
  is guaranteed to be up-to-date and to describe the use of globals, all input
  and output should be via parameter lists and return values.

- ○ People should not write code that relies on undocumented or unofficial
  side-effects of functions. If it's not documented, the behavior may change.

Redoing underlying data structures and access methods.   At times we may
wish to redesign and reimplement the underlying data structures or access methods.
If we decide to do this, we want to have to change the minimum number of modules. This implies that knowledge of something be isolated to as few modules as
possible.

Letting new people take over.   The main requirement here is that the code
take the minimum amount of time to learn and understand so that changes can be
made quickly and safely. This implies that:

- ○ Modules have descriptive names.

- ○ The code consists largely of well-named function calls that show the code
  flow in an obvious way.

- ○ No module should do too much.

- ○ Modules do only one logical thing.

- ○ What is done in one module has no effect on other modules, except
  through well-defined and well-controlled interfaces.

- ○ It should be easy to understand the input and output of a module. No one
  should have to read the code to understand this. Unless the documentation
  is guaranteed to both be up-to-date and to describe the use of globals, all
  input and output should be via parameter lists and return values.

Reusability of software.   I have broken this out into its own section, rather than put it in the enhancements section, because it is a topic worth considering in its own right. Creating reusable software means that you don't have to write things from scratch, and thus don't have to retest things. Reusable software implies:

- No global variables. If a piece of software is going to be reusable over time, you can't insist that all calling software use globals of a given name. All passed and returned data should be via parameters and return values.

- A module should do a single logical thing. If a module does unrelated things, it is of little use as a general, reusable module.

- Only the data required should be passed, rather than passing a larger data structure with the relevant piece of data inside. Modules that call the reusable module should not be required to concern themselves with irrelevant data structures just so they can make function calls. If you want a date validation routine, pass the date by itself, not as part of a data structure that has meaning only to one application.

Portability.   The main requirements of portability are that the software can be ported with a minimum of changes, and when there are changes they are easy to locate and make.

- Code that is machine-specific should be put in separate modules.

- Data structures that are machine-specific should be put in separate modules.

Optimization.   The main requirement of optimization is that things be easy to optimize, should it be necessary. Anything that you feel may later need to be optimized (e.g., rewrite in assembler, change the data structures, change the access methods) should be isolated into separate modules.

What general conclusions can you draw from all this?

- Modularization should make the system/program easier to understand.

- Modules should be short enough to be comprehensible and to test easily.

- Modules should not be able to affect other modules except through well-defined, well-controlled interfaces. Thus, modules should not use global variables.

- Modules should have short parameter lists.

- A module should deal with a single logical concept.

- A given piece of functionality should be handled in a single module.

    ○ Information should be hidden in as few modules as possible so that changes affect the minimum number of modules. Modules should not be made to know about something unless there is a conceptual reason that they should know. This is known as "information hiding."

Further Reading

Myers, Glenford. 1978. *Composite/Structured Design*. New York: Van Nostrand Reinhold.

Summary

The main reason for modularizing software is that it allows us to break down large problems into small parts and solve each small problem in isolation. By the process of "divide and conquer," it allows us to develop systems of far greater complexity than if we didn't modularize.

    Unfortunately, modularization is often ineffective in reducing software complexity because modules are made to do too many related but different functions; common functions are not identified in the design, resulting in their distribution among many different modules; and modules interact on shared or common data in unexpected ways.

    This chapter starts from first principles and develops some general rules for creating "good" modules.

15

Reusable Software

What is reusable software?

Reusable software is software that can be used again and again. It's off-the-shelf software, software that you can just take and use rather than having to create and test it yourself. The C function library is an example of reusable software: if you want to find an occurrence of a character in a string you just call "strchr"—you don't have to write a new routine each time.

Software engineering consists largely of putting together building blocks to solve problems. The more building blocks you have available to you, the easier it is to create those solutions. If you've written a b-tree manager once, you should be able to take it with you from project to project, never having to write another one. If you've got a good error-reporting function, you should be able to use it on project after project.

Building blocks come in all sizes, from the simple function that checks a date, up to databases and window/form manager packages. Some, such as the date-checking routine, will probably never change, while others, such as the error-reporting function, will probably change in an evolutionary way. Packages such as database managers will probably change in a revolutionary way; you'll use the same software until the day when you decide to replace it completely with a more powerful database. But regardless how the software changes, it is all reusable; you don't have to write a new piece of code every time you want to perform a particular function.

It has been said that reusable software is the single largest factor in improving productivity, and yet it takes most software engineers years to develop an apprecia-

141

tion for it. Desire for reusable software tends to be an emotional reaction to the frustration of being given tough deadlines that you know would be easy to meet if there were a few more standard routines and standard building blocks around.

Is there much reusable software you can buy?

Yes, but the amount and price generally depend on the hardware for which you are developing. The PC probably has the largest number of reusable software libraries available. As a general rule, you can probably find vendors who will sell libraries to manipulate databases, windowing environments, graphics, and memory-resident data structures such as b-trees and linked lists. You may also be able to find disk file utilities and general utilities such as date manipulation routines. To find out exactly what is available, look at the magazines and periodicals for your platform.

What do you do with the software?

If it's externally purchased software, such as a set of database routines, or a window manager package, you'll probably do what the vendor suggested. This will probably mean that it has its own object library that you link with your software.

I put all general routines written by the organization in an organization-specific object library. I also insist on strict naming and documentation conventions. For example, let's use the prefix org_ to denote routines that are general purpose routines specific to our organization. The object library module might be org_lib, and source files might have names such as org_check_date.c or org_print.c. The individual functions would have names such as org_if_check_date() and org_if_print(). To get prototypes for the functions, and perhaps to get certain defined values, the caller would have to include header files such as org_date.h and org_files.h. The function header documentation would specify the header file to include.

There may also be routines that are general to a particular project or product. These I'd put in a project/product-specific object library. Again, all the names will reflect the name of this project or product.

How does reusable software affect software quality?

If you write code once, test the hell out of it, and put it in a library, then everyone can use it without worrying about its quality. Of course, there still may be bugs, but they will get worked out. No longer does each software engineer have to recreate and test (with varying degrees of completeness) the software every time that particular functionality is needed.

But it goes beyond that. Reusable, easy-to-use, standard building blocks make it easier to present a consistent, high-quality product to the user. Everything uses the same user interface, everything uses the same database, everything works in a predictable way. Of course, there will always be exceptions, but they should be exceptions.

Having standard building blocks that you can use without having to design, write, and test them means one of two things: you have more time for the rest of the project, in which case you can create a better-quality product; or the product will be completed more quickly, in which case you have increased productivity.

What about the quality of third-party software libraries?

Obviously you don't have the same level of control. However, there are some things you can do. You can ask for prerelease defect information and for a list of known defects. If you're getting the source code ask for the test suites used to test the software. Whether you'll get any of these things depends on whether they exist and on how keen the vendor is to sell to you.

How do you write reusable software?

You have to develop the mindset for it. Constantly ask yourself: "Is this routine useful enough that everyone could use it? Is it general enough that it could be used by more than this project?" Try to generalize things. Think about how you could use this functionality in the future in other situations. Sometimes it may mean taking a block of code and breaking it up into several general-purpose functions that you then call.

It's easier to write reusable software in an object-oriented environment because objects lend themselves to reuse more than modular decomposition does. But while it's not so easy using a procedural language, the increase in quality and productivity is worth the effort.

Doesn't it take extra time and effort to write reusable software?

In the short term, yes. It takes longer to generalize the routine you need and to test all the possibilities. However, next time you or someone else needs to perform that particular action, it will take vastly less time. Over time you and others in the organization will build up an increasingly rich set of routines, which means that over time, you will need to write less and less code to do these common functions. You and the organization will be able to spend a larger percentage of time on more interesting and more profitable problems.

How do you know that what you write will be useful to other people?

Therein lies one of the biggest problems of reusable software. Some people suggest that you shouldn't make anything reusable the first time you write it. The second time you write it, go back to the original code, make it reusable, then reuse it. The assumption being that if you need something twice, you'll probably need it again. And if you need it only once, why make it reusable? There's a lot of value to this suggestion, but it has the major flaw that it's hard to know if something has already been written (unless you also wrote it the first time). So most potentially reusable software doesn't get reused because no one knows about it. Design and code reviews help overcome this limitation because people can point out similar needs or solutions. Otherwise, the best we can usually do is to "think general-purpose" and create routines that might be reusable.

What about documenting the software?

Documentation is vital. If you have a useful piece of code, other people should be able to use it without having to pore through the code to understand what it does and what parameters it expects. The routine header documentation should describe what the routine does, what parameters it expects, the acceptable values or range of values, and what it returns under what conditions. It should describe the "contract" between the caller and the routine. It should also describe whether it's reentrant, i.e., whether it can be called by anyone, any place, any time, or whether it remembers its context. An example of a routine that is not reentrant might be a file-reading function, in which the next chunk of data depends on the last data it got. An example of this function header documentation might be:

```
/*----------------------------------------------------------------------------
FUNCTION int  org_if_date_convert (void *vpr_in_date, int ir_in_format,
                                   void *vwp_out_date, int ir_out_format)

This function converts a date in one format to a date in another format.
Formats include string, integer, and quad based date formats. The pointers are
defined a void pointers so that the caller doesn't have to cast the dates to
any particular type. For a full list of formats, see org_date.h. Note that
there is a format option to convert today's date into any of the formats.

KEYWORDS:    DATE CONVERT

FUNCTION OBLIGATIONS:

        Check the pointers to ensure they are not NULL.
        Check the formats to ensure they are both valid.
        Check the input date for validity.
        Use today's date as the input date if so requested.
        Convert the input date to the output date format.
```

```
CALLER OBLIGATIONS:
          Pass valid pointers to the appropriate data structures.
          Include "org_date.h" for prototypes and format defines.

PARAMETERS:
   Read:    vpr_in_date          Pointer to date to convert.
            ir_in_format         Format of input date.  Defined in org_date.h.
            ir_out_format        Format of output date.  Defined in org_date.h.
   Write:   vwp_out_date         Pointer to data area for converted date.

GLOBALS:    None.

RETURNS:    SYS_SUCCESS          Good date, successfully converted.
            SYS_INVALDATE        Invalid input date.
            SYS_NULLPTR          Null pointer passed as parameter.
            SYS_INVALPARAM       Invalid format passed as a parameter.
-----------------------------------------------------------------------------*/
```

This documentation should also be printed out and distributed to all the software engineers so that they have a page of documentation about every organization-wide function. Software engineers would have a loose-leaf binder of organization-written functions that they can refer to, just as they probably have books about the language being used and manuals about the operating system level routines.

How do you get other people to use these organization-written routines?

The first step is obviously to write routines or functions that people will find useful. The next step is make it easy for people to find the information about the reusable software.

The larger the organization, the more likely it is to have tools to help maintain this information. A useful tool is a search tool that allows you to specify keywords and that will find all functions with the keywords in the keyword section of the header documentation. You can then browse through all the functions, looking at the descriptions and parameters and possibly the code. If the tool is well integrated, it will search the various libraries available to you—product, product family, organization.

However, most organizations don't have tools like these, in which case you need to document all functions and routines in a single document that is easy to reference. All the functions and routines should be organized into categories, with a one- or two-line description of the function, and a reference to where a full description can be found. As new functions are written, the list can be updated, with the new functions also listed at the bottom. Date the list, and distribute a new one whenever it makes sense.

Because the NIH syndrome can be strong, you may also have to provide some additional incentives, such as doing code reviews and requiring that some code be replaced with calls to library functions.

Can you give me an example of what a list of routines would look like?

Here's an abbreviated list, showing some ANSI C functions and some organization-written functions.

FUNCTIONS

Code:	C	C language (ANSI C)
	ORG	ORG_LIB. Organization-wide library.

Code	Function	Description

Data Structure Management

Code	Function	Description
ORG	org_vpf_dll_add	Add a member to a doubly linked list.
ORG	org_vpf_dll_insert_after	Insert a new member after an existing member.
ORG	org_vpf_dll_insert_before	Insert a new member before an existing member.
ORG	org_if_dll_delete_member	Delete a list member and free all memory associated with it.
ORG	org_vpf_dll_get_first	Get first member of the linked list.
ORG	org_vpf_dll_get_last	Get last member of the linked list.
ORG	org_vpf_dll_get_next	Get next member of the linked list.
ORG	org_vpf_dll_get_prev	Get previous member of the linked list.
ORG	org_vpf_dll_create_list	Create a doubly linked list.
ORG	org_if_dll_clear_list	Clear a doubly linked list.
ORG	org_if_dll_delete_list	Delete a doubly linked list and free up all associated memory.

Date/Time

Code	Function	Description
ORG	org_if_date_check	Check a date in one of several formats for validity.
ORG	org_if_date_convert	Convert a date from one format to another.
ORG	org_if_date_add	Add some number of days to a date.
C	asctim	Converts time from tm structure to a string.
C	clock	Returns the elapsed processor time in number of ticks.
C	ctime	Converts time from type time_t to a string.
C	difftime	Computes the difference of two values of type time_t.
C	gmtime	Converts time from type time_t to a tm structure which corresponds to GMT.
C	mktime	Converts time from a value of type time_t to a tm structure which corresponds to the local time. Not supported in VAXC.
C	strftime	Prepares a string with date and time values from a tm structure, formatted according to a specified format. Not supported in VAXC.
C	time	Returns the current date and time as a value of type time_t.

Error Reporting

ORG	org_err	Report an error, either to logfile, stderr, or store in linked list.
ORG	org_if_err_clear	Clear the linked list of stored error messages.
ORG	org_if_err_close_logfile	Close the logfile for error logging. org_err will now use stderr for logging.
ORG	org_if_err_open_logfile	Open a logfile for logging error messages to. If not opened, org_err will log to stderr.
ORG	org_cpf_err_next	Get next stored error message.
ORG	org_cpf_err_prev	Get previous stored error message.
C	strerror	Returns a string containing the system error message for a given error number.
C	perror	Prints an error message to stderr from your message and the system message associated with errno.
C	assert	Prints a diagnostic message and aborts program if a given logical expression is false.

But isn't maintaining and distributing this information a waste of a programmer's time?

If you have fancy tools, they should be able to extract the information from the function headers in the code in the library. If you don't have the tools, all the programmer has to do is provide information about new general-purpose functions he has written. The master list would be maintained by one person—perhaps an entry level trainee or an administrator—who would also be responsible for distributing the list.

I imagine standards are useful with reusable software.

Of course. Standards should probably be defined for documentation, keywords, examples, naming conventions, libraries for specific languages, and test suites. To help people conform to standards, provide a template that makes it obvious what is needed.

```
/*------------------------------------------------------------
int _if_

DESCRIPTION:

KEYWORDS:

EXAMPLES:

FUNCTION OBLIGATIONS:

CALLER OBLIGATIONS:
```

```
PARAMETERS:
    Read:
    Modify:
    Write:

GLOBALS:
    Read:
    Modify:
    Write:

RETURNS:
------------------------------------------------------------*/
int _if_
{
    static char  ca_version[] = "$version$: _if_ 1.0";
    int          i_status;


    return (i_status);
}
```

How do you make sure you have the right version of the routine?

One way is to have all functions include a static variable that contains a well-defined character string:

```
static char ca_version[] = "$version$: function_name 1.0"
```

When you make a change that requires a change to the documentation, update the version number. Numbers to the right of the decimal point are incremented when the change doesn't require a change to the documentation. If the documentation changes, the integer part is incremented and the decimal part is reset to zero. For example:

1.23 → 1.24   No documentation change
1.23 → 2.0   Documentation changes

It's simple to write a program that searches an executable and looks for the string "$version$:", printing out the function name and the version number. Of course, the documentation should also contain the integral version number if you are to reconcile the documentation and code.

How do you ensure the software is well tested?

You'd usually require that each routine submitted have a test suite, which is maintained and run when the routine is changed. Since it's so important for reusable software to be bullet-proof, I'd also insist on design reviews, code reviews, and test plan reviews.

How do you enforce the rules?

Reusable software libraries work best when each library has an owner (a developer, not a manager), who enforces the rules. There should also be a formal, documented procedure for adding a routine to the libraries, with things that must be checked off. For example:

```
Routine name:
Description:

_____    Requirements review
_____    Design review
_____    Test plan review
_____    Code review
_____    Test suite run
_____    Documentation okay
_____    Keywords okay
_____    Examples okay
_____    Naming conventions followed
_____    Passes lint (if C code)
```

Besides an owner of the library, each routine should have an owner (usually the person who originally wrote it). Incidentally, reusable libraries tend to work best when they are started by a developer, rather than by a manager.

Are there any other types of reusable software?

Yes, there are the skeleton program and the standard program. A skeleton program is one where all the structure and function calls are in place, and you just fill in the blanks. The standard program is very similar, but it's already complete, and you strip out what you don't need, replacing it with your code. Either way, there will be comments showing you where to make changes.

These types of program work well in situations where you are likely to have many programs that are similar in concept but differ in the details. Examples might be reports, editing database files, or reading data from an external feed. While you still will have to test them, skeleton and standard programs make it easier to get things right, thus increasing quality and productivity. They are very successful reuse techniques.

Further Reading

Biggerstaff, Ted. 1989. *Software Reusability. Volume 1: Concepts and Models; Volume 2: Applications and Experience*. ACM Press.

Freeman, Peter (editor). 1987. *Software Reusability*. Los Alamitos, CA: IEEE Computer Society Press.

Tracz, Will (editor). 1988. *Software Reuse—Emerging Technology*. Los Alamitos, CA: IEEE Computer Society Press.

Summary

Reusing software can increase quality and productivity: quality because the software has already been well tested, and productivity because you don't have to write and test the software. Reusable software includes third-party function libraries and in-house function libraries. Semi-reusable software includes skeleton programs, in which the basic structure has already been created, and you fill in the appropriate sections with code specific to your application. Some of the biggest barriers to reuse are:

- People would rather write their own software to solve particular problems.
- People don't trust software written by others.
- People are under too much time pressure to generalize the code sufficiently so it can be used by other people in other situations.

Reusable software libraries work best when they are started and maintained by one person, who takes responsibility for the library, makes sure that the functions put in the library conform to all the appropriate standards for code and documentation, and distributes information about the library and its contents.

The promise of object-oriented development is that it makes it much easier to reuse software and thus gain the increase in quality and productivity.

16

Methodologies

What is a methodology?

For our purposes, a methodology is a formal language for describing some aspect of the system we are describing or the solution we are proposing. For example, data flow diagrams describe the way that data flows around the system. State transition diagrams describe the possible states and changes of state in a software system. Other people have defined methodology as the process used in software development, or the models and practices used, but, in the end, most discussions of methodologies come down to discussions about formal languages and diagramming techniques. That tends to be where the controversies and disagreements lie.

Various methodologies have been created and refined to describe the different types of software systems. Now, methodology is a dirty word among some software developers who feel that using a methodology restricts their creativity. In reality, a methodology is simply a language that happens to be good at describing a system, and is useful for communicating your ideas and thoughts to other people.

Methodologies are languages that have evolved to solve the problems of writing down the way that systems work or should work. Languages like English are too verbose and imprecise to be good at communicating the way systems work, and they don't provide a framework for doing things consistently. Use a methodology when you can't afford to have things misunderstood.

So a methodology is a tool?

The act of writing things down (requirements, design, etc.) forces you to think clearly and helps you notice holes and inconsistencies in your thinking. Once you have something written, you can pass it around and others can review it. Methodologies are simply an effective tool for that writing. And, like any tool, methodologies can help you create a good product if you use them well, but they won't prevent you from creating a poor product. A methodology won't compensate for poor requirements or poor design.

To build a house, you need a range of tools. To build a good house you also need a good design and good materials. The quality of the software product depends on the quality of the requirements and the design, and the appropriateness of the tools for the job. No one methodology will work for all situations; you need a repertoire of methodologies so that you can use the correct one for the job. The more fluent you are with a range of methodologies, the easier it is to jot down ideas using one of the diagramming techniques.

Are there any dangers in using a formal methodology?

The biggest danger is that it's easy to get carried away and make conformance to the methodology, rather than the product, the main goal. As long as you approach it from the perspective that the methodology is a tool to help build the product, you should be okay.

How do methodologies relate to CASE?

CASE tools rely on methodologies, although you don't need CASE to use a methodology. CASE makes it easier to control and make changes to the descriptions of large systems; unfortunately, CASE also makes it easier to get carried away with the methodology, to the detriment of the product.

What are the different methodologies?

There are an incredible number of them, although some are just refinements on others. I'll list some of the methodologies and diagramming techniques.

- Action diagrams
- Control flow diagrams
- Data flow diagrams
- Decision tables
- Entity relationship diagrams
- HIPO charts
- Jackson structured design
- Modern structured analysis
- Petri nets
- Program design language
- Problem statement language

- Real-time structured analysis (Hatley and Pirbhai)
- Real-time structured analysis (Ward and Mellor)
- Statecharts
- State transition diagrams
- Structured analysis (DeMarco)
- Structured analysis (Gane and Sarson)
- Structured analysis (Yourdon)
- Structured analysis and design techniques (SADT)
- Structured analysis and system specification (SASS)
- Structured requirements definition
- Warnier-Orr diagrams

Then there are the object-oriented analysis and design techniques, some of which I've listed:

- CRC cards (Ward Cunningham)
- Hierarchical object-oriented design
- Object modeling technique
- Object-oriented analysis (Peter Coad)
- Object-oriented analysis (Sally Shlaer and Stephen Mellor)
- Object-oriented design (Grady Booch)
- Object-oriented requirements specification (Bailin)
- Object-oriented systems analysis (Hewlett-Packard)
- Object-oriented structured design
- ObjectOry (Ivar Jacobson)
- Synthesis/Analysis (Meilir Page-Jones and Steven Weiss)

How on earth do you decide which one you need?

I agree, it's rather bewildering. One of the biggest reasons people don't use methodologies is they don't know how. I've worked at various places where every requirements document was different, every design document was different. There were no standards on what information should be in them or how it should be represented.

The best advice I can give is to read up on the different methodologies and choose one that seems to work with your type of software. Then implement it. It's not a trivial task—learning how to speak in a new language is never easy—and it can seem overwhelming at first. Some books that may help are listed at the end of this chapter. Other things you might do include:

- Bring in a consultant who is an expert on different methodologies to advise on what methodology to use and to help get you started.

- Read books, such as the ones following, to get some ideas on different methodologies.

○ Start with a single small project, just so that you can learn how to use the methodology.

○ Send a few people to a course that deals with analysis and design methodologies.

○ Talk to other people in your line of software about what they do.

○ Post to one of the bulletin boards where people discuss software engineering and methodologies. The newsgroup comp.software-eng in the Usenet bulletin board (rn on Unix) is one such place.

If you still have no idea where to start, use the "Ready, Fire, Aim" technique to get off dead-center. Choose a methodology, start using it, then learn its strengths and weaknesses. Once you have the knowledge that comes with using it, you can look at other methodologies and ask the right questions of them. If you can't think of a better methodology to start with, choose Data Flow Diagrams.

Further Reading

Davis, Alan. 1990. *Software Requirements: Analysis and Specification*. Englewood Cliffs, NJ: Prentice-Hall. Includes a survey of the various methodologies, and uses them with three different types of problems.

Martin, James, and Carma McClure. 1985. *Diagramming Techniques for Analysts and Programmers*. Englewood Cliffs, NJ: Prentice-Hall. A comprehensive survey of diagramming notations for analysis and design.

Martin, James, and Carma McClure. 1988. *Structured Techniques for Computing: The Basis for CASE*. Englewood Cliffs, NJ: Prentice-Hall. Describes many of the techniques of structured analysis and design, and analyzes and compares their various strengths and weaknesses.

Summary

This chapter discusses a methodology as a formal language for describing some part of the system we are developing. Methodology is often considered a dirty word by developers who feel that using a methodology restricts their freedom. However, a methodology is just a language that has evolved to solve the problems of describing a system—natural languages generally being too wordy and imprecise.

No one methodology is perfect for all problems, so developers should be familiar with a range of methodologies, and able to select the right one for the particular task.

17

Specifications and Documents

Tell me more about the documents.

Before we look at the content of the documents, let's try to understand why we are creating them. Who needs the information? Why do they need it? Who are the right people to review the information? What is the best way to organize and present the information. Here are some possible purposes of documents:

- ○ Help concentrate on the problem you are trying to solve.
- ○ Provide something to test against.
- ○ Provide something for reviewers to look at.
- ○ Help get quick feedback on what is being built.
- ○ Inform other groups about the product:
  - QA (purpose is to help them focus their testing):
    - – What user interface has changed.
    - – What functionality has changed.
    - – What modules have changed.
    - – What tests have been run.
  - Support (purpose is to help them know how to install, what has changed, what bugs have been fixed):
    - – What must be installed with this.
    - – What installation procedures have changed.
    - – What else must happen at installation (what programs must be run, etc.).
    - – What new functionality is there.

- – What bugs have been fixed.
- – What bugs have been introduced.
- Sales:
  - – What is new.
  - – What are the benefits.
- Training:
  - – What is new.
- User Documentation (purpose is to tell them what documentation must be written or has changed, and when new documentation is needed):
  - – What new functionality is there.
  - – What functionality has changed.
  - – What user interface changes are there.
  - – How things are done.
  - – Examples of what users want to do.
- ○ Provide a reference about the product and its history of decisions.

Some documents may have sufficiently different audiences that you should create two documents instead of one. For example, if you are writing a user guide for translating all existing messages into other languages, you have several audiences: the developers who will make the changes to the existing software, the people who will be doing the actual translations, and the people who will be building and installing the language files. You may need several user guides.

What do you want to see in a requirements spec?

Here's a list of topics you might want to see in a requirements document. Based on the product you develop, you may need to remove some and add others.

- ○ Audience and reason they want to see this
- ○ Problem statement
- ○ Product overview
- ○ Goals/non-goals
- ○ Scope
- ○ Glossary
- ○ User involvement
- ○ Constraints
  - Development cost
  - Unit cost
  - Timeframe
  - Implementation priorities
- ○ Functional requirements
- ○ Space requirements
  - Memory usage
  - Disk usage

- Performance requirements
  - Response times
  - Number of operations per second
  - Data flow volumes
- Exception handling
- Maintainability
- Reliability
- Security
- Compliance to standards
- Training
  - Ease of learning
  - Self-paced training
- Ease of use
  - Help
  - Beginner/Expert mode
  - Consistency of user interface
  - Predictability of results
- Ease of tailoring
  - User profiles
  - Group profiles
  - System profiles
- Installation
  - Ease of installation/setup
  - Ease of configuration
- Support
  - Ease of support
  - Ease of recovery
- Hardware platforms
  - Vendor
  - Hardware
  - Operating system
  - Terminals/workstations/PCs
  - Color/monochrome
- Hardware interfaces
- Communications interfaces
- Database requirements
- Programming languages
- International capabilities
  - Translated text and error messages
  - Input/recognition of accented characters, etc.
  - Date/time formats and separators
  - Numeric separators
  - Sorting sequences

- ○ Testing/validation requirements
- ○ Acceptance criteria
- ○ Possible future requirements
- ○ Sources of information

Remember that the attribute requirements (such as maintainability, performance, and ease of use) should be specified separately from the functional requirements. In general, the attribute requirements should have planned-level values and worst-case values so that you can test and measure to see if the requirements were met. If you can't measure them, they become motherhood and apple pie—everyone agrees about them but there's no special attention paid to them. People work hardest to meet the requirements that are measurable, so if a requirement is important, make it measurable.

There are several formal requirements specifications. For example, as part of the software process defined in DOD-STD-2167A, the Department of Defense standard for software contractors, DI-MCCR-80025A defines the software requirements specification. Another organization that defines standards is IEEE, the Institute of Electrical and Electronics Engineers. The *IEEE Guide for Software Requirements* (IEEE/ANSI 830-1084) is the IEEE and ANSI standard for requirements. It offers several outlines for an SRS (software requirements specification), each tailored for a different type of problem. Let's look at them and their differences.

Common Start

1. Introduction
    1.1   Purpose of SRS
    1.2   Scope of product
    1.3   Definitions, acronyms, abbreviations
    1.4   References
    1.5   Overview of rest of SRS
2. General description
    2.1   Product perspective
    2.2   Product functions
    2.3   User characteristics
    2.4   General constraints
    2.5   Assumptions and dependencies
3. Specific requirements
    Appendices
        History
        Cross-references
        Sample formats for input
        Sample formats for output
    Index

There are four different versions, differing in section 3.

Version 1

Main points of difference:

- External user interface is the same for all functional requirements.
- Attributes (maintainability, performance, constraints, etc.) are the same for all functional requirements.

3. Specific requirements
   3.1 Functional requirements
      3.1.1 Functional requirement 1
         3.1.1.1 Introduction
         3.1.1.2 Inputs
         3.1.1.3 Processing
         3.1.1.4 Outputs
      3.1.2 Functional requirement 2
        ...

        ...

   3.2 External interface requirements
      3.2.1 User interface
      3.2.2 Hardware interfaces
      3.2.3 Software interfaces
      3.2.4 Communications interfaces
   3.3 Performance requirements
   3.4 Design constraints
      3.4.1 Standards compliance
      3.4.2 Hardware limitations
      ...
   3.5 Attributes
      3.5.1 Availability
      3.5.2 Security
      3.5.3 Maintainability
      3.5.4 Transferability/conversion
      ...
   3.6 Other requirements
      3.6.1 Database
      3.6.2 Operations
      3.6.3 Site adaption

Version 2

Main points of difference:

- External user interface is different for each functional requirement.
- Attributes (maintainability, performance, constraints, etc.) are the same for all functional requirements.

3. Specific requirements
   3.1 Functional requirements

3.1.1 Functional requirement 1
    3.1.1.1 Specification
        3.1.1.1.1 Introduction
        3.1.1.1.2 Inputs
        3.1.1.1.3 Processing
        3.1.1.1.4 Outputs
    3.1.1.2 External interfaces
        3.1.1.2.1 User interfaces
        3.1.1.2.2 Hardware interfaces
        3.1.1.2.3 Software interfaces
        3.1.1.2.4 Communications interfaces
3.1.2 Functional requirement 2
    ...

3.2 Performance requirements
3.3 Design constraints
3.4 Attributes
    3.4.1 Availability
    3.4.2 Security
    3.4.3 Maintainability
    3.4.4 Transferability/conversion
...
3.6 Other requirements
    3.6.1 Database
    3.6.2 Operations
    3.6.3 Site adaption

Version 3

Main points of difference:

- External user interface is the same for all functional requirements.
- Attributes (maintainability, performance, constraints, etc.) are different for each functional requirement.

3. Specific requirements
  3.1 Functional requirements
    3.1.1 Functional requirement 1
      3.1.1.1 Introduction
      3.1.1.2 Inputs
      3.1.1.3 Processing
      3.1.1.4 Outputs
      3.1.1.5 Performance requirements
      3.1.1.6 Design constraints
        3.1.1.6.1 Standards compliance
        3.1.1.6.2 Hardware limitations
        ...
      3.1.1.7 Attributes
        3.1.1.7.1 Availability
        3.1.1.7.2 Security

3.1.1.7.3   Maintainability
3.1.1.7.4   Transferability/conversion
...
3.1.1.8   Other requirements
3.1.1.8.1   Database
3.1.1.8.2   Operations
3.1.1.8.3   Site adaption
...
3.1.2   Functional requirement 2
...
3.2   External interface requirements
3.2.1   User interfaces
3.2.1.1   Performance requirements
3.2.1.2   Design constraints
3.2.1.2.1   Standards compliance
3.2.1.2.2   Hardware limitations
...
3.2.1.3   Attributes
3.2.1.3.1   Availability
3.2.1.3.2   Security
3.2.1.3.3   Maintainability
3.3.1.3.4   Transferability/conversion
...
3.2.1.4   Other requirements
3.2.1.4.1   Database
3.2.1.4.2   Operations
3.2.1.4.3   Site adaption
...
3.2.2   Hardware interfaces
...
3.2.3   Software interfaces
...
3.2.4   Communications interfaces
...

Version 4

Main points of difference:

○   External user interface is different for each functional requirement.
○   Attributes (maintainability, performance, constraints, etc.) are different for each functional requirement.

3.   Specific requirements
3.1   Functional requirement 1
3.1.1   Introduction
3.1.2   Inputs
3.1.3   Processing
3.1.4   Outputs

3.1.5 External interfaces
    3.1.5.1   User interfaces
    3.1.5.2   Hardware interfaces
    3.1.5.3   Software interfaces
    3.1.5.4   Communication interfaces
3.1.6 Performance requirements
3.1.7 Design constraints
    3.1.7.1   Standards compliance
    3.1.7.2   Hardware limitations
    …
3.1.8 Attributes
    3.1.8.1   Availability
    3.1.8.2   Security
    3.1.8.3   Maintainability
    3.1.8.4   Transferability/conversion
    …
3.1.9 Other requirements
    3.1.9.1   Database
    3.1.9.2   Operations
    3.1.9.3   Site adaptation
    …

3.2   Functional requirement 2
…

The IEEE requirements standards are designed to cover a wide variety of software problem types, so you should be able to find one that roughly matches your needs. Here's an example of a somewhat abbreviated and incomplete requirements document, modified to meet some specific needs.

Requirements Document

System/Subsystem:	Multi-Language
Release Number:	5.0
Project Number:	C32
Document Revision:	4
Date:	4/30/91
Author:	Wendy Smith

1. INTRODUCTION

    1.1   Audience and Reason

       ◦ Software developers
         • To define what the solution must provide
         • To help think through the requirements
         • To give something to test against
         • To give reviewers the information they need to review the requirements
         • To provide historical information to future developers

- ○ Foreign distributors
  - So they can understand what we are doing and how it may affect their operations
  - To help get feedback on the requirements
- ○ Documentation
  - To give them a feel for changes that may happen in documentation
- ○ Quality Assurance
  - To give them a feel for changes in the software
  - To provide something to test against
- ○ Support
  - To give them a feel for changes in the software that may affect their jobs

1.2 Problem to be solved

Our software is English-based. This makes it difficult to sell software in countries where a different language is spoken. We want to modify our software so that it can be used by people who speak a different language.

1.3 Overview

We anticipate that we can earn another $6 million a year from the European market if we have European-language-based software. Japanese and Chinese language capability is worth about $4 million per year. (From International Business Analysis paper BA-0482, by Fred Jones.)

Currently, menu and message text is all hard coded in the programs. To modify our software to solve the problem requires two things. First, all text must be in external files that can be easily translated by foreign distributors. Second, all programs must get the text they need from the external files.

1.4 Project Scope

The project is limited in scope. In this release we plan to address only the languages that can be represented by a single-byte character set. In a future release we may address multibyte character sets; however, this is not scheduled, so the current project must provide a solution that will work for at least the next three years.

1.5 Resource constraints

It should be possible to fully implement the solution within two person-years, and in the next software development cycle of six months elapsed time (from Sue White, based on profit/loss analysis).

1.6 User Characteristics

There are several different types of user:
- ○ The end user will use the workstation, and may on occasion change the language in which he or she is working. These users are familiar with our software, but may not be computer-literate.
- ○ Software developers will modify the existing software to obtain all character strings, currency symbols, etc., from a file rather than using hard-coded values.
- ○ Translators at foreign distributors will translate the text and will build new language files from the translations. The translators will probably not be computer-literate.
- ○ Installation people at foreign offices will install the software. These people are computer-literate.

1.7 Assumptions and Dependencies

2. REQUIREMENTS

2.1 Functional Requirements

2.1.1 All text must be stored in a program-independent file or files so it can be translated.

    2.1.1.1 messages
    2.1.1.2 menus
    2.1.1.3 selection characters

2.1.2 Other country-dependent data must be stored in a file or files so that it can be modified by overseas people.

    2.1.2.1 currency symbol
    2.1.2.2 numeric separators
    2.1.2.3 date/time format

2.1.3 It must not be possible for the translators to end up with missing messages, etc.

2.1.4 All errors related to translation process must be caught before they would show up during program execution.

2.1.5 The software must get all text and selection characters from the translated files.

2.1.6 The software must get all knowledge of currency symbol, numeric separators, and date formats from the modified files.

2.1.8 It must be possible to install multiple languages on a network, and have any invocation of the program choose its own language.

2.1.9 It must be possible for all nodes to share a language file across the network, rather than require that each node has its own language files.

2.1.10 It must be possible to set up each workstation so that the software comes up in the chosen language.

2.1.11 t must be possible, with no more than five keystrokes, to change from one language to another.

2.2 Quality Requirements

2.2.1 Verifiability

    2.2.1.1 It must be possible to determine if messages, menus, etc., are coming from the translated files.

2.2.2 Supportability

    2.2.2.1 It must be possible to install language files on a node or network ...
        2.2.2.1.1 ... with no more than six commands.
        2.2.2.1.2 ... in no more than 10 minutes (from internal paper Human Factors in Installation, HF-0045, by Sam Ellis).

    2.2.2.2 It must be possible to set up a program invocation to use a language file ...
        2.2.2.2.1 ... with no more than three commands.
        2.2.2.2.2 ... in no more than five minutes (from internal paper Human Factors in Installation, HF-0045, by Sam Ellis).

    2.2.2.3 If a message is missing, or has a serious error, the software must give information about the message and its error sufficient to track down the message and fix it.

2.2.3   Maintainability

    2.2.3.1   It must be possible to add new messages and menus without requiring that translated text be retranslated.

2.2.4   Translatability

    2.2.4.1   The translators must have some context to help them translate the messages. At a minimum, they must know:
        2.2.4.1.1   If the text is a message, menu, or selection character.
        2.2.4.1.2   The application to which the message belongs.

    2.2.4.2   It must be possible for translators to add comments and notes to the individual messages in the text files.

    2.2.4.3   Translators should be able to use either standard editors available on their workstations, or a specific editor provided as part of this project.

2.2.5   Extensibility

    2.2.5.1   It must be possible to extend the scheme to a multi-byte scheme with no more than six person-months of effort (from Sue White, based on profit/ loss analysis).

2.3   Performance Requirements

    2.3.1   The user interface software must run no more than five percent slower because of the translated text (from Al McManus).

    2.3.2   It should take no longer than 15 seconds to change from one language to another (from Al McManus).

2.4   Portability Requirements

    2.4.1   The functions written must be portable without changes to the following platforms:

        2.4.1.1   Apollo/Aegis
        2.4.1.2   HP-UX
        2.4.1.3   Sun
        2.4.1.4   Ultrix

    2.4.2   The translated files must be readable across the network, by workstations running any of the following:

        2.4.2.1   Apollo/Aegis
        2.4.2.2   HP-UX
        2.4.2.3   Sun
        2.4.2.4   Ultrix

2.5   Design Constraints

    2.5.1   The new way of handling text must require less than 1 megabyte of additional swap space or paging space (from Al McManus).

    2.5.2   The new way of handling text must require less than 1 megabyte of additional disk space (excluding any additional swap space). (From Al McManus.)

    2.5.3   It should not be required that every node in a network have translated text files.

2.6   Possible Future Enhancements

    2.6.1   We may add multi-byte processing for Asian countries.
    2.6.2   We may add a Motif-style user interface.

What do you want to see in a functional spec?

The purpose of the functional spec is to detail the solution, showing what the product will do, how it will do it, and what the underlying data and control flows will be. It should demonstrate that the developers understand the requirements. What goes in the functional spec and what goes in the design spec is often a matter of individual taste; some people may put the data flows in the functional spec, while others prefer them in the design spec.

- Audience and reason (at whom is this directed, and why?)
- Glossary of terms
- Product Overview
  - Purpose of product
  - Scope of project
  - Product goals
  - Product non-goals
- External interfaces
  - Context
  - User screens
  - Report formats
  - User commands summary
- Internal data flows, etc.
  - Diagrams (data flow, state transition, etc)
  - Data dictionary
  - Database/data file access
- Performance
- Exceptions conditions/exception handling
- Requirements traceback (a table that links each item in the functional spec to a specific requirement)

What do you want to see in a design spec?

It's difficult to give a definitive answer, because there are many levels of design and thus of design spec. Things that one person might consider part of the low-level design are part of another person's high-level design. And the documents you'd create for a new system may be different from those you'd need for maintenance work. So the formats I'll show are mainly to give you ideas of things to include and aren't necessarily the best way for your software. You can improve your documents over time by thinking about design problems that weren't covered in the design document, then modifying the template.

Let's start with an architectural design spec. An architecture is the way a system fits together, so this document shows the relationship between the high-level components. This document format could also be used to describe software at lower and lower subcomponent levels.

System/Subsystem:
Release Number:
Project Number:
Document Revision:
Date:
Designer's Name:

1.0 INTRODUCTION

    1.1   Audience and Reason
        [At whom is this directed, and why?]
        • Original developer—to help think architectural design through
        • Other developers—to review the architectural design

    1.2   Design goals
        [Is your goal maintainable software? Platform-independent software? Performance? There is probably more than one goal, so list them in order of priority.]
        • Maintainability/extendibility
        • Performance

    1.3   Product overview/Background
        [An overview of the product being designed and the scope of the architecture. Why are you doing this?]

    1.4   Glossary/terminology
        [Lists the terms used]

    1.5   Risks and issues
        [Describes the risks inherent in the design, things that may not provide necessary performance, etc., or which may delay schedules.]

2.0 DESIGN

    2.1   Architecture
        [Show the major components of the design, and their relationships to each other.]

    2.2   Component functionality breakdown
        [Describe the functions that are performed by each major component. Describe whether these are new components or modified components.]

    2.3   Requirements traceback
        [This is a table that links the functionality provided by each component to a specific item in the Requirements spec or the Functional spec.]

    2.4   Control and data flow
        [Show the control and data flow between the major components. This may include data flow diagrams, etc.]

    2.5   Component interfaces
        [Show the interfaces between components, showing both input and output data.]

2.6   Interface data structures
[Show the detailed data structures used for communicating between components.]

2.7   Global data
[Show any global data that is shared between components.]

2.8   Internal data structures
[Show the major internal data structures, their relationships to each other, and the methods used to access them (array, linked list, b-tree, etc.).]

2.9   Sequencing/Timing
[Show any sequencing, timing, or interrupt processing required when communicating between components.]

2.10 Data Dictionary and database/file design
[Describe the data dictionary and the database or data file structure, showing access types and relationships between files and records. Describe the database/file record layout.]

2.11 Exception/error conditions
[Describe the exception/error conditions and how they will be handled.]

2.12 Initialization procedures
[Describe the initialization procedures for the overall system and for the individual components.]

2.13 Subcomponents
[List and describe the subcomponents of each major component. The document showing the design of the subcomponents could take the form of another document similar to this, or might be a more detailed design document, depending on the size of the subcomponent.]

2.14 Software to be reused
[Describe any components, subcomponents, and modules that can be reused here.]

2.15 Components no longer used
[List any components or modules that are no longer used, and why. List any source files if appropriate.]

2.16 Regression/automated testing
[Describe any built-in testing mechanisms for playing repeatable test cases and doing regression testing.]

What would you see in a more detailed design?

Module/routine/function name:
Release Number:
Project Number:
Document Revision:
Date:
Designer's Name:

1.0   Audience and reason
[At whom is this directed, and why?]

2.0 Module description

2.1 Obligations
[What does the module do? What are its obligations to the caller?]

2.2 Assumptions/dependencies
[What assumptions does the module make about the state of the world, or about what the caller has done? What does the module depend on?]

2.3 Limitations
[What are the limitations of the module?]

3.0 Interface specifications

3.1 Input parameters
[What parameters are passed in to be used?]

3.2 Legality checks
[What checks are done on the input parameters to ensure they are legal? What checks are done on pointers for output values?]

3.3 Output parameters
[What data do we return through the parameter list?]

3.4 Global data
[What global data is read? What global data is modified? Under what conditions? Why?]

3.5 Return values
[What values are returned? Which ones signify errors? Under what conditions are the different values returned?]

4.0 Algorithms
[What special algorithms are being used in the module? Where did the algorithm come from? Describe it.]

5.0 Main data structures
[What are the main data structures used internally? What are the access methods to the data structures (array, linked list, b-tree, etc.). What data structures retain their values between invocations?]

6.0 Code to be reused
[What library routines can be used? What code can be cut and pasted from somewhere else?]

7.0 Pseudocode
[Give the module's pseudocode.]

For single routines, all of the information in sections 2.0 through 5.0 could be placed in the routine header block and printed out for the review. That way the information would be preserved in the code for future developers. I've also included a section for the pseudocode for those who like to see pseudocode. My preference is for the detailed design to *not* include pseudocode, because I'd rather review the other sections as part of the detailed design, then review the real code to see if it implemented the detailed design. I'd also review critical algorithms separately, to emphasize their importance.

You will probably need to modify these examples to meet your own needs. When you do so, remember that for any type of software system there is always a key element that is at the heart of the system. For most software systems, the key element is the data structures, so however you modify these documents, make sure that you keep a section that describes the data structures.

What do you want to see in a test document?

There are several different types of test document. There is a test plan, which describes the whole test environment and the types of testing you'll be doing. Test procedures detail the steps needed for a particular test. Test cases describe the actual test data for a test. The most general of these is the test plan, and you might consider the others as detail of the test plan. Different types of product need different types of testing, so before showing some test plan outlines, let's list some of the things you might want to include in a test plan.

- ○ Objective of the test (test feature, function, algorithm, etc.).
- ○ How the test will be run (test driver, automated keystrokes, by hand, etc.).
- ○ Tools and techniques to be used.
- ○ Machine configuration.
- ○ Test assumptions.
- ○ Requirements being tested against.
- ○ Items from functional spec being tested against.
- ○ A unique number to make it easy to trace back to the requirements.
- ○ Functionality Tests
  - • Default values
  - • Normal inputs
  - • Boundary conditions
  - • Troublesome conditions: missing or empty files, 0, 1, etc.
- ○ Performance Tests
  - • Response time
  - • Execution time
  - • Throughput
  - • Memory use

Here are examples of three types of test plan templates, with descriptions for each heading.

EXTERNAL TEST PLAN
(Keyboard/image level testing)
[Test Number]
[Release #]
[Project#]
[Date]
[Name]

[This test plan covers external (keyboard-level) testing. Description and text in square brackets are for your use when creating the test plan. It is not needed in the final output and can be deleted.]

Audience and Reason
[At whom is this document directed, and why?]

Original developer	To help think test cases through
Other developers	To review the test plan and test cases
QA	To make QA aware of the changes and the testing that will be done

Requirements/Functional Specification and Item Numbers:
[Give the number/location of the Requirements spec and/or the Functional spec and the item number within the spec that this software should be tested against.]

Requirements Specification:
Requirements Spec Item #:
Functional Specification:
Functional Spec Item #:

Scope/Purpose
[What is the scope and purpose of this testing? On what platforms should the tests be run? Are we testing functionality, performance, or some other attribute of the software?]

Description/overview of software changes
[Give an overview of the software and state what the software is supposed to do.]

Other areas that may be affected
[List other areas that may be affected by the changes and that should be tested.]

Routines/files modified
[List the routines that were modified and the files where they live.]

Routines/files added
[List the routines that were added and the files where they live.]

Routines/files deleted
[List the routines that were deleted and the files where they live.]

Test cases with the results that should happen
[In the following categories, list the various test cases that will be tested and that should work. List also the results that should be seen. List any keystroke logs, data files, etc., that are used in the test cases.]

Default values
[Check that the default values give the expected results.]

Representative data
[Test cases with data that should work with no problem; cases that the software expects as the "right" way to do things.]

Too little data/data missing
[Check for situation where there is data missing, or not enough information has been given, empty or missing files, etc.]

Too much data
[Check for too many records or fields, fields with too much data, etc.]

Boundary values
[Check for boundary conditions such as fields one less than maximum size, max size, one greater than max size, zero-length data, data with length one.]

Troublesome data
[There are certain values, such as spaces, 0, 1, -1, that cause more than their fair share of problems.]

You should be able to test for conformance to each requirement or functional spec item. So there should be a table showing which requirements and functional spec items are tested by which test.

BUG FIX TEST PLAN
(External/keyboard-level testing)
[Bug Number]
[Release #]
[Date]
[Name]

[This test plan covers external (keyboard-level) testing of bugs. Description and text in square brackets is for your use when creating the test plan. It is not needed in the final output and can be deleted.]

Audience and Reason
[At whom is this document directed, and why?]

Original developer	To help think test cases through
Other developers	To review the test plan and test cases
QA	To make QA aware of the changes and the testing that will be done

Platforms
[What platforms should the tests be run on?]

Description/overview of software changes
[Describe the bug and how you solved the problem.]

Other areas that may be affected
[List other areas that may be affected by the changes and that should be tested.]

Routines/files modified
[List the routines that were modified, and the files where they live.]

Routines/files added
[List the routines that were added, and the files where they live.]

Routines/files deleted
[List the routines that were deleted, and the files where they used to live.]

Test cases with the results that should happen
[In the following categories, list the various test cases that will be tested, and that should work. List also the results that should be seen. List any keystroke logs, data files, etc., that are used in the test cases.]

INTERNAL TEST PLAN
(Function/subsystem/driver-level testing)
[Test Number]
[Function/Subsystem]
[Source file name (if applicable)]
[Date]
[Name]

[This test plan covers testing that can be done at the function/subsystem level. This includes such things as test drivers for function. It does not include keyboard testing of the whole image—this is covered in the External Test Plan.]

Audience and Reason
[At whom is this document directed, and why?]

Design Specification and Item Numbers:
[Give the number/location of the Design spec and the item number within the spec that this function is being tested against.]

Design Specification:
Item number:

Overview of the function
[Description/overview of the function, describing what it is supposed to do.]

Input parameters/globals
[List the input parameters and globals variables used. Show the acceptable and unacceptable values.]

Input parameters/global values not handled
[List the values of any input parameters or global values that the software simply doesn't handle. Examples include NULL pointers, or pointers out of range.]

Output parameters/globals
[List the output parameters and globals variables used. Show the acceptable and unacceptable values.]

Return values
[List the return values and the conditions that cause these values.]

Test cases, with the results that should happen
[In the following categories, list the various test cases that will be tested and that should work. List also the results that should be seen. List any files, etc., that are used in the test cases.]

Equivalence classes
[List the equivalence classes. These are groups of values that should perform in a similar fashion. For example, in the statement "if a < 2", the equivalence classes are "everything less than 2," and "2 and greater."]

Representative data
[Give a test case using representative data for each equivalence class.]

Boundary values
[Check for boundary values in each equivalence class. For example, in the case of: "if a < − .5 ‖ a > .5," the boundary values are − .5 and .5.]

Troublesome data (e.g., 0, 1, − 1)
[There are certain values that cause more than their fair share of problems, values such as spaces, 0, 1, − 1. If you are dealing with a char variable type, values such as 127, − 127, 128, − 128, 255, 256 typically cause problems, depending on whether the variable is signed or unsigned.]

What do you want to see in a user guide?

Since every user guide will be very different, let's just list what it should contain. Giving this information helps developers find any holes in their solution or design.

- Product overview and rationale
- Glossary/Terminology
- Summary of screens and reports
- Overview of the likely flow, showing things the user may want to do.
- How to do the various tasks a user would want to do; i.e., sample runs.
- Description of the commands (if command-driven).
- Error messages.
- Scenarios/examples (plenty of these—these are how we learn and understand).

There's a lot of effort involved in creating these documents.

If you have a template or example document from which to start, it doesn't take much time to type the information. The difficult part is determining the correct information, and that has to be done anyway. Having a document act as a starting-point in which you have to enter the information simply makes it easier.

I would also put together a notebook for developers, devoting two chapters to each document that we've talked about. The first chapter, at most 10 pages, should describe that particular document and how to create a useful example. It should define the target audiences for the document and the information they need. If appropriate, it should also define the role of prototypes, i.e., when they are required and when optional.

The second chapter, again about 10 pages, should describe how to review the document (and the prototype, if one is created). The chapter should have pointers on what makes a good document, and a checklist of issues to consider and types of errors to look for.

A word of caution though when creating documents. Creating a product can be a difficult and stressful time, having to deal with difficult developers who don't agree with designs, with people who don't want to conform to standards, and with seemingly impossible schedules. There's a great temptation to focus on the documents and try to perfect them—they don't answer back, you can control them. They are comfortable and safe. But the documents aren't the goal—high quality software is the goal. The documents are simply a tool to help you reach your goal. In so far as they help you reach the goal, the documents are valuable. In so far as they detract from the effort, the documents are a hindrance. Always ask yourself "What is the purpose of this document, and how does it satisfy that purpose?"

Software development is very iterative. How do you make sure that documents are kept up-to-date?

This is one of the classic problems of high-pressure software development. Requirements and design always change, but developers are under too much pressure to produce, so they rarely update the requirements and design documents. Stating the importance of accurate documentation does no good—even when developers agree it's important, they often don't keep it accurate.

The problem is basically structural, and can only be solved by structural change, not by exhortation. Look at the reward/punishment side of keeping the documentation up-to-date that is discussed in Chapter 5. What are the consequences of keeping the documentation up to date?

NIC	Have to write documentation
NIC	Spend less time programming
NFU	Schedules may slip
?FC	Documentation will be better for future developers
PFU	Managers will be happy

Given these consequences, it's not surprising that documentation is rarely kept up-to-date. To overcome this structural problem, you might change the organization structure, and have a person whose job is to help the developers keep documentation up-to-date. The developer is still responsible (the documentation person doesn't always know when something needs to be updated), but doesn't have to do all the work. The documentation person also maintains the project notebook, which contains the latest versions of all the specs, plus a historical notebook, which contains all the previous revisions of the documents.

What is the full job description of this documentation specialist?

The responsibilities of this person are to:

- Assist developers in creating requirements, functional, and design specifications.
- Assist in updating documentation when designs or requirements change.

- ○ Assist developers with code-level documentation.
- ○ Maintain the specifications part of the project notebook.
- ○ Maintain internal documentation templates.
- ○ Assist design teams by recording designs that are created on white boards.

The skills needed are:

- ○ Good communication skills.
- ○ Good writing skills.
- ○ Knowledge of software development and design.
- ○ Ability to work well with developers.

How do you organize the master documents so people can use them?

Let's split this question into two parts: what sort of template should you use, and where do you keep the templates.

What sort of template to use.   There are several different types of templates, some better than others.

- ○ A template with headings
- ○ A template with headings and a description under each heading that tells people the type of information to put there
- ○ A real example that is as complete as you can make it—people learn and understand things best from examples

Fill in as much default information as possible, for example, the audiences will generally be the same for all requirements specs. As you think of more or different things that you'd like to see in the document, modify the template. If you want to ensure that new specs don't retain parts of the descriptions or examples, create all the descriptions and example text in a different font, in italic, or surround it with brackets or braces.

Where to keep the templates.   I'd keep them in a special directory on disk so people can copy them when needed. Let's look at a few examples of how you might name the various documents.

example.reqs_intlf	Requirements spec using an example in Interleaf format on workstation
example.reqs_ascii	Requirements spec using an example in ASCII format on workstation
template.func_intlf	Functional spec using a template in Interleaf format on workstation
example.hl_design_ascii	High-level design spec using an example in ASCII format on workstation
template.ll_design_ascii	Low-level design spec using a template in ASCII format on workstation
example.int_test_intlf	Internal test document using an example in Interleaf format on workstation
template.ext_test_ascii	External test document using a template in ASCII format on workstation
example.rsw	Requirements spec using an example in Word format in DOS
template.rsa	Requirements spec using a template in ASCII format in DOS

example.fsw	Functional spec using an example in Word format in DOS
template.hsa	High-level design spec using a template in ASCII format in DOS
template.lsa	Low-level design spec using a template in ASCII format in DOS
example.itw	Internal test document using an example in Word format in DOS
template.eta	External test document using a template in ASCII format in DOS

When you've created a document from an example or template, you'd change the example or template part of the filename to the project number, project name, or something that uniquely identifies the document.

Why do some of the documents have numbers for every item?

So that you can easily test to make sure that every item has been satisfied. You must be able to test against each specific requirement or piece of functionality, and you must be able to say categorically that this requirement is satisfied, or that item is not satisfied.

But you shouldn't have to wait until testing to make sure requirements are met. Every item in the functional spec should be in response to a particular requirement, and every aspect of the design in response to some requirement or functional item.

Correspondingly, there is no reason to have items in the functional spec if they do not satisfy a requirement. There is no point to include design features if they are not in response to a requirement or functional spec item.

How do you make sure that the functional spec covers all the requirements?

In each functional item described by the functional spec, put the tag of the requirement that the item satisfies. If you do this, you will be sure that you have no non-required items, that you are not doing unnecessary work. For example:

4.2.3   A menu selection will allow the user to delete a process (3.5.2.2)

But it's not easy to make sure you covered all the requirements this way, so you also need a cross-reference section in the functional spec that lists the tags of all the requirements and shows which functional spec items satisfy which requirements. For example:

Requirement	F.S. Item
...	
3.5.2.2	4.2.3
3.5.2.3	5.1.6
3.5.2.4	5.4.1
3.5.3	4.2.2, 4.2.3, 5.2.1
...	

What should the tags look like?

Tags can be either names—make them uppercase or give them another font or some other emphasis to distinguish them—or numbers such as 2.3.2.1. The advantage of numbers is you can easily find them in the document, and you don't have to think up a great many descriptive name tags. The disadvantage of numbers is that they change when new things are added or deleted. This is especially troublesome when the functional spec has a requirements cross-reference section and the requirements tags change. With numbers, you also lose the ability to track how an item has changed through the revisions. Try one approach and see how it works for you.

Tag each specific requirement or piece of functionality so that it can be referred to easily. Don't group requirements or functional items under a single tag—make a separate tag for each one. (If you are using names, you can group items and give them a tag in GROUP.TAGNAME format.)

Is there anything else to consider?

Yes. These documents serve two main functions. First, they make you think. Second, they communicate information to others. Make your document easy to understand. If it is difficult to understand, people are likely to misunderstand it—assuming they even manage to work through it. Einstein used to say that if you can't explain what you are doing to an eight-year-old, you obviously don't know what it is. Allowing for a little poetic licence, it's a useful thought to consider.

There's a case to be made that anything that won't fit on a single sheet of paper can't be easily understood; it's easier to grasp something if it's all present at once. Try to modularize your document in a way that to review any aspect of it takes only a single sheet. Obviously reality doesn't care about your desire to put things on a single page, so it shouldn't be an unbreakable rule, but it does make things easier to understand.

For example, keep functions to about a single page, or keep the function header documentation on one page, and the function code on another page. Keep the high-level design diagram to a page. Keep the exploded view of a process to about a page. It will help the reviewers and it will help your thinking. If you have a laser printer, print in a smaller font or print two pages to a sheet. Despite the increased density of information, being on one sheet still makes it easier to grasp.

Further Reading

Davis, Alan. 1990. *Software Requirements: Analysis and Specification.* Englewood Cliffs, NJ: Prentice-Hall.

Dorfman, Merlin, and Richard Thayer (editors). 1990. *Standards, Guidelines, and Examples on System and Software Requirements Engineering*. Washington, DC: IEEE Computer Society Press.

IEEE Software Standards. Washington, DC: IEEE Computer Society Press. Catalog number 1001 covers all the IEEE software standards.

Summary

The various specifications and documents involved in the software development process serve two purposes. First, writing things down forces you to clarify your thinking and consider all the possibilities. Second, having a document allows you to share the information with other people.

This chapter discussed the various audiences for the information in these specifications and documents, then gave sample templates for the different documents.

PART 4

Programming

18

Naming Conventions

A consistent use of names in a project has multiple benefits. First, it makes it more obvious if you are using a variable incorrectly. Second, it makes it easier for someone else to pick up the program and understand what you are doing.

Give me an example of the first point.

Suppose you have:

```
temp = funcaaa (window);
```

You can't tell if this is correct without looking at all the declarations. On the other hand, if you see:

```
d_temp = dc_if_funcaaa (s_window);
```

you would notice that the result of an integer function is being placed in a double-precision number. You would also notice that a structure was being passed to the function and would probably guess that you were meant to pass a pointer to the structure.

Or if you are programming in assembler you might have:

```
MOVL   XXX, R6          ; move the longword at XXX into
                        ; register 6
```

If XXX is a two-byte variable, you'll be moving garbage data into the high two bytes of R6.

On the other hand, it would be more obvious that you are doing something wrong if you saw:

```
MOVL   W_XXX, R6        ; move the longword at XXX into
                        ; register 6
```

If you are reviewing someone else's code you would probably think it was okay if you saw the line:

```
new_count = old_count + 1;
```

However, if new_count is a two-byte word, and old_count is a long integer, there may well be future problems if the top two bytes are truncated. It would be much more obvious the data was being truncated if the line looked like:

```
w_new_count = l_old_count + 1;
```

You could then ask why the variables are of different sizes. Similarly, it would be easier to spot occasions when someone is assigning a signed variable to an unsigned or vice versa (these are subtle potential problems for the future, when someone modifies the code, not realizing that information is stripped at certain times).

Since we are trying to eliminate rework, we should embrace anything that helps people get things right before the program is run.

Do you have an example of the second point—it is easier for people to pick up the program?

Suppose you see the line:

```
incoming = setup
```

You don't really have a clue what is happening, especially in a language like Pascal, where setup could be a function. You'd get a much quicker and clearer idea if the line looked like one of the following:

```
l_incoming    = l_setup      (both long integers)
sp_incoming   = dc_spf_setup (setup is a function that allocates a structure and returns a
                              pointer to it)
```

I see the idea, but I'm not sure what all the extra letters mean.

Here's an example of how you might name variables. I use this scheme when writing in C. Bear in mind that it's not complete, and that the specific language you choose may have more or fewer variable types, or your application may have more or fewer types. The general idea is as follows:

{ module-prefix_ } < type > [sign][constant][function][array][indirection][parameter] { life } _-variable-name

The bracketing convention used here is:

<>   Required

[ ]   Used depending on type of variable. Always appears after the thing it is describing.

{ }   Used depending on type of variable. Appears in the position shown.

MODULE PREFIX: The acronym of the module (for example a Data Capture module might have the acronym "dc"). This is used only when the variable is an external global variable.

TYPE:
b	bit
B	BOOLEAN (typedef or #define in C)
c	character
d	double
e	enum variable
E	enum type
f	float
F	FILE (typedef or #define in C)
i	integer
l	long integer
s	structure
u	union
v	void
w	short integer. I use w for word since s means structure (even though these days words are usually the same as a long integer).
x	system defined type of variable or typedef (take special care)

SIGN: u   if type is unsigned; else signed.

CONSTANT: k   The constant k suffix goes immediately after whatever it is describing as constant. Thus a constant int might be ik_max, a pointer to a constant int might be ikp_max, and a constant pointer to an int might be ipk_max.

FUNCTION: f   if function name; else omitted.

ARRAY: a   if array name; else omitted, e.g., ia_ is an integer array. In C a ca_ would be a character array or string.

INDIRECTION: p   if a pointer to the specified type; else omitted. Note that the indirection can go more than one level. A pointer to a structure would be sp_ while a pointer to a pointer to a structure would be spp_, etc.

PARAMETER: Used only with parameter variables within a function. Parameter variables in the function have extra identifiers to show whether the parameter is read, written to, or read and written to. I use the following convention:

r   read-only variable

w   write-only variable

m   modified (read-and-write)

These identifiers are placed after the thing they are describing.

LIFE: g   module scope (static) global

s   function scope static

(External scope globals are distinguished by a module prefix.)

Now give me some examples of all this!

int	i_count;	Integer
int	*ip_sum;	Pointer to integer
int	*ipp_sum;	Pointer to pointer to integer
unsigned int	iua_counts[6];	Unsigned integer array
unsigned int	*iuap_counts;	Pointer to unsigned integer array
unsigned int	*iupa_counts[6];	Array of pointers to unsigned integers
int	iaa_counts[3][4];	Array of arrays of integers
short	w_length;	Short (word) integer
static int	is_type;	Function level static integer
static long	lg_type;	Module scope global long
unsigned char	cu_terminator;	Unsigned character
struct window	s_window;	Structure
struct window	*sp_window;	Pointer to structure

What about the x_ variable type?

This is a variable of "unknown" type. For example, in C, the value returned by the function time() is of type time_t. To know how time_t is defined, you'd have to look in the system include file time.h. Even then, you can't guarantee that this won't change in the future. To cover all these situations, I use a variable type of x_. In effect, it's a warning to the programmer to be careful when dealing with this variable. So if I want to use the function time(), I'd declare the variable as:

```
time_t x_time;
..
x_time = time(NULL);
```

What if you have particular structures you use all the time?

If a structure is in common use, such as a "window" in graphical user interface software, figure out a way to specify that a variable is a window structure variable. The purpose of naming conventions is to make the function of a particular variable obvious. You might include the window information in the variable prefix, or you might make it a suffix.

```
s_main_win
sw_main
xwin_main
win_main
```

Just make sure that your scheme allows the name to be uniquely identified as a window, without conflicting with the main naming convention. There must be no possibility that someone might think it's some other type of variable. I've always kept things simple and specified the type of object in the name rather than the prefix. Thus window objects are s_main_win, s_this_win, s_that_win.

How about some examples of functions?

In C, there are two types of functions: static functions, callable only within the source module, and external functions, callable from anywhere. But for practical use, I differentiate between four different types:

- Static (module scope)
- Subsystem (externally callable, but should not be called from outside the subsystem)
- Library (externally callable)
- Library internal (externally callable, but should not be called except by library functions)

Static (module scope) functions have no module prefix. Subsystem functions have a module prefix. Library functions have a module prefix (we assume you know whether a particular prefix is a subsystem prefix or a library prefix). Library internal functions have the module prefix plus an i for "internal" to show that you shouldn't be calling them.

static int	if_read_file();	Module-level (static) integer function
static char	*cpf_get_version();	Module-level (static) function returning pointer to a character string
int	dc_if_read_file();	Subsystem scope external integer function
struct win	*dc_spf_create_window();	Subsystem scope external function returning pointer to structure
int	win_if_change_border();	Library integer function
int	wini_if_translate_coords();	Library internal integer function

And some examples of globals?

C has two types of global variables: *external global*, referencable by any module, and *module level global* (static global), referencable only by functions in the source file. Again, I prefer to differentiate between several different types of global variables:

- ○ Module scope (static)
- ○ Subsystem
- ○ Library
- ○ Library internal

Module scope globals have a ''life'' identifier of ''g''—an alternative way of denoting module scope globals might be to capitalize the first character of the name part of the variable. Subsystem globals have a module prefix. Library globals that are used by callers of the library routines have module prefixes. Globals internal to the library routines have module prefixes plus an ''i'' to denote ''internal.''

```
static long     lg_bad_rec_count;       Module scope long integer.
static int      ig_trans_processed;     Module scope integer.
```

or

```
static long     l_Bad_rec_count;        Module scope long integer.
static int      i_Trans_processed;      Module scope integer.

short           dc_w_state;             Subsystem short integer.
char            dc_ca_name[32];         Subsystem character array.

int             win_i_errno;            Library externally available integer.
struct window   *wini_sp_window;        Library internally used structure pointer.
```

I prefer not to use dashes in my variable and function names to save space. Instead I capitalize the first letter of distinct words or abbreviations.

If you do this, you obviously won't be able to use a capital letter to indicate a module scope variable. The above examples would look like:

```
static long     lg_BadRecCount;             Long integer module global
static int      if_ReadFile();              Module-level (static) integer function
struct window   *dc_spf_CreateWindow();     External function returning pointer to
                                            structure
```

or

```
static long     lgBadRecCount;              Long integer module global
static int      ifReadFile();               Module-level (static) integer function
struct window   *dc_spfCreateWindow();      External function returning pointer to
                                            structure
```

The disadvantage of using capital letters to distinguish words is that if you are programming Windows- or X-based software, you may come into conflict with other similar-looking but different conventions. If you use underscores to separate the words, you know that when you see words distinguished by uppercase first characters, you are looking at a variable or function defined by an external package.

Can you give some examples of the parameter variables?

```
int     ir_count;        Integer value that is read
int     *iwp_count;      Pointer to integer—contents written to
char    *camp_name;      Pointer to character array—contents read and written to
```

In the case of a language like C, you can pass only by value and not by reference. To modify a variable you have to pass its address, and then modify the memory at that address. So in a function you might be modifying both the pointer and the variable pointed to. To accommodate this, I use the parameter attributes as follows:

```
int  *ipr_xxx;  (or irpr_xxx)    The pointer is not modified; the value pointed to is not
                                 modified
int  *ipw_xxx;  (or irpw_xxx)    The pointer is modified; the value pointed to is not
                                 modified
int  *iwp_xxx;  (or iwpr_xxx)    The pointer is not modified; the value pointed to is
                                 modified
int  *iwpw_xxx;                  The pointer is modified; the value pointed to is modified
```

Note that I take a shortcut in my usage. I use ''w'' to specify exactly what is being written to, but don't bother with the ''r'' unless nothing is written to, in which case I use a single ''r'' just to show that it's a function parameter. If this gets to be too much, a fairly safe convention is to use ipr_ if the data pointed to is not modified, and ipw_ if you do modify the data pointed to. This does lose some precision though.

How do you name a parameter that is a pointer to an array?

In C, you can't pass arrays as parameters; you can only pass a pointer to the array. The name I give to an array pointer depends on how I will use that variable, whether as a pointer or as an array. I use the following convention:

```
if_function (int *iapr_xxx, int iar_yyy[]);
```

The first parameter is used as a pointer and the second is used as an array.

Why do you use prefixes rather than suffixes?

Personal preference. I've worked on projects where we've used suffixes for both the module and the variable type, and where we've used a prefix for the module and a suffix for the type. I found that I sometimes forget to add the suffix, but I rarely forget the prefix.

Some linkers need the first six or eight characters to be unique for global variables. Check the linker documentation for your computer. For truly portable code, use suffixes for everything. So for example, dc_i_count would be count_i_dc in suffix notation.

But it really doesn't matter whether you use all prefixes, all suffixes, or a mixture, provided it works for you and it's consistent with what everyone else uses. If you use link maps a lot, you might choose prefixes or suffixes based on how you like to see the variables grouped in the map.

I've heard of Hungarian notation. What is that?

Hungarian notation is another naming convention. It was invented in 1972 by Charles Simonyi, one of Microsoft's chief architects, and was given the name Hungarian because people thought it looked like a foreign language; in this case Hungarian since Simonyi was born in Hungary. If you want more information, look at the August 1991 issue of *BYTE* (pages 131 to 138), where Simonyi and Martin Heller wrote an article describing Hungarian notation. It's widely used at Microsoft, and you will have seen it if you have done any work with Microsoft Windows or Presentation Manager. Hungarian notation is probably the only generally known naming convention, and at least one software tool, CodeCheck from Abraxas Software, will check for Hungarian notation conformance.

But the important point is not which convention you use, but that you use a convention. Having everyone on the project or in the company use the same naming convention means that when you pick up and modify any piece of code, you get a better picture of what is going on, and are less likely to make mistakes.

Summary

The value of a naming convention is that it makes it easier to spot mistakes in assignments, parameters, or assumptions about the lifetime of a variable. It also reduces the necessity to constantly refer to the top of the function or file or an include file to learn the type of a variable. This chapter gives a particular naming convention as an example.

19

Documentation

At various points in their careers, most software engineers waste hours trying to understand the implications of a piece of code or the intentions of another programmer, simply because there is no documentation to give them the information. If a software engineer is trying to understand code in order to fix it or enhance it, good documentation will save time and will ensure a greater likelihood that the new code will do what it is supposed to do.

Wouldn't incorrect documentation be worse than no documentation?

Obviously it would be preferable if the documentation was correct, and there's no reason why the program shouldn't start with correct documentation. Over time it may become out-of-date, although there's no reason why it can't be kept correct. Even if the documentation is no longer correct, it will still give you an idea of what the program is trying to do, even if some of the details are wrong. If you are reading the documentation in order to modify the code, you'll soon notice if the documentation and code don't match.

Because documentation should start correct, can be kept up-to-date, and is seldom of serious consequence if out-of-date, I'd rather have documentation and take my chances that it may be out-of-date than have no documentation.

How do you prevent documentation and code getting out of synchronization?

It's very difficult to keep program documentation current if it doesn't live in the program. We try to avoid synchronizing two identical sets of data in our software, so we should do the same with our documentation. The first step is good documentation in the program files themselves.

What should be documented?

Anything that will make life easier for future software developers. Let's make a list.

- ○ Files
  - • Revision history describing the changes and the reasons for the changes.
  - • Instructions on how to "build" the file—how to create the object and possibly the executable.
  - • Description of the general nature of the functions in the file or the purpose of the file.
  - • List of the functions in the file.
- ○ Functions
  - • Function overview.
  - • Obligations of function: what will it do?
  - • Obligations of the caller: what does the function expect the caller to have done.
  - • Parameters: what they are, how they are used, and acceptable and unacceptable values.
  - • Global variables used.
  - • Return values.
  - • Notes to future programmers:
    - – Potential problems
    - – Limitations
    - – Assumptions
    - – Dependencies
    - – Impact of changes on other modules
  - • Where this function is called from (for non-library functions).
  - • Functions called.
  - • Error reporting done (displayed, logged to file, added to linked list, etc.).
- ○ Structures
  - • What their purpose is.
  - • Type of each field.
  - • Purpose of each field.
  - • Typical values.
- ○ Message types/command types
  - • What they are.
  - • How they are used.
  - • Appropriate values for different situations.

- ○ Blocks of code
  - • Intention of programmer (it's important to describe what you are trying to achieve because it makes it easier for future programmers to suspect a bug if the code is not doing what the intention describes).
  - • What the code is doing.
  - • Notes about complex algorithms.
  - • Notes about potential problems.
  - • Notes about future possible enhancements.
  - • Notes to distinguish quick fixes from well-thought-through, well-tested changes.

What about "self-documenting programs"?

There is tremendous value to self-documenting programs. I'm not talking about sloppy programs written by programmers who say that any decent programmer can understand the program. I'm talking about programs that are self-documented by virtue of the names given to variables and constants. Some people use the term "self-documenting programs" to refer to programs with in-line documentation, but nowadays that is the norm rather than the exception, so it makes more sense to define self-documenting programs as programs in which the names themselves provide documentation.

```
switch (sp_msg_rcvd->i_record_type)
{
    case DC_STOCK_RECORD:
        ...
        break;
    case DC_STOCK_CORRECTION:
        ...
        break;
    case DC_BOND_RECORD:
        ...
        break;
    case DC_BOND_CORRECTION:
        ...
        break;
    case DC_MUTUALFUND_RECORD:
        ...
        break;
    case DC_MUTUALFUND_CORRECTION:
        ...
        break;
    default:
        err_vf ("Received unexpected record type %d\n",
                sp_msg_rcvd->i_record_type);
        break;
}
```

Code that is self-documenting like this looks almost trivial. But contrast it for comprehension effort with:

```c
switch (msg->typ) {
case STK:
    ...
    break;
case STC:
    ...
    break;
case BND:
    ...
    break;
case BC:
    ...
    break;
case MFND:
    ...
    break;
case MFC:
    ...
    break;
default:
    err_vf ("Bad message\n");
    break;
}
```

And if you think this is exaggerated, let me assure you that the truth is even worse. So yes, self-documenting programs are immensely useful. But they can't possibly explain everything, so you need to put in additional documentation.

How do you document files?

An example of a program file might be:

```
/*************************************************************************
File name:      dc_parse.c
Project:        Weather Information Processing (WIP)
Facility:       Data Capture (DC)
Build Instruct: This file and its dependencies are included in the make
                file "dc.make". "dc.make" is executed from the file "wip.make".
                To make the Capture executable, execute "wip.make".

This file contains functions for parsing incoming data. The external functions
contained here are:

        dc_if_parse_header
        dc_if_parse_record
        dc_if_parse_trailer
```

```
History:

{0}    90/11/11    Joe Smith.    Created.
{1}    90/12/12    Joe Brown.    Rel 3.1.
       Objective:   Need to allow more than one record type.
       Edit:        Modified dc_if_parse_record(). The code now looks at
                    i_rec_type and does a switch/case block.
{2}    90/12/16    Joe Brown.    Bug 336.
       Objective:   Fix bug where standard record can have a record type of
                    'space' (hex 20) as well as a type of 0.
       Edit:        Added case DC_STANDARD_SPACE to the switch (i_rec_type)
block
                    in dc_if_parse_record().

***********************************************************************/
```

I've never seen a list of the functions at the top before. Why do you include them?

Because it's a lot faster to get an idea of what's in the file if all the names are listed in one place. It's up at the top, so if you add or delete a function, you can easily make this change when you make your change comments. Of course, if you have only one external function per file, the list is unnecessary.

Speaking of change comments, what is your philosophy behind them?

My philosophy is that I'd rather the programmer spend 3 extra minutes making the revision comments complete than the next person spend 15 minutes figuring out what happened.

The number in curly brackets is the revision number. I would expect the programmer to put the same number in brackets where he made the code changes. That way future programmers can just search to the revision number, or if they see the revision number, they can refer back to the history to see why the change was made.

The date and name are obvious. If you are making major changes for a new software release, rather than making lots of small history comments with a date, an alternative is to put the release number instead of the date, then describe all the changes. Thus, one number in curly brackets can be used for all the changes.

The next information is the bug being fixed or the software release that the enhancement is for. It can be extremely useful to know more of the background behind a change. By tracking the bug number, a future programmer can go back to the original bug report for a greater understanding.

The main body of the comment contains two pieces of information. The first piece is the intention behind the change. What was the programmer trying to achieve? This is useful because when fixing a bug there's a 20-to-50 percent chance of introducing another bug. Knowing the intention makes it easier to determine if the change was complete and to correct it if problems are found later. The second piece is detail of what was done to implement the change. This gives future programmers an overview, which is especially important if the change required code modifications in more than one place.

A lot of this information is available from your source code control system.

That's true if you're using a source code control system. It's partly a matter of taste where you record the information, but I find the information in the file more useful, especially when I'm looking at a piece of code that's been changed, and I want to know why and when. Also, some source code control systems limit the amount of information you can record in a comment. But if you find that using the source code control system is more useful, make sure everyone knows how to record and find the information.

How do you document functions?

A good function is like a black box. You shouldn't need to understand its internal workings to use it. That means the header documentation should describe what the function does, the input it expects, and the output it creates.

Functions should document what they expect from the calling function and what they don't deal with. As Bertrand Meyer says about functions in Eiffel, there is a "contract" between the caller and the function. This contract is actually enforced in Eiffel, whereas in most languages the function has to check that the contract is honored. Documentation helps both you and future software engineers understand the contract and ensure that the code honors it.

```
/*-----------------------------------------------------------------------
int dc_if_open_log_file (char *capr_name)

This function opens a log file for logging data capture messages.

FUNCTION OBLIGATIONS:
    If we were passed a NULL pointer, set the file pointer to NULL.
    If there is a log file already open, close it.
    Open log file for write access.
    If we opened the file, store the file pointer in a external global.
    If we failed to open the file, set the file pointer to NULL.

CALLER OBLIGATIONS:
    Pass a valid pointer to the file name, or a NULL pointer.

PARAMETERS:
    Read:        capr_name           Pointer to name of file to open
GLOBALS:
    Write:       dc_Fp_log_file      File pointer for log file
```

```
RETURNS:        SYS_GOOD            File successfully opened
                SYS_FAILURE         File not opened, or pointer NULL.
                                    Errors are printed to stderr


CALLED FROM:    dc_if_parse_data
                dc_if_check_header
CALLS:          fopen
NOTES:          None.
-------------------------------------------------------------------*/

    int dc_if_open_log_file (char *capr_name)
    {
        ....
    }
```

What is that "called from" section?

I like to document where the function is called from, on the principle that it's quicker and more useful if you can see immediately which functions call this one. It's more reliable to use library tools that give you this information, or to use a link map, but it's generally far more time-consuming. If you plan to change parameter lists, you should definitely use these methods to ensure that you haven't forgotten anything, but for many purposes it's useful to quickly see where a function is called. A lot of people don't like this section because it's difficult to keep up-to-date, but if you are the only person that works on a piece of code, it can be useful.

Note that the "called from" section can be done only with functions that are local to the application. For general library functions, a programmer should be able to use them without going into the function and changing the documentation.

If you use tools such as ctags or DEC's SCA (source code analyzer), where you can press a button and see all the files that reference this function, you obviously don't need to record this information.

Can you give me an example of how to document a function that has structures in the parameter list?

I'll give you an example of a function that uses a pointer to an array of structures. In C, there is a problem from the perspective of the calling routine in that you simply pass the address of the first structure. There's no way of telling whether the routine will do something with one structure or several.

I've seen interesting errors where the calling function allocates space for one structure but the function it's calling assumes it can write data into the full array of structures. We want programmers to be able to use functions as black boxes—the programmer shouldn't have to understand each function before using it. Therefore the documentation should be good.

```
/*----------------------------------------------------------------
int dc_if_fill_process_strucs (struct proc_struct saw_process[])
```

This function sends inquiries to the other processes and fills in process
structures for each of the processes. It expects an array of DC_MAX_PROC_
STRUCS
to be allocated, and when filling in the data it indexes into the array using
the internal process ID it receives from each process.

FUNCTION OBLIGATIONS:
    Fill in the data structure for each process, if the process exists. It sets
      w_state = DC_EXISTS, and fills in the fields
      i_mailbox
      i_proc_id
      ca_proc_name
    Initialize the data structure for non-existent processes. It sets
      w_state = DC_NONEXISTENT, and sets the other fields to 0.
    Ensure that we haven't been passed a NULL pointer.

CALLER OBLIGATIONS:
    Pass a valid pointer to the array of DC_MAX_PROC_STRUCS process
structures.

PARAMETERS:
    Write: saw_process[]   Pointer to an array of DC_MAX_PROC_STRUC
                                 process structures.

GLOBALS   None

RETURNS: SYS_GOOD   Successful
                SYS_NULLPTR   Passed a NULL pointer as a parameter.
                                No error reporting.
                Anything else   Error. Error is logged to current error log
                                 file.

CALLED FROM: dc_if_init
CALLS: dc_if_send_msg, dc_if_rcv_msg, err_vf

NOTES: To allow for future expansion of the structure, we start by
                initializing the entire array of structures to zeros using
                memset.
```
----------------------------------------------------------------*/
```

**It seems that the function header documentation can easily get out of sync
with the detailed design documentation.**

That's true, if you have different documents. One approach is to combine the low-
level design and the function header documentation, and make them the same document. Put everything you want to see in the low-level design into the function
header, and write a tool that can extract it from the file and print it out as a design
document.

What about documenting the function code?

Besides documenting the function as a black box, you should also document the code in the function. Any time you have a block of code that performs a specific, single thing, document the intention of the code. Document interesting algorithms, code that is particularly obscure, code that makes use of little-known facts. In short, document anything that the next programmer may have difficulty with.

It's also important to document reasons for technical decisions; if the circumstances change, it may be appropriate to change the decision, but you'll have to understand the reasons for the decision.

Think of the program as being made up of two separate programs, one an action program, and one an intention program. The action program is the actual code, the "what." The intention program is the comments that describe what you are trying to do, the "why." There should be a match between the two; if not, you should suspect a bug.

In some ways it's more important to document intentions than the code itself. Much code commenting ends up being a repetition of the obvious. Except in poorly written code or complicated algorithms, it's pretty obvious what each line is doing. Where documenting becomes difficult is in helping you to understand the relationship of that line to the problem being solved. What exactly does this variable contain? What are you trying to do? Why does this variable need to be modified?

When do you document?

I try to document while I'm coding because that way I have the best idea of what I'm trying to do. It tends to be an iterative process though, because as I'm documenting, I realize things that I overlooked and have to add code to take care of things.

Another time to consider documentation is when you are working through a piece of obscure code to fix a bug. Once you've figured out what's going on, document what you learned so that the next person in doesn't have to spend the same time learning the answers.

Often, software engineers are under pressure to produce and can't afford to document.

Under pressure from whom? From the project manager. One of the responsibilities of the project manager is to ensure that things are done right because it will save a lot of work in the long run.

But what is more important, if the pressure is high enough that the software engineer is coding away furiously, you've almost certainly got problems. If the emphasis is on furious coding, the project manager is not putting enough emphasis on ensuring high quality. You're probably not doing sensible things like reviewing the code—if you were, you'd find that some high-quality documentation would save more time in the code review than it took to write the documentation.

The only other real possibility is that this is a rush for a trade show or for a single customer, in which case the thing is a prototype. Once the prototype is delivered, go back and fix it up and make it into a real product.

Of course, this is sometimes too idealistic. We *are* under pressure, and once this piece of software is done, we're under pressure to move on. In this situation I will try to do the documentation while I'm coding because once there are more than a few functions, it gets too difficult psychologically to go back and document everything well.

I'll create good, complete documentation for major functions, general-purpose library functions, and other functions that I think other people may have difficulty with. For shorter and more simple functions, I'll sometimes skip doing full header documentation if I'm under pressure. However, even then I'll document what the function does, what the parameters and return values are, and what external scope global variables it uses. I also make sure I provide good documentation about the major data structures because these are the heart of the software. Beyond that, I don't document the obvious if I'm under a lot of time pressure.

You've only talked about documentation in the programs themselves. Surely you also need documentation about how the system fits together?

Of course you do. Systems are becoming increasingly complex, so it's increasingly hard to understand them without excellent documentation. Besides the in-program documentation, you also need external documentation that describes things that are not specific to individual program files. This list would include items such as:

- How the system fits together
- How and when the parts of the system communicate
- How to set up a system
- How to test a system
- What can go wrong and what to do if it does
- Possible enhancements and how to make them
- What key structures are used and where to find them defined
- What key values are used and where to find them defined

Without this type of documentation, it takes a person a long, long time to learn how programs fit together and how the information and commands interact and are processed. But it's just not worth wasting their time and your time when the information and understanding could be easily available.

But it can often be hard to find information that's scattered throughout lots of separate documentation files.

All information that doesn't fit tidily into program files should be in a single document with a very good index and table of contents. People may read the document from start to finish, but its real use will be when they need to find out information relating to their current problem, and for this they need to know where to look in the document.

If you want to make your documentation really good, put in lots of examples. People are good at extracting general rules from examples, and poor at creating examples from general rules. As Edmund Burke said: "Example is the school of mankind, and they will learn at no other."

Okay, how about some examples then!

One of the areas that's very important to document well is commands and responses to commands. Let's use the example of a system with multiple processes. Most of them run as detached processes, and there is a main administrator process that interacts with the user. The particular process on which we are working has two functions for communicating: dc_if_send_mail and dc_if_rcv_mail. For the sake of this discussion, they reside in separate files. Let's look at dc_send_mail.c.

```
/************************************************************************
File name    :  dc_send_mail.c
Project      :  Weather Data Processor
Facility     :  Data Capture
Build Instr  :  make wdp

History:
(0) 90/11/11  Joe Smith Created

Functions contained in this file include:
   dc_if_send_mail

This file contains functions to send mail to other processes. The following
describes the messages that can be sent, the situation in which they are sent,
and the data the messages contain.

The message structure is "struct mail_msg," as described in dc_i_mail.h.
All #defines for the fields in the structure are defined and described in
dc_i_mail.h.

Note that all mail messages are routed via the Admin process, which is the only
process with a fixed mailbox. All processes sign in with Admin, and all
processes request other people's mailboxes from Admin.

Some commands expect an acknowledgment, while others do not. An acknowledgment
will have the same command, with a status that has specific meaning. For the
acknowledgment information, see the documentation in dc_rcv_mail.c.
```

Fields other than those specified should be initialized to null; however, the code ignores these values.

Command:

DC_TABLE_CREATED

This command goes to the DATA CONSOLIDATE process when we have seen and processed a "unit" of data from the incoming data. It instructs the DATA CONSOLIDATE process to look for the data in the FIFO file and get to work on it. This command expects an acknowledgment.

i_dest_mbox	Mailbox to send to
i_process_id	Process ID of this process
i_process_type	Process type of this process

DC_SIGN_IN

This command is sent to ADMIN and requests to be signed in. It expects an acknowledgment.

i_process_id	Process ID of this process
i_process_type	Process type of this process
i_my_mbox	Mailbox of this process

DC_SHUTTING_DOWN

This command goes to the ADMIN process, either as a response to a shutdown command, or because an internal error is causing the process to shut down of its own accord. It does not expect a response.

i_status = DC_RESPOND_TO_REQUEST	If we are shutting down in response to external request.
= DC_SELF_INITIATED	If we are shutting down because of an internal error.
i_process_id	Process ID of this process.
i_process_type	Type of this process. Types are defined in wdp_proc_types.h.

DC_SEND_STATISTICS

This command is sent in response to a request for statistics. It does not expect a response.

i_bytes =	Number of bytes of data being appended onto end of mail_msg structure. Note that this should equal the number of statistics bytes minus 1.
data_c =	First byte of statistics data.

DC_REQUEST_MAILBOX

This command is sent to the Admin process to ask for the mailbox of another process.

i_my_mbox =	Mailbox of this process
i_proc_type =	Type of process we want mailbox of
i_proc_id =	ID of process we want mailbox of

```
**********************************************************************/
```

I notice that you put lines of asterisks or dashes above and below blocks of documentation. Is there any significance to these symbols?

Yes, there is. I use a tool to extract documentation from source files, and I have a standard way of denoting the beginning and ending of the block of documentation. For C programs, I start the block with a particular three-character sequence and end with the same three-character sequence in reverse. The tool treats everything between them as documentation. The standard that I use is:

`/**`	`...`	`**/`	File header documentation
`/*-`	`...`	`-*/`	Function header documentation for externally callable subsystem or library functions
`/*=`	`...`	`=*/`	Function header documentation for library functions that should not be called by library users
`/*^`	`...`	`^*/`	Function header documentation for module scope functions callable only within the source file

Here's an example of using the UNIX ''sed'' command to extract the function header documentation.

```
sed -n '/\/\*-/,/-\*\//p' <filename>
```

It's easy enough to write a similar tool for other operating systems, or modify it for languages other than C. Obviously, you can extend the convention to any type of documentation that you'd like to be able to extract from the source files. The documentation of particular interest to me is that extracted for externally callable library functions. Now, by definition, the only up-to-date parameter/obligation documentation is documentation extracted by my program.

Further Reading

Straker, David. 1992. *C Style, Standards, and Guidelines.* Englewood Cliffs, NJ: Prentice-Hall.

Summary

This chapter discussed the value of documentation, and gave several examples of documentation. Some of the points made are:

- ◦ Good documentation can save a programmer hours of effort when he is trying to understand a piece of code that he has to make changes to.
- ◦ Documentation in the source files themselves makes it less likely that the documentation and source will get out of synchronization.

- ○ Using descriptive variable and function names can help make the programs self-documenting.
- ○ When documenting changes to a program, the comments should include both the purpose behind the change, and a description of the change. There should be an easy way to find the code changes that are related to each change comment, and vice versa.
- ○ Documentation in the code should describe what the programmer is trying to achieve, rather than what the code is doing. There may be a bug in the code that will be obvious to someone who is attempting to match the intentions to the code actions.
- ○ Function header documentation should describe all the information passed in and out. This includes parameters, globals used, and return values. It should also describe any obligations on the part of the caller. Function header documentation should be marked in a way that makes the documentation easy to extract from the source file and put in a loose leaf folder.

20

Functions

As we've seen in Chapters 13 and 14, "The Solution" and "Modularization," functions help us break down complex problems into a hierarchical set of smaller problems. As we saw, to help with testing, debugging, and maintenance, functions should deal with a single, cohesive concept, should be "black boxes" with well-defined interfaces, and should be short enough to be understood easily.

So we've talked about what a function should do and how it should react to the world around it. Let's look now at the internals of the function. We'll start with four examples of the same function. To save space, the function is incomplete. The goal simply is to show various ways of coding the function.

```
/* ---------- Use "return" any time we get a bad status ---------- */

FUNCTION int dc_if_do_things (...)
{
    int   i_status;

    i_status = dc_if_do_thing_1 (...);
    if (i_status != SYS_SUCCESS) {
        err_vf (...);
        return (i_status);
    }

    i_status = dc_if_do_thing_2 (...);
    if (i_status != SYS_SUCCESS) {
        err_vf (...);
        return (i_status);
    }

    i_status = dc_if_do_thing_3 (...);
    if (i_status != SYS_SUCCESS) {
```

```
            err_vf (...);
            return (i_status);
        }

    i_status = dc_if_do_this ();
    if (i_status != SYS_SUCCESS)
    {
        err_vf (...);
        return (i_status);
    }

    i_status = dc_if_do_that ();
    if (i_status != SYS_SUCCESS)
    {
        err_vf (...);
        return (i_status);
    }

    return (i_status);
    }


/* ---------- Use "goto" any time we get a bad status ---------- */

FUNCTION int dc_if_do_things (...)
{
    int  i_status;

    i_status = dc_if_do_thing_1 (...);
    if (i_status != SYS_SUCCESS)
    {
        err_vf (...);
        goto Exit;
    }

    i_status = dc_if_do_thing_2 (...);
    if (i_status != SYS_SUCCESS)
    {
        err_vf (...);
        goto Exit;
    }

    i_status = dc_if_do_thing_3 (...);
    if (i_status != SYS_SUCCESS)
    {
        err_vf (...);
        goto Exit;
    }

    i_status = dc_if_do_this ();
    if (i_status != SYS_SUCCESS)
    {
        err_vf (...);
        goto Exit;
    }

    i_status = dc_if_do_that ();
    if (i_status != SYS_SUCCESS)
    {
        err_vf (...);
```

```
            goto Exit;
        }

Exit:
    return (i_status);
}


/* ---------- Do things only if we have a good status ---------- */

FUNCTION int dc_if_do_things (...)
{
    int  i_status;
    i_status = dc_if_do_thing_1 (...);
    if (i_status != SYS_SUCCESS) {
        err_vf (...);
    }

    if (i_status == SYS_SUCCESS) {
        i_status = dc_if_do_thing_2 (...);
        if (i_status != SYS_SUCCESS) {
            err_vf (...);
        }
    }

    if (i_status == SYS_SUCCESS) {
        i_status = dc_if_do_thing_3 (...);
        if (i_status != SYS_SUCCESS) {
            err_vf (...);
        }
    }

    if (i_status == SYS_SUCCESS) {
        i_status = dc_if_do_this (...);
        if (i_status != SYS_SUCCESS) {
            err_vf (...);
        }
    }

    if (i_status == SYS_SUCCESS) {
        i_status = dc_if_do_that (...);
        if (i_status != SYS_SUCCESS) {
            err_vf (...);
        }
    }

    return (i_status);
}


/* ---------- Indentation ---------- */

FUNCTION int dc_if_do_things (...)
{
    int  i_status;

    i_status = dc_if_do_thing_1 (...);
    if (i_status != SYS_SUCCESS)
    {
        err_vf (...);
    }
```

```
        else
        {
            i_status = dc_if_do_thing_2 (...);
            if (i_status != SYS_SUCCESS)
            {
                err_vf (...);
            }
            else
            {
                i_status = dc_if_do_thing_3 (...);
                if (i_status != SYS_SUCCESS)
                {
                    err_vf (...);
                }
                else
                {
                    i_status = dc_if_do_this ();
                    if (i_status != SYS_SUCCESS)
                    {
                        err_vf (...);
                    }
                    else
                    {
                        i_status = dc_if_do_that ();
                        if (i_status != SYS_SUCCESS)
                        {
                            err_vf (...);
                        }
                    }
                }
            }
        }
    return (i_status);
}
```

The first two examples are similar in that they both decide to leave the function as soon as they find something wrong. The difference is that the first example leaves via an immediate return, while the second example exits only from a single exit point, which it reaches via a goto.

Two "rules" of structured programming suggest that we avoid using goto, and that we write functions with a single entry point and a single exit point. The first example violates the "single exit" rule, and the second example violates the "no gotos" rule.

The third and fourth examples satisfy both rules, but to me they tend to be harder to follow. The first two examples have the virtue of being simple-minded; it's obvious what the function is doing. The third example seems backwards from the way that most people think.

The fourth example suffers from two flaws: we can end up so far over to the side of the paper that what should take one line now takes several lines to type, and it can be difficult to remember how we got to a particular block of code. The difficulty of remembering context information increases non-linearly as the number of indentation levels climbs, and above about three levels of indentation you seriously increase the chances of other people making errors when working with the code.

Given the four examples, my preference is for either the first or the second. There's not much in it; in the first example you don't have to ensure that the value of i_status is always set, whereas in the second example you can very easily set a debugger breakpoint at the exit from the function. I suspect that consistency is the greatest virtue here, that we shouldn't mix the returns and the gotos.

If there is some clean-up that needs to be done when we encounter an error, often it can be simpler to use the goto version and do the cleanup in one place only. It is the same if we are doing exit tracing. The single exit point adds some clarity because it is obvious what we are returning and what we are doing just before returning. And ''goto Exit'' can be easier to see than ''return (i_status).''

If there aren't too many levels of indentation, style four is probably the best. But in these examples, I find that styles one and two are both clearer than example four. Which style to use is a matter of personal or project preference. Clarity is all.

Isn't the use of ''goto'' rather controversial?

There are some people who feel that ''gotos'' should never be used, that their use is the cardinal sin of programming. A poor use of gotos can certainly mean poor code, but my feeling is that gotos can make code easier to understand and maintain if you obey two rules.

- Never goto a label above your current location in the program.
- Use gotos only in one of the following situations:
  - To goto an exit label at the end of the function.
  - To jump cleanly out of a complex set of embedded loops by going to a label at the end of the block of code. The alternative is to have complex if-then-else and flag setting-checking code. Sometimes it's better to cut the Gordian knot and use a goto to exit the whole block cleanly.

Are there any easy ways to clean up when things go wrong?

There are probably many variants, but here are a couple of things you can do. Suppose you are opening two files and allocating two blocks of memory. To save space, I'll ignore all the error reporting.

```
...
FILE          *Fp_file1   = NULL;
FILE          *Fp_file2   = NULL;
struct abc    *sp_struct1 = NULL;
struct abc    *sp_struct2 = NULL;
...
if ((Fp_file1 = fopen ("file1", "r")) == NULL)
    goto Error_exit;
```

```
        if ((Fp_file1 = fopen ("file1", "r")) == NULL)
            goto Error_exit;

        if ((sp_struct1 = malloc (SIZE1)) == NULL)
            goto Error_exit;

        if ((sp_struct2 = malloc (SIZE2)) == NULL)
            goto Error_exit;
        ...
Error_exit:
        if (Fp_file1 != NULL)
            (void) fclose (Fp_file1);
        if (Fp_file2 != NULL)
            (void) fclose (Fp_file2);
        if (sp_struct1 != NULL)
            free (sp_struct1);
        if (sp_struct2 != NULL)
            free (sp_struct2);
        ...
```

The other way is to call a cleanup function when necessary. I've shown the example using immediate returns, but the concept can work with any type of function structure.

```
...
FILE        *Fp_file1;
FILE        *Fp_file2;
struct abc  *sp_struct1;
struct abc  *sp_struct2;
...
if ((Fp_file1 = fopen ("file1", "r")) == NULL)
{
    err_vf_cleanup ("%F", Fp_file1);
    return (SYS_FAILURE);
}
if ((Fp_file2 = fopen ("file2", "r")) == NULL)
{
    err_vf_cleanup ("%F %F", Fp_file1, Fp_file2);
    return (SYS_FAILURE);
}
if ((sp_struct1 = malloc (SIZE1)) == NULL)
{
    err_vf_cleanup ("%F %F %M", Fp_file1, Fp_file2, sp_struct1);
    return (SYS_FAILURE);
}
if ((sp_struct2 = malloc (SIZE2)) == NULL)
{
    err_vf_cleanup ("%F%F%M%M", Fp_file1, Fp_file2, sp_struct1, sp_struct2);
    return (SYS_FAILURE);
}
....
```

Here is an example of the err_vf_cleanup function. It's fairly primitive, and handles only file pointers and memory allocations, but it would be easy to extend. You could also enhance it to check that the pointers are non-NULL, and you could pass the addresses of the pointers so that the function also zeros out the pointers. The function works a bit like printf—it's a variable list function, and you pass a control string that uses %F and %M to indicate that a file pointer or memory pointer is being passed.

```
FUNCTION void err_vf_cleanup (char *capr_string, ...)
{
    va_list    x_arg_ptr;

    va_start (x_arg_ptr, capr_string);

    if (capr_string == NULL)
        goto Exit;

    for ( ; *capr_string != '\0'; capr_string++)
    {
        switch (*capr_string)
        {
            case '%':
                switch (*(++capr_string))     /* Look at the next character */
                {
                    case 'F':                     /* FILE, opened with fopen */
                        (void) fclose (va_arg (x_arg_ptr, FILE *));
                        break;
                    case 'M':                     /* Allocated memory   */
                        free (va_arg (x_arg_ptr, void *));
                        break;
                    default:     /* Unknown character. Terminate processing */
                        goto Exit;
                }
                break;
            case ' ':                 /* Space or tab.  Just ignore it */
            case '\t':
                break;
            default:                  /* Unknown character.  Terminate processing */
                goto Exit;
        }
    }
Exit:
    va_end (x_arg_ptr);
    return;
}
```

What is that word FUNCTION at the start of the function? That's not standard C, is it?

No, it's not part of C. It's just something I use so that it's easy to search through a source file for the start of each function. In my system-wide include file I have a line that looks like:

```
#define FUNCTION
```

When the preprocessor sees the word FUNCTION in the source file, it simply removes it completely.

How much code should you have in a function?

There are several guidelines. As we discussed in the chapter on Specifications and Documents, there's a lot of value in keeping things to a single page, because they are a lot easier to grasp and understand if you can see everything on one page. In the chapter on Modularization, we talked about the value of keeping functions simple and having them do just one thing.

Studies have shown that our short term memory can keep in mind only about seven different things at once, sometimes knows as the Rule of Seven (and often modified to seven plus or minus two). If you apply this rule, a function might have up to seven blocks of code, with each block consisting of up to seven lines of code. As a guideline, I'd say that if a function can do its job with less code, that's great. But if it needs more than about seven blocks, and if the blocks are more than about seven lines of code, you should split the function.

Some languages, such as COBOL, give you pseudo-functions, such as PERFORM blocks. It can be very hard following such code.

COBOL PERFORM blocks allow you to do some of the worst things in programming: every variable is a global variable, and PERFORM blocks are often poorly documented, and are often scattered around the source file. It's not unusual to have to use many fingers or pieces of paper to follow the logic of a COBOL program.

Despite the limitations of PERFORM blocks, you can control things by following a few standards. Every variable is a global, but you can make things a lot easier to understand by documenting each PERFORM block, describing what it does, what variables it reads, and what variables it changes. You can also use naming standards to make the blocks easier to find. When PERFORMing a block of code, you have two choices:

```
PERFORM LABEL1.
```
or
```
PERFORM LABEL1 THROUGH LABEL2.
```

In the first example, the PERFORM terminates at the next label it sees. To protect against unintended side effects should someone decide to put a label in the middle of a block of code, it is always safer to use the second approach, e.g.:

```
PERFORM COMPUTE-STATE-TAX THROUGH COMPUTE-STATE-TAX-EXIT.
```

To aid programmers in finding the PERFORM block, it makes sense to prefix labels with a number:

```
PERFORM 1000-COMPUTE-STATE-TAX THROUGH 1000-COMPUTE-STATE-TAX-EXIT.
```
or
```
PERFORM 1000-COMPUTE-STATE-TAX THROUGH 1099-COMPUTE-STATE-TAX-EXIT.
```

If the PERFORM blocks are laid out in numerical order in the source file, it will be much easier to follow the code.

Summary

This chapter described four different versions of code flow through a function, showing different ways of exiting from the function when things go wrong:

- Immediate returns
- Goto a label
- Blocks of code only when the status is good
- If-then-else indentations

It made the point that the most important thing is that the code be easy to understand and modify. We then showed some ways of cleaning up when things go wrong in a function.

21
_____
Files

We've talked a lot about functions. How do functions relate to source files?

It depends on what tools you have, but as a general rule, there are three things that should determine the names of functions. The function name should tell you:

- What the function does.
- The function type. Does the function return an integer? A pointer? Nothing?
- The file where you can find the function.

At one extreme, you can have one externally callable function per source file, with the names being virtually identical; e.g., dc_if_parse_item() would live in file dc_parse_item.c or dc_if_parse_item.c. I prefer to drop the _if_ because it doesn't add anything, and it just confuses things if you ever have to change a function from one type to another. If you put the _if_ in the file name, and dc_if_parse_item later changes from a function returning an integer to one returning a character pointer, what do you do? Change the file name, with all the attendant makefile, option file, and library consequences, or have dc_cpf_parse_item residing in file dc_if_parse_item.c?

If the externally callable function uses some support functions that are not used by any other function, you can put the support functions in the same source file and restrict their scopes to that file (making them static in C).

The "make" facility described in Chapter 6, "Software Tools," makes it easy to put functions in separate files. You no longer have to worry about what needs to be compiled; make takes care of all that for you.

What is the other extreme?

The other extreme is to have all the functions in a single file. To make it easy to find the file, you might put all the dc_ functions in a file called dc.c or dc_functions.c. You would have some naming convention that told you what the name of the file was.

However, if you put several externally callable functions in the same file, your executable will contain all of these functions, even if only one function was called by your code. An object module is indivisible. Link one function from an object module and you get the whole object module.

Is there anything in between these two extremes?

Of course. The typical development environment consists of many source files, some containing one function, and some containing several related functions. It's fairly common to put related functions in the same file when they rely on global data. By putting them in the same file, you can restrict the scope of that global data to only the functions in the file. The question is how to name the functions and files in the situation where you have several functions in a source file.

The best situation is one in which the name of the file is obvious from the name of the function. The second-best situation occurs when displaying a directory will tell you the name of the file containing any particular function. The worst is if you have to search the files or use a link map to find out the file name. Let's look at a few ways you might relate functions to files.

The idea that makes most sense is to put related functions in the same file. For example, dc_if_parse_item and dc_if_parse_header could logically reside in dc_parse.c. A strict naming convention could tell you the name of the file immediately, or a directory display would allow you to make an educated guess.

However, it's sometimes difficult to follow strict standards. Let's look at some of the functions you might use in an administrator program: adm_if_read_setup_info, adm_if_write_setup_info, adm_if_create_process_table, and adm_if_log_session. Perhaps the commonality among these functions is that they all read and write files, so let's put them in the file adm_files.c. To have a relationship between the function and file names, the function names now become adm_if_files_read_setup_info, adm_if_files_write_setup_info, adm_if_files_create_process_table, and adm_if_files_log_session. I fear that the names now have become sufficiently long that there will be a tendency to not bother with the _files_ part of the name.

How do you get around that?

One way around this problem is to use a number. dc3_if_parse_item resides in dc3.c. tmm7_if_check_duplicate resides in tmm7.c. Of course this has a disadvantage because you can't tell anything about the relationships of the functions in dc3.c or tmm7.c. Does dc3.c contain functions to parse data, or functions to control the user interface? You can't tell.

You might modify this a little so that dc3_if_parse_item and dc3_if_check_ header reside in dc3_parse.c. You know from the file name that the functions in dc3_parse.c are all for parsing. Of course, if you're looking for the name of the file containing dc3_if_check_header, you'll have to do a directory display to find out the full name of the dc3 file, but it's a lot easier to be consistent in the naming of the files.

I've used this method to good effect, but a lot of people have an aversion to seeing numbers in the function and file name.

I know people who use tools that cross-reference all the functions and files.

Some development environments have tools that allow you to build relationships between functions, variables, and files. When you are in a source file, you can position the cursor on a function, press a key, and see the file where the function is defined or where it is called. Position the cursor on a variable, press a key, and you can see where it is declared and where it is used. In UNIX, you can use ctags with the vi editor to do this, or etags with emacs.

If you use tools like these, the relationship between file and function names becomes much less important. The relationship is important for people who don't have tools to do the work for them.

How do you name any internal support functions?

Under the naming convention described in the chapter on Naming Conventions, functions that are internal support functions for an externally callable function don't have to worry about names if they reside in the same source file as the externally callable function. A function with no module prefix is, by definition, a function local to the file it's in.

How do you organize the functions in a single file?

Again, you should be motivated by the goal of helping the programmer spend as little time as possible finding information correctly. In general, my inclination is to organize functions alphabetically with page breaks between functions. That way there's no doubt where something will be found. I might make exceptions in a special case, but only if I was convinced it was a more effective method in that instance.

What about include files? How do you name them?

There are two types of include file:

- ∘ Internal
  - Used only by the files within a subsystem
- ∘ External
  - Contains subsystem information that is needed by users of the subsystem (e.g., function prototypes)
  - Contains project information that is common across subsystems in the project
  - Contains system-wide information that is common across projects

I would give slightly different names to these two types of include file. Let's look at an example of a library of database functions. If you have a single include file for external modules that call the database functions, and several include files that are of local scope, you might name the files as follows:

```
External:    db_external.h    or    db.h

Internal:    db_error.h
             db_proto.h
             db_structure.h
```

The external include file name should be such that you can use a similar name for all external include files across libraries and modules. You might name external include files xxx_external.h, xxx_global.h, xxx.h, or whatever makes sense to you. If you have multiple external include files for a subsystem, you would need a stricter naming convention, and so you might name the files:

```
External:    db_error.h          Internal:    db_i_error.h
             db_proto.h                        db_i_proto.h
             db_structures.h                   db_i_structures.h
```

or

```
External:    db_e_error.h        Internal:    db_error.h
             db_e_proto.h                      db_proto.h
             db_e_structures.h                 db_structures.h
```

Whatever the naming convention, the important point is to be consistent so that it's obvious from the name whether the include file is internal or external.

How would you name project- and system-wide include files?

If I wanted all system-wide information in one file, I'd probably call it:

```
sys.h
```

Or if there was a lot of system information, I might split it into several include files:

```
sys_defines.h
sys_macros.h
sys_structs.h
...
```

I'd try to prefix the system-wide defines, structures, etc., with SYS_ to make it obvious where the information came from. However, I'd also make an exception for some things. I'd probably define TRUE, FALSE, MAX, MIN, and a few other useful defines and macros without the SYS_ prefix.

For project-wide information, I'd do the same as for system-wide information, but I'd use prefixes of prj_ and PRJ_ instead of sys_ and SYS_.

What do you put in include files?

The main purpose of include files is to store common information that would otherwise be defined in several places. If a piece of information changes, you only have to change it in one place, which is a lot safer than having to make sure you found all the places. For example, if several places in the Capture system need to know the buffer length being used, you'd do a #define. For example,

```
#define  CAP_BUFFER_SIZE     5000
```

You'd also include structure templates, external global declarations, prototype functions, and so on.

Incidentally, I include an include file called debug.h in every source file. That way you can affect all source files simply by adding or changing things in the debug.h file. I also use a prefix for #defines that are local to single source files with LOC_. For example:

```
#define  LOC_BUFF_SIZE       256
```

How do you treat external and global declarations?

In the C language, global variables are supposed to be defined once (have storage assigned), and every other file should reference them explicitly as extern variables. Many C compilers actually allow external variables to be referenced as globals everywhere, but that's not particularly good practice.

I like to put all the global definitions in one place, and have an include file that contains all the extern references. The obvious choice would be to have a file, such as dc_globals.c, that contains only the definitions and storage allocation for all global variables. dc_extern.h contains the corresponding extern declaration for the variables. Any module that wants to reference any of the global variables simply includes dc_extern.h.

However, this method of putting all externs in a single file violates scope rules. All global variables are available to any function that has access to the include file. My personal feeling is that I'd rather have the minimum number of globals and make them easy to find than worry about scope rules, but if this concerns you, you can easily extend this idea to take scope of variables into account.

One caveat about putting all the globals into a file by themselves: I have worked with linkers that will not get such an object file from a library, but will resolve all the variables, giving them zero values. I ended up putting the global variables in a file that contained functions guaranteed to be linked in.

I've heard of using putting all the globals in an include file, and using #defines to make them either global or extern. How does that work?

That is another way of doing it, and may be a better way if you have lots of global variables because the more globals, the more likely it is to get the global.c file and the extern.h file out of sync. The standard way of doing this is to have something like the following in an include file called, say, global.h.

```
#if defined (MAIN)
    #define GLOBAL
#else
    #define GLOBAL extern
#endif
```

In global.h, or in the appropriate subsystem include files, you would write the global/extern variables as:

```
GLOBAL int  dc_i_thingummy;
GLOBAL char dc_caa_whatsits[DC_WHATSIT_COUNT][DC_WHATSIT_LENGTH];
```

You would have a #define MAIN at the top of the main source file, and so GLOBAL would evaluate to nothing in the main source file, and to extern in all the other source files. You can extend this to also initialize the variables.

```
#if defined (MAIN)
    #define GLOBAL
    #define INIT(x) = (x)
    #define INITSTART = {
    #define INITVAL(x) x,
    #define INITEND }
#else
    #define GLOBAL extern
    #define INIT(x)
    #define INITSTART
    #define INITVAL(x)
    #define INITEND
#endif
```

The INIT macro is used to initialize a single variable, and the INITSTART, INITVAL, and INITEND are used to initialize arrays and structures. For example, you might have:

```
GLOBAL int dc_i_thingummy  INIT(3);
GLOBAL int dc_ia_whatsits[DC_WHATSIT_COUNT]
          INITSTART
              INITVAL(3)
              INITVAL(2)
              INITVAL(1)
          INITEND;
```

Do you put everything in one include file, or do you split things up?

Since you should be using make or some equivalent to rebuild things as necessary, I recommend splitting things up into logical include files. For example, you might have:

```
#include dc_structures.h     /* Structure definitions      */
#include dc_defines.h        /* # defines                  */
#include dc_externs.h        /* External globals           */
#include dc_protos.h         /* Prototype functions        */
```

You might split up the include files into smaller files, such as

```
#include dc_structures.h        /* Structure definitions          */
#include dc_msg_defines.h       /* message # defines              */
#include dc_defines.h           /* other # defines                */
#include dc_externs.h           /* External globals               */
#include dc_parse_protos.h      /* Prototypes for parsing functions    */
#include dc_process_protos.h    /* Prototypes for processing functions */
```

I would have one include file per system for things common to the whole system, such as TRUE, FALSE, BOOLEAN, etc.

Why so many files in the second example?

Because you don't want to rebuild everything just because one line changes in an include file. If you separate out the include files, the chances are that you'll only rebuild a few files when one of the include files changes. But I can't give a hard and fast number for how many files to use because it must also be obvious in which file you can find things. You want to strike a balance between creating a proliferation of include files, and recompiling every source file when an irrelevant change is made to an include file.

What are those "protos.h" files?

They are files containing prototype functions as defined for ANSI C. A prototype function is a definition of a function and its parameters. C compilers will look at the prototype function and compare it with calls to the function and with the function declaration, then give you errors if things are inconsistent. In fact, the C compilers I've worked with let a lot of inconsistencies through, but lint picks them all up.

Prototype functions are very useful for ensuring that you haven't made a mistake with parameters. It's a lot quicker to find these errors with the compiler and lint than waiting until the program is compiled and linked and then testing the program. Sometimes you won't catch parameter errors until the program is being used by customers.

Give me an example of what an include file might look like.

```
/**************************************************************************

     File name:      db_errors.h
     Subsystem:      DataBase.

     Description:    This file contains error statuses for use by external programs
                     when they are calling the database functions. Note that
                     database errors have the range 5000 - 6000.

     History:

     {0}   90/11/11   Joe Smith.  Created.
     {1}   90/12/12   Dave Smith.  Rel 2.0.
           Objective: Distinguish between no-more-records and no-records-in-file
                      error returns.
           Edit:      Added an error status DB_NO_RECS_FOUND.


**************************************************************************/

#ifndef DB_ERRORS_H
#define DB_ERRORS_H


#define   DB_OPENED_EXCLUSIVE   5000
#define   DB_OPEN_FAILED        5010
          ...
#define   DB_NO_MORE_RECORDS    5150
#define   DB_NO_RECS_FOUND      5160    /*{1}*/
          ...


#endif
```

What is the #ifndef for?

To ensure that the file is included only once. (You could also have `#if !defined` `(DB_ERRORS_H)`.) This technique is useful when include files include other include files. Generally, I'm not in favor of doing that, but perhaps a project-wide include file, project.h, might do nothing but include prj_defs.h, prj_structs.h, and prj_errs.h. The #ifndef/#endif prevents the file being included twice should a programmer include, say, prj_err.h directly into the program.

The #ifndef tells the preprocessor: "if this variable is not defined, include what follows." The next line defines the variable, so the information in the include file won't be included a second time.

If you have a large system with many files, it may take the compiler too long to open all the include files before deciding not to include the data. To avoid the file opening time, you can put #ifndef in the program source file (and in include files that include other include files). For example,

```
#ifndef DC_DEFINES_H
#include "dc_defines.h"
#endif

#if ! defined (DB_ERRORS_H)
#include "db_errors.h"
#endif
```

Even if you use similar code in your source and include files, I would still put the #ifndef/#endif code in the include file as a fail-safe measure.

Why aren't you in favor of include files including include files?

Mainly because I believe information should be explicit. I'd rather see exactly what include files are used, rather than having them hidden. Secondly, there's a danger on some operating systems that you won't get the include file dependencies right if they are not all explicit. Lastly, hidden include files make it possible for a program to have more include files than it needs, which means it may be compiled unnecessarily if one of those files changes.

Summary

This chapter talked about the relationship between functions and files and described various ways of putting functions into files. It also described some include file naming-conventions and showed what an include file might look like.

22

Coding

What is there left to say about coding?

A couple of things.

Most software developers consider themselves above average and, of course, half of them *are* above average. On the other hand, half of them are below average. If software developers would just take their feelings of being above average to the logical conclusion, the state of software development would be much improved. If one is above average, there is a greater-than-50-percent chance that the person who eventually takes over the code will be of lesser ability than oneself, and therefore in need of well-documented code that follows standards and naming conventions.

The second point is that when a piece of code has been modified so many times that it has become messy and unintelligible, it's a good idea to rewrite it (assuming you know what it does and understand all the side effects). A clean, well-structured piece of code is easier to maintain and modify correctly than a messy, unintelligible piece. Obviously, the more frequently you rewrite something, the more expensive it becomes, but if you follow all the suggestions in this book, rewriting will be less frequent, with the consequent savings of time and money.

You use C in your examples, and I know C has a lot of useful control structures. What do you do if your language doesn't have these?

The main control structures are:

- ◦ IF-THEN-ELSE blocks
- ◦ DO-WHILE loops

- ○ REPEAT-UNTIL loops
- ○ FOR-NEXT loops
- ○ SELECT-CASE blocks

Let's see how we can duplicate them in a language which has only GOTOs. We'll also emulate the loop control statements "continue" and "break." Break means break out of the loop. Continue means ignore the rest of this block and continue with the next iteration of the loop.

We'll start with the IF-THEN-ELSE structure.

```
start_if_else_100:
      if (condition is true) goto if_100
      if (condition 1 is true) goto else_if_1_100
      if (condition 2 is true) goto else_if_2_100
      goto else_100
if_100:
      ...
      goto end_if_else_100
else_if_1_100:
      ...
      goto end_if_else_100
else_if_2_100:
      ...
      goto end_if_else_100
else_100:
   ...
end_if_else_100:
```

DO-WHILE loops evaluate the condition at the top of the loop, and do the block of code if the condition is true.

```
start_dw_loop_200:
      if (condition is not true) goto exit_dw_loop_200

      ...

      /* if we want to break, we do the following */
      goto exit_dw_loop_200

      /* if we want to continue, we do the following */
      goto start_dw_loop_200

      ...

      goto start_dw_loop_200
exit_dw_loop_200:

      ...
```

REPEAT-UNTIL loops evaluate the condition at the bottom of the loop, and then repeat the block of code if the condition is true. The loop will be done at least once.

```
start_ru_loop_300:
```

```
    . . .

    /* if we want to break, we do the following */
    goto exit_ru_loop_300

    /* if we want to continue, we do the following */
    goto end_ru_loop_300

    . . .

end_ru_loop_300:
    if (condition is not true) goto start_ru_loop_300
exit_ru_loop_300:

    . . .
```

FOR-NEXT loops set an initial count, then at the top of the loop they compare the count with a boundary value and execute the loop if the count is within the boundary value. At the bottom of the loop we increment or decrement the count and go back to the top. FOR-NEXT loops allow you to specify starting values, how much to change the count, and whether it is incremented or decremented. For example:

```
    FOR I = 1 TO 30 STEP 3
    FOR I = 30 TO 2 STEP -2
```

This is the standard FOR-NEXT loop. Some languages, such as C, allow multiple values to be initialized, evaluated, and changed. It's straightforward to extend this example to give these capabilities.

```
    control = start_value;
start_fn_loop_400:
    if (end_value >= start_value AND control > end_value) goto exit_fn_loop_
400
    if (end_value < start_value AND control < end_value) goto exit_fn_loop_
400

    . . .

    /* if we want to break, we do the following */
    goto exit_fn_loop_400

    /* if we want to continue, we do the following */
    goto end_fn_loop_400

    . . .
end_fn_loop_400:
    control = control + step_value
    goto start_fn_loop_400
exit_fn_loop_400
    . . .
```

SELECT-CASE blocks allow you to execute one of several blocks of code based on the value of a particular variable. If you've never seen one before, you'll get the idea from the following example.

```
        if (value equals value1) goto case_500_value1
        if (value equals value2) goto case_500_value2
        if (value equals value3) goto case_500_value3
        if (value equals value4) goto case_500_value4
        if (value equals value5) goto case_500_value5
        goto case_500_default

case_500_value1:
        ...
        goto case_500_exit
case_500_value2:
        ...
        goto case_500_exit
case_500_value3:
        ...
        goto case_500_exit
case_500_value4:
        ...
        goto case_500_exit
case_500_value4:
        ...
        goto case_500_exit
case_500_default:
        ...
        goto case_500_exit
case_500_exit:
        ...
```

Note that with each one of these self-contained units, the labels are all consistent, and we never goto a label outside the unit. Provided we stick strictly to this discipline, we have a high-quality method of writing structured code with a language that supports only gotos.

Note also the use of numbers in the labels. Using numbers like this allows you to have multiple similar loops in a function. Thus you could have two REPEAT-UNTIL loops one after the other by giving them separate numbers, such as 100 and 200.

These methods allow you to move from one language to another, while keeping up the same style of programming. It also keeps all the code obvious, while a method such as COBOL's PERFORM VARYING requires you to look at some other part of the code to see what is happening in your FOR-NEXT loop.

I read that indentation has a big effect on code readability.

Indeed. Studies have shown that well-indented code can have a major impact on people's ability to understand the code. Let's give a few examples of indentation using meaningless code.

Example 1—all code at the same level:

```
        if (i_count < i_max)
        {
```

```
if (i_count < DC_ARRAY_SIZE)
{
i_value = ia_array[i_count];
B_from_array = TRUE;
}
else
i_value = 0;
}
else
{
i_value = (-1);
}
```

Example 2—seemingly arbitrary indentation:

```
if (i_count < i_max)
{
    if (i_count < DC_ARRAY_SIZE)
  {
  i_value = ia_array[i_count];
    B_from_array = TRUE;
      }
else
    i_value = 0;
}
    else
     {
 i_value = (-1);
}
```

Example 3—regular indentation:

```
if (i_count < i_max)
{
    if (i_count < DC_ARRAY_SIZE)
    {
        i_value = ia_array[i_count];
        B_from_array = TRUE;
    }
    else
        i_value = 0;
}
else
{
    i_value = (-1);
}
```

Which indentation style can you follow the most easily? Indentation and bracketing style is one of the more passionate subjects in programming, so instead of requiring that code be in a particular style, you can define a standard style, then use code formatters to translate to the standard style before reviewing or storing the code, and let people reformat checked-out code into the style they like to work with.

I noticed that you surrounded some single lines with curly brackets.

You mean code like the following:

```
else
{
    i_value = (-1);
}
```

Coding like this is generally a good idea because when you add extra statements in the "if" section, it's easy to forget to add the braces. Suppose you had the following:

```
if (i_count == i_max_value)
    B_maxed_out = TRUE;
....
```

and you decided that, as well as setting the flag, you needed to zero out the counter. If you forget to add the braces, you have:

```
if (i_count == i_max_value)
    B_maxed_out = TRUE;
    i_count = 0;
....
```

which has a very different meaning than the one that you were trying to achieve. Putting braces around single lines makes it just about impossible to get it wrong when you add extra statements.

Further Reading

Bentley, Jon. 1986. *Programming Pearls*. Reading, MA: Addison-Wesley.

Bentley, Jon. 1988. *More Programming Pearls*. Reading, MA: Addison-Wesley.

Bentley, Jon. 1982. *Writing Efficient Programs*. Englewood Cliffs, NJ: Prentice-Hall.

Kernighan, Brian, and P.J. Plaugher. 1978. *The Elements of Programming Style (2nd Edition)*. New York: McGraw-Hill.

Straker, David. 1992. *C Style, Standards, and Guidelines*. Englewood Cliffs, NJ: Prentice-Hall.

Yourdon, Ed. 1976. *Techniques of Program Structure and Design*. Englewood Cliffs, NJ: Yourdon Press.

Summary

In this chapter we looked at ways of simulating the main program control structures (IF-THEN-ELSE, DO-WHILE, REPEAT-UNTIL, FOR-NEXT, SELECT-CASE) in a language that doesn't support them. We also looked at indentation styles as a way to improve the understandability of the program.

PART 5

Finding, Preventing, and Removing Errors

23

Error Reporting

Error reporting is a critical but mainly overlooked part of a project. When things go wrong and the error reporting is cryptic, two things happen. Users become frustrated, and programmers spend a lot of unnecessary time figuring out what went wrong.

So what should be done?

User-level error reporting should clearly tell the user what is wrong and what action to take. If you can validate data when it is first entered, do so. If you can only validate data later, and on validation it turns out the data is incorrect, give the user an error message that describes exactly what is wrong and instructs the user how to fix the problem.

But what if the error is one that needs to be fixed by a programmer?

If the error is due to a coding error, the error message should tell the user that the problem is a coding problem and tell the user whom to get in touch with. Additionally, it should provide enough information in a coherent fashion that the programmer will be able to find and fix the problem in the shortest possible time. Ideally, the type of error message directed at the programmer should give the following information:

- Enough information to set the context
- The name of the function where the error occurred

    ○   Where in the function the error occurred
    ○   The values of useful variables
    ○   The version number of the software
    ○   The date and time when the error occurred
    ○   The severity of the error
    ○   The error number
    ○   Instructions to the user

Give me an example of an error report.

```
Received unexpected command 33 while waiting for Startup command.
Error code 56 - UNEXPECTED COMMAND RECEIVED
WARNING reported in function: dc_if_first_command
Process name: CAPTURE    Version: 2.1    Monday, Dec 31, 1990  09:43:32.59
Please give this error log to your System Manager.
```

In fact the message might be expanded on. Perhaps the command comes in a structure with other data; in this case, providing the other data in the structure could help the programmer.

As for the error number, there are three approaches to take. The first approach says that every error number should be unique, so that when a particular error code is reported, it could be reported from only one place. The second approach gives unique error numbers within a function, so that if you know the function name, you can find the exact location of the error. The third approach says that identical errors get the same number, and some other piece of information tells you in which of the potential locations the error actually occurred. For example, a file-open failure on a non-existent file could report the same error code every place that the file open failed. The third approach can often give more useful information because, for example, there are various reasons for a file open failure to occur. If you consolidate all possible reasons into a single unique error code for that particular call, you lose information.

In C, you can use the __LINE__ and __FILE__ values in each error call to identify the line number and file. You could either pass them as parameters to the error routine, or use a macro to report errors and have these two values passed to the routine behind the scenes.

Should all errors be reported?

In general, yes. Murphy's Law ensures that if you don't report on an error, sooner or later it will come back to bite someone.

Would you use separate functions for the user and programmer messages?

No, I'd use a single function. The obvious thing to do is pass a flag that tells the function whether this message should be written to a file, go to a user, or both. You could also extend the idea and have a flag that tells you to send a message to an operator console.

Where should the message be logged? Where it's first found, or later on?

As a general principle, you should log messages from where they are found, all the way out until you reach a place that allows you to continue or you have exited the program.

It's important to remember that not every bad status is an error. For example, you call a function to retrieve a database record but the function can't find the record. The function cannot determine if the non-existence of the record is an error because you may have called it just to see if the record exists or not. A bad status is an error only if the function that sees it can determine that it's an error.

If a function does notice an error, it should log the error then propagate the error status outward.

Give me an example.

Let's use the above database example.

```
int prc_if_process_data (...)
{
    static char   ca_fname[] = "prc_if_process_data";
    int           i_status;
    ..
    ..
    i_status = prc_if_consolidate_data (...)
    if (i_status != SYS_SUCCESS)
    {
        err_vf (i_status, ca_fname,
            SYS_PLEASE_INFORM_SYS_MANAGER,
            "Error on call to prc_if_consolidate_data");
        return (i_status);
    }
    ..
}

int prc_if_consolidate_data (...)
{
    static char    ca_fname[] = "prc_if_consolidate_data";
    int            i_status;
    ..
    i_status = db_if_read_rec (....)
    if (i_status != SYS_SUCCESS)
    {
```

```
                    err_vf (i_status, ca_fname,
                           SYS_PLEASE_INFORM_SYS_MANAGER,
                           "Error on call to db_if_read_rec");
                    return (i_status);
               }
               ..

          }
```

If this was real code, I would also report the values of key variables. The exact method of doing this would depend on the language you use. In a language like C you could build up a string containing all the relevant values, or you could use the ANSI C variable list functionality and send a variable number of parameters to print.

All this error checking takes a lot of space.

There are ways to reduce the space if you have a macro capability in the language you use. For example, in C you might define macros such as the following: The first one checks the status and returns if not good; the second checks the status and goes to the exit.

```
#define ERR_CR(i_stat, ca_name, ca_msg)                          \
     if (i_stat != SYS_STATUS_OK) {                               \
          err_vf (i_stat, ca_name,                                \
                    SYS_PLEASE_INFORM_SYS_MANAGER, ca_msg);       \
          return (i_status);                                      \
     }

#define ERR_CG(ca_msg)                                           \
     if (i_status != SYS_STATUS_OK) {                             \
          err_vf (i_status, ca_fname,                             \
                    SYS_PLEASE_INFORM_SYS_MANAGER, ca_msg);       \
          goto Exit;                                              \
     }
```

In the first macro, you pass all the values explicitly. The second macro has been set up to assume that the status variable is called i_status, and the function name is called ca_fname. The code above would now look like:

```
int prc_if_process_data (...)
{
     static char   ca_fname[] = "prc_if_process_data";
     int           i_status;
     ..
     i_status = prc_if_consolidate_data (...)
     ERR_CR(i_status, ca_fname, "Error on call to prc_if_consolidate_data");
     ..
}

int prc_if_consolidate_data (...)
{
```

```
        static char     ca_fname[] = "prc_if_consolidate_data";
        int             i_status;
        ..
        i_status = db_if_read_rec (....)
        ERR_CR("Error on call to db_if_read_rec");
        ..
    }
```

Neither macro can handle the variable list parameters that err_vf is capable of dealing with. Let's look at how you might do the macros to handle variable list arguments. The macro will assume that the caller is setting i_status and ca_fname.

```
#define ERR_CG(args)                                \
    if (i_status != SYS_STATUS_OK) {                \
        err_vf (i_status, ca_fname,                 \
                SYS_PLEASE_INFORM_SYS_MANAGER,      \
                err_cpf_build_string args);         \
        goto Exit;                                  \
    }
```

You need the following function in your library:

```
char  *err_cpf_build_string (char *capr_format, ...)
{
    va_list         xp_variable_list;
    static char     ca_scratch_buff[500];    /*  Must be large enough to handle
                                                 any error message  */

    va_start (xp_variable_list, capr_format);
    vsprintf (ca_scratch_buff, capr_format, xp_variable_list);
    va_end (xp_variable_list);

    return (ca_scratch_buff);
}
```

And you use the macro as follows:

```
i_status = db_if_read_rec (ca_empno)
ERR_CG(("Error calling db_if_read_rec with employee number <%s>\n", ca_
empno));
```

Note the double parentheses; they are needed because of the way C does macro substitution.

What would you do if you had a function returning a pointer, but there is the possibility of several different types of errors in the function?

This is a specific instance of the more general problem of "if you have a function that returns a value, how do you also return error values?" Another example might be: if you have a function that returns a count of something, how do you return one of several possible error statuses?

Returning a status value.   As a general principle, if there is a possibility of errors, the function should return a status value. Any other values that you are interested in would be passed back as return parameters. For example,

```
i_status = dc_if_get_count (..., &i_count);
```

Using impossible return values as error codes.   Another approach is to use the return value for both the status and the value that you are interested in by returning an impossible value if an error occurred. For example, if there will never be a negative count, you might use negative numbers for errors.

```
if ((i_count = dc_if_get_count(...)) < 0)
    do_error_stuff();
```

The disadvantage of this approach is that each function has a different range of valid returns, so there is no consistency in what denotes an error.

Consolidating errors into a single exceptional value.   Another approach is to bundle many errors into one. This is useful if you don't care about differentiating between the different types of error. In the above example, if we regard getting an error as no different from getting a count of zero, we might have:

```
if ((i_count = dc_if_get_count(...)) != 0)
{
    ...
```

Another example would be if you are using a linked list, and you are getting the first member of a doubly linked list, passing a pointer to the list header.

```
sp_first = dll_vpf_get_first (vp_list_header);
```

There are three possible situations, and we might use a NULL return for all three cases:

- Everything is okay and we get a pointer to the first member of the list.
- The list is empty.
- The pointer passed is invalid.

Consolidating all errors and exceptions into a single exception condition has most value when you are able to do something repetitive until the exception condition occurs. An obvious example is seen when you work through a linked list.

```
while ((sp_widget = dll_vpf_get_next(sp_widget)) != NULL)
{
    ...
```

Using a global variable to contain the error code.   The problem with consolidating all errors into a single return value is that information is lost. If a single return value gives you benefits, but you'd still like the additional information, you could use a global variable to contain the specific cause of failure. If the function returns a failure, you would examine the global variable to find out why it failed. In our previous example,

```
sp_first = dll_vpf_get_first (vp_list_header);
```

if sp_first == NULL, we would look at dll_i_errno to discover if the list was empty, if we are at the end of the list, or if there was a problem with the pointer to the list header.

In terms of naming your global error variable, I'd have one error variable for each subsystem; so the dll_ subsystem has dll_i_errno, while the dc_ subsystem has dc_i_errno.

Make sure there are no errors.   It's often useful to use the return value from one function as a parameter in another function. In this case you want a function that's guaranteed not to return an error code. For example,

```
strcpy (ca_process_name, sys_cpf_get_proc_name());
```

makes it easy to get the process name and copy it into your variable in one statement. In situations like this, you would require that the function could not break. In this case it might return a pointer to the string "NO NAME" if an error occurred.

But whatever approach you take, try to be consistent and document the return values and return conditions well.

How would you report errors in a screen-oriented environment, where you don't want error messages splattered all over the screen?

If an error occurs in a fairly deep function in this environment, I would propagate the error outward, storing the messages as I went, until I reached a point where it made sense to show them to the user.

A way that I particularly like is to have an error function that allocates memory to store the error message. It keeps track of a linked list of error messages that can be reported whenever the application sees fit.

Show me how.

Our basic error reporting function, err_vf(), calculates the length of the function name, instruction string, and error message string, and allocates memory. You would have a structure that contained:

```
structure
{
    forward pointer
```

```
            backward pointer
            status that was passed in
            function name string
            instruction string
            error message string
    }
```

In a variable-length string environment, such as C, you would have a slightly different structure. At the point the application wants to display the messages, it could put up a small window and allow the user to scroll through the messages. The available functions in this scheme might be:

- `err_vf (function name, error status, flag, instructions, error message);`

  This function either prints the error message to a log file or stores it in a linked list of errors for later reporting.

  flag would be one or many of:

`ERR_STORE`	Store this error in the linked list.
`ERR_PRINT`	Print this error to the error log.
`ERR_CLEAR`	Clear the linked list before storing this error.

- `err_if_next (flag, pointer to a structure);`

  This function gets the next error message in the linked list. The application program would call the function when it wants to report the errors that have been stored up.

  flag would be 0 for the first message in the list and non-zero for the next one.

  The structure might be:

```
struct
{
    int    i_status;            /* Status value               */
    char   *cap_fname;          /* Pointer to function name    */
    char   *cap_instructions;   /* Pointer to instructions     */
    char   *cap_message;        /* Pointer to error message    */
}
```

- `err_if_prior (flag, pointer to structure);`

  As for err_if_next() but starts at the end and works backwards.

- `err_vf_clear();`

  Clears up the linked list of messages and deallocates any memory that was allocated.

- `err_if_open_logfile (name);`

  Opens a named logfile. It's probably just as easy for the application to open the file, but we want to hide superfluous information about the file from the application. All the application needs to know is whether the file was opened successfully.

- `err_vf_close_logfile();`

  Closes the logfile that was previously opened.

What other ways are there to track errors?

There are many other ways to track errors, some of which are:

○ Give each possible error point in a function a unique number within the function, between 1 and, say, 10. Each time, multiply the error number you have accumulated by 10, and add the current error number. As you progress outward, you have a track of all the unique error numbers by function. It's not at all user-oriented, but can help a programmer track inward, following the path of the error. If you think 10 is too small a number to track all the unique error locations in a function, choose a larger number and multiply by this each time. Zero out the number after reporting it, and at every innermost error situation.

○ If you have too many functions to keep adding numbers and multiplying by 10 and still remain with the maximum value of an integer, you could allocate an array of, say, 100 bytes, and accumulate the error values in the array, each value you report taking the next available zero-filled position. Whenever you report on the error values or record the innermost error that will be tracked outward, clear out the array.

○ Allocate a string of, say, 256 bytes. This string would be passed in and out of every function. If the string is "OK", or perhaps a null string, the code continues on its path. Otherwise the function appends its name and returns. The innermost function where the error occurred would also print the error or failure in the string before appending its name. Some languages have expensive string comparisons, so you might use a global Boolean value to determine if there is an error or not, and manipulate the string only if there is an error.

How about a listing for an error-reporting system?

Okay. To save space, I've left out all the header documentation, and I've hidden some of the details in function calls.

```
/*  This is the main error reporting function */

FUNCTION void err_vf (int  ir_errno, char *capr_function, int ir_flags,
                      char *capr_instr, char *capr_format, ...)
{
    static char  ca_procname[SYS_PROCNAME_LEN] = '\0';
    char         *cp_temp;
    char         ca_scratch_buff[MAX_BUFF_LEN];
    char         ca_err_lookup[MAX_MSG_BUFF];
    int          i_status;
    va_list      xp_variable_list;

    /* Get process name the first time through. */
    if (ca_procname[0] == '\0')
        strcpy(ca_procname, sys_cpf_proc_name());

    /*  If it's a C runtime error, the user has passed 'errno' so we look
        it up and print the message as well.  If it's not a C runtime error,
```

```
                    we create a null string if it's 0.  Otherwise we look up
                    the system error message facility to get the string. */

            if (ir_errno == 0)
                ca_err_lookup[0] = '\0';
            else if (ir_flags & ERR_CRTL)          /* C Runtime Library */
            {
                if (strerror (ir_errno) == NULL)
                    sprintf(ca_err_lookup, "Error %d - NO TEXT", ir_errno);
                else
                    sprintf(ca_err_lookup, "Error %d - %s", ir_errno, strerror(ir_errno));
            }
            else if (ir_flags & ERR_NOLOOKUP)      /* No Lookup */
                sprintf(ca_err_lookup, "Error %d.  No error text", ir_errno);
            else
                strcpy (ca_err_lookup, sys_cpf_get_msg(ir_errno));

            /* CREATE A STRING WITH THE VARIABLE LIST ARGUMENTS */
            if (capr_format == NULL)
                ca_scratch_buff[0] = '\0';
            else
            {
                /* Create a string from the variable list */
                va_start (xp_variable_list, capr_format);
                vsprintf (ca_scratch_buff, capr_format, xp_variable_list);
                va_end (xp_variable_list);
                /* Set temporary pointer to last char in string before \0 terminator */
                cp_temp = ca_scratch_buff + strlen(ca_scratch_buff) - 1;
                if (*cp_temp != '\n')
                {
                    cp_temp++;              /* Move to the  \0   terminator */
                    /* Append a newline at the end if there isn't already one */
                    *cp_temp++ = '\n';
                    *cp_temp   = '\0';
                }
            }

            /* CLEAR THE LINKED LIST IF INSTRUCTED TO DO SO */
            if (ir_flags & ERR_CLEAR)
                err_vf_clear();

            /* PRINT OUT THE MESSAGE IF SO INSTRUCTED. THIS IS ALSO THE
               DEFAULT IF MESSAGE IS NOT STORED.  */
            if ((ir_flags & ERR_LOG) || !(ir_flags & ERR_STORE))
                vf_print_msg (capr_function, ir_flags, ca_procname, capr_instr,
                            ca_scratch_buff, ca_err_lookup);

            /* STORE THE ERROR MESSAGE IF SO REQUESTED.  */
            if (ir_flags & ERR_STORE)
                vf_store_msg (capr_function, capr_instr, ca_procname,
                            ca_scratch_buff, ca_err_lookup);
        }


FUNCTION static void vf_print_msg (char *capr_function, int  ir_flags,
                                   char *capr_procname, char *capr_instructions,
                                   char *capr_errmsg, char *capr_err_lookup)
    {
```

```
    time_t  x_time;          /* x_ signifies system defined type */

    /* IF NO LOG FILE IS OPEN, WE'LL PRINT TO STDERR */
    if (err_Fp_log == NULL)
        err_Fp_log = stderr;

    /* Get the system time */
    x_time = time(NULL);

    /* Print a newline */
    fprintf (err_Fp_log, "\n");

    /* Print the error message */
    if (capr_errmsg != NULL)
        fprintf (err_Fp_log, capr_errmsg);

    /* Print the level of the error and the function name */
    if (ir_flags & ERR_I)
        fprintf (err_Fp_log, "INFORMATION ");
    else if (ir_flags & ERR_W)
        fprintf (err_Fp_log, "WARNING ");
    else if (ir_flags & ERR_F)
        fprintf (err_Fp_log, "FATAL ERROR ");
    else              /* Anything else is ERROR */
        fprintf (err_Fp_log, "ERROR ");

    if (capr_function != NULL)
        fprintf (err_Fp_log, "reported from: %s\n", capr_function);
    else
        fprintf (err_Fp_log, "reported from unknown function\n");

    /* Print process name and time */
    fprintf (err_Fp_log, "Process name: %s.   Date/time: %s",
             capr_procname, ctime(&x_time));

    /* Print system lookup error message */
    if (capr_err_lookup != NULL && capr_err_lookup[0] != '\0')
        fprintf (err_Fp_log, "%s\n", capr_err_lookup);

    /* Write instructions to user */
    if (capr_instructions != NULL)
        fprintf (err_Fp_log, "%s\n", capr_instructions);

    fflush (err_Fp_log);
}


FUNCTION static void vf_store_msg (char *capr_function, char *capr_instructions,
                                   char *capr_procname, char *capr_errmsg,
                                   char *capr_err_lookup)
{
    static char   ca_fname[] = "vf_store_msg";
    char          *cp_data;
    unsigned int  iu_size   = 0;

    /* If we don't have a list header, create one */
    if (err_vp_list_head == NULL)
    {
        err_vp_list_head = dll_vpf_create_list();
        if (err_vp_list_head == NULL)
        {
            vf_print_msg (ca_fname, ERR_E, capr_procname,
```

```
                                err_ca_please_inform,
                                "Error in error func creating list\n",
                                "NULL pointer");
                return;
        }
    }

    /* Calculate the size of the memory to allocate.  Each string gets
       an additional 1 byte for the null terminator.   */
    if (capr_function != NULL)
        iu_size += strlen(capr_function) + 1;
    if (capr_instructions != NULL)
        iu_size += strlen(capr_instructions) + 1;
    if (capr_errmsg != NULL)
        iu_size += strlen(capr_errmsg) + 1;
    if (capr_err_lookup != NULL)
        iu_size += strlen(capr_err_lookup) + 1;

    /* Add to the end of the linked list */
    cp_data = dll_vpf_add (err_vp_list_head, iu_size);
    if (cp_data == NULL)
    {
        vf_print_msg (ca_fname, ERR_E, capr_procname, err_ca_please_inform,
                    "Error in error function on call to dll_vpf_add\n",
                    "NULL pointer");
        return;
    }
    else
    {
        /*  Concatenate the strings, putting NULLs at the end of each one */
        cp_data = sp_member;
        if (capr_function != NULL)
        {
            strcpy (cp_data, capr_function);
            cp_data += strlen(capr_function);
        }
        *cp_data++ = '\0';

        if (capr_instructions != NULL)
        {
            strcpy(cp_data, capr_instructions);
            cp_data += strlen(capr_instructions);
        }
        *cp_data++ = '\0';

        if (capr_errmsg != NULL)
        {
            strcpy (cp_data, capr_errmsg);
            cp_data += strlen(capr_errmsg);
        }
        *cp_data++ = '\0';

        if (capr_err_lookup != NULL)
        {
            strcpy (cp_data, capr_err_lookup);
            cp_data += strlen(capr_err_lookup);
        }
```

```
        *cp_data = '\0';
    }
}
```

Summary

In this chapter we discussed the value of reporting errors, and talked about several ways to log any errors discovered in the program. We showed some macros that reduce the amount of space taken in the program file to check and report errors. We then showed a sample error-reporting function.

24

Testing

The goal of software engineering is to create software that does what it's supposed to do, never breaks, and is easy to modify. Testing is one of the methods used to achieve this goal. We test so that we can find and eliminate the errors in the software.

Testing is the process of trying to show that the software *fails* to work as required; it is about trying to *break* the software. If you want to find and eliminate all the errors, you have to devise tests that will find all the errors. Thus, a successful test is one that produces a failure in the software. This is an important point because the type and quality of testing you do depends on your view of testing. If you're trying to show that the software works, you'll probably run through the mainstream code a couple of times and discover few bugs.

On the other hand, if you're trying to break the software, you'll find lots of interesting things to check out. A good tester will always be trying to demonstrate that the software doesn't work as required.

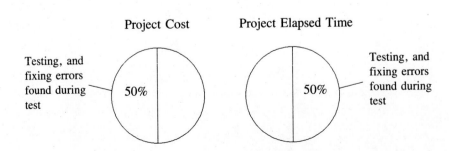

Testing is a strange part of the software development process. Testing and fixing the errors found typically consumes 50 percent of the cost and 50 percent of the elapsed time of a project, but it is the part of the development process that organizations pay the least attention to. We typically leave it up to the individual software engineers to test their software, but we don't teach them how to test, and we don't review their test methods, plans, and test cases.

Testing is difficult, creative work. If you thought designing and coding the program was hard, "you ain't seen nothing yet." And the difficulty is compounded by two things. First, software engineers are often under a lot of pressure to get the thing built, and the obvious place to save time is on testing. Second, it's psychologically difficult to spend time and emotional energy creating something, and then to turn around and try to destroy it. We don't want our software to fail.

Most organizations start by trying to get the software engineers to thoroughly test their software. After the cost of fixing bugs in the shipped software becomes too high, they develop a test organization to make sure that the software is fully tested before it is shipped.

Unfortunately, inspections never improve quality. They only detect the lack of quality. Automobile manufacturers used to inspect all incoming parts, but the Japanese revolutionized the process and improved the quality of the incoming parts so that inspections were no longer necessary. So it should be with software. The effort must always be to push quality back as far as possible with the goal of eliminating the need for Quality Assurance (QA) inspections.

QA organizations often work against quality in other ways. Normally deadlines are tough and developers have to hustle to meet them. They work late into the night or over the weekend to meet the deadline, without regard to conforming to naming, documentation, or coding standards. Once QA people have tested the code, they don't want the software engineer adding documentation or changing code style or variable names because that would mean a whole new round of retesting.

But programmers are notoriously bad at testing their own software. They know how it's supposed to work, and they don't really want it to fail.

Testing can be boring, tedious work and some people are better suited to it than others are. Even when a programmer has tested his code exhaustively when first written, he's unlikely to put in the same effort after making modifications. So you're right.

But, as Deming pointed out, most quality problems stem from problems in the system rather than in the individual. The system must be such that it becomes difficult to do a poor job of testing. The system should be designed around the premise that there will be bugs and that we need well-thought-out procedures for finding them.

So what do we do?

There are seven aspects of software testing to consider:

1. Reduce the number of errors in the software.
2. Do software reviews.
3. Do test plan reviews.
4. Develop good test methods.
5. Develop good test cases.
6. Develop reusable test cases.
7. Design testing into the system.

Let's look at each one in turn. The first one is addressed throughout the book and there is a separate chapter about Reviews, so let's look at the fourth aspect, developing good testing methods.

How much code should you write before testing it?

The basic answer is: test each logical unit, whether it is an algorithm, a function, or whatever. The trouble with coding too much before testing is that if you have too much to test, your attitude tends to shift from trying to break the software, to demonstrating that it works. So add one component at a time, and test each component as you add it.

When you write a test driver to test a component, write a separate test for each thing you want to test. Combining tests suffers from two disadvantages: it's easier to overlook tests you should make, and it's easier to misinterpret the results. A single test for a single piece of functionality gives the best results.

When testing, you should make sure that you know what results you expect and try to build that knowledge into the driver. The test program should be able to report errors it discovers.

I've heard about top-down and bottom-up testing. Which is best?

Let's look first at the top-down approach. You code the first (top) level module, including all the calls to the second level modules. Then you create stubs for the second level modules and put in enough code to allow them to return useful data. You'll notice at once that if the module is supposed to perform anything complex, you'll have to write a lot of code in the stub to be able to return enough values and conditions to test the top level module.

Once the top level module is tested fully, you code the second level modules and stub the third level modules in the same way. You slowly work your way down until everything is fully functional. As you work down, you are testing the integrated module. So you will be much less likely to have serious integration problems.

However, the problems with top-down testing are manyfold. First, to really test the upper modules, you have to create stubs that will return the full range of values that you'll get in the production software. If you are going to do that much work, you might as well write the modules themselves.

Second, as you implement the code, you will inevitably find errors in the design, or discover better ways to do things. If you have already tested the top-level code, you will either resist making those sensible changes, or you won't adequately test the changes.

Third, and most devastating, it's impossible to fully test lower-level modules using the upper-level code. After all, the upper-level software will be manipulating good data, so you'll never be able to test the lower level modules with invalid data. At first glance this may not seem too bad, but the goal is to make the lower level bulletproof because you don't know how it will be called in the future.

How about bottom-up testing then?

In the bottom-up approach, you start at the lowest-level functions. You code the function, then write a driver program for it. The driver will call the function with a variety of values, carefully devised to exhaustively test the function with data it should be able to handle and with data it should reject. You test the function until you can't break it any more, then write the function that calls this one. You now have to create a driver for the new function. And so you work slowly upwards.

Bottom-up testing also has its disadvantages. First, you can lose sight of the overall product, and can end up in an integration nightmare. Second, it assumes that you have done a detailed design all the way down to the lowest-level modules. This completely ignores the prototyping aspect to software develop-ment. It also ignores reality by assuming that everyone will do detailed designs that are reviewed before implementation. It's important to get things right as quickly as possible, but it's also important to stay in touch with reality!

What is the best way to develop and test then?

You'll notice that the disadvantages of top-down testing relate to the testing itself, while the disadvantages of bottom-up testing relate to the coding. In general, the best way to develop software is to use a mixture of top-down and bottom-up coding, combined with exhaustive bottom-up testing. This gives you the best of both worlds. You can prototype, modify the design as appropriate, but still test exhaustively.

But once the software seems to be working, there's less incentive to test exhaustively.

That's true, but if you don't want to test, it's easy not to test. The approach I've described is the most effective. It's up to you to decide if you want to test the software, or just try a few simple test cases. If you don't want to really test the software, no approach is going to change that. You should recognize that testing is not complete until you have done exhaustive and complete bottom-up testing.

It seems that a good modular design will help the testing effort.

No question. There are various attributes a software module should have if you are going to be able to test it effectively. First, getting information in and out should be through well-defined interfaces—having global variables complicates the interface and makes a module more difficult to test. There shouldn't be too many parameters, otherwise the number of possibilities becomes too large to manage effectively. Second, the module should be "cohesive"—it should concern itself with just one concept. If it does too many unrelated things, it becomes too complicated to test well.

In reality, there is never enough time to test things properly. You are always under pressure to get the next thing done.

That's often true. If you work for an organization that stresses good testing, you'll have the opportunity to test. If you work for an organization that continually pushes for progress, it's hard to test thoroughly. It's also difficult to maintain test drivers for routines if no one else is doing so. In the end you tend to adapt to the prevailing style.

If you feel under too much pressure to be able to test every module to exhaustion with all the test drivers that entails, there are a few things you can do to help in the quest for quality.

One technique I really recommend is stepping through the code in a source code debugger. As you step past each line, things occur to you that you missed before. You see cases that you haven't considered, and get new ideas for things to test. You also see immediately where you are having problems. Constantly examine the contents of variables to see if the values are what you expect. I think it's invaluable to step through the code several times.

Another thing is to do test walkthroughs by yourself. A walkthrough is where you walk a test case through the code, acting as though you are the computer. Based on the data in your test case, you make the appropriate decisions and follow the appropriate flows. Again, you will probably see things that you missed when doing the design and coding.

A third option is to use as many library routines as possible, on the assumption that a library routine has been thoroughly tested. I try to generalize my software.

When I need to write a new routine, I think: "How can I generalize this routine so that it will be useful to other people or to the future me?" Then I write a general-purpose library routine with simple input and output and no globals and build test drivers to test the hell out of it. It takes longer to write a routine this way, but over time I've built up a library of useful routines that save me having to recode and retest that functionality.

These ideas seem to require a lot of work.

It's not as much as you might think. It really doesn't take that long to step through the code, either in the debugger or in a walkthrough. It's a lot more effective than desk debugging, and you'll probably discover bugs or situations you didn't consider, and which would take a lot longer to discover any other way.

The alternative is to just let the software run. If it fails, you'll probably have to go to the debugger anyway. If it succeeds, then what? There is a limit to how many situations you can create, and without watching how the code behaves, you'll never be in a position to develop hunches about potential problems. If the software then fails six months later at a customer site, the organization will spend days to get the problem fixed.

Incidentally, if you're testing interactive software by changing values and going back into the screen to make sure that the values were stored, go into other screens between times. If you go back immediately into the screen you are testing, it may use the same area of memory, with all the old values. You want to make sure that stack memory is reused before going back into the screen.

Should people write test plans?

I think it's a very good idea to write down test plans and test cases. The act of writing forces you to think and to clarify your thinking. You're a lot more likely to cover all the bases with a test plan. If you review test plans, it's essential to write them down. In fact, it's a good idea to create two test plans: the developer creates one, and a test person creates the other. Both plans are reviewed, then they are combined to form a single test plan. The idea is that two people working independently will come up with more ideas than would either person working alone.

What about the next aspect—developing good test cases?

It's sometimes thought that if you devise tests that execute every unique path through a module, the module will be thoroughly tested. Not only is this generally impossible because of a prohibitively large number of unique paths, but it is wrong for several reasons. First, there may be specific data dependencies; second, there may be paths missing; third, the module may be perfectly coded to do something other than what it is supposed to do!

How do we design test cases then?

Test case design is probably the most difficult and creative part of testing, so we use our intelligence and creativity. The goal is to come up with a set of test cases that give us the best test coverage in the most effective manner.

The test cases you create will depend on two things. First, they depend on what the module is trying to do. This information should be in the module header documentation; in fact, it's likely to be an iterative process of updating the documentation as you refine your notion of what the module is supposed to do. Second, the test cases will depend on the actual code in the module.

A function module consists of sequentially executed lines of code and decisions (if, for, while, etc.). If there are no decisions, any test case will execute all the code. So the interesting cases involve the decisions. At a minimum you should design enough test cases to cover every possible outcome of each decision. For example, if you have a decision of the form:

```
if (i_a > i_b)
```

you need a case where i_a is greater than i_b and a case where i_a is not greater than i_b. If you have a decision such as:

```
if (i_a > i_b AND i_c < 10)
```

you need the following test cases:

```
i_a > i_b          and     i_c < 10
i_a > i_b          and     i_c >= 10
i_a <= i_b         and     i_c < 10
i_a <= i_b         and     i_c >= 10
```

These are just the minimum cases as we will soon see.

But the range of possible values you use is infinite. How do you choose what values to use?

You split the possibilities into "equivalence groups," and choose one value from each group. Then you choose values to test the boundary conditions and add in troublesome values and conditions that are notorious for producing more than their fair share of errors.

What are equivalence groups?

Let me give you some examples. If you are testing for single alphabetic character input, you might decide on the following equivalence classes.

Single alphabetic character

Single non-alphabetic character
Less than one character (perhaps just pressing Return)
Greater than one character

If you suspect that members of an equivalence group may be treated differently, split the equivalence group into smaller groups. In this case, we might split the single alphabetic character group into:

Single lowercase alphabetic character
Single uppercase alphabetic character

If you know you are dealing with ASCII characters, you might split the single non-alphabetic character group into:

Character below "A"
Character above "z"
Character between "Z" and "a"

As you can see, there's no right way to create the equivalence groups. It depends on your imagination and feel for where errors may lie. Another example might be the decision line

```
if (i_x < -1 OR i_x > 1)
```

The equivalence groups would probably be

```
i_x < -1
i_x > 1
i_x is between -1 and 1 inclusive
```

Where do the boundary conditions come in?

The boundaries of the equivalence groups are where the errors are most likely to occur. Since the purpose of testing is to show that the software doesn't work, it's important to stress the boundaries. In the first case, if you are dealing with ASCII, the boundaries would be @ A Z [' a z {.

In the second example, the boundaries are -1 and 1, so although both -1 and 1 fall into the third equivalence group, you would devise separate cases for those two values. If you were dealing with floating-point numbers, you might also include -1.00001, -0.99999, 0.99999, 1.00001. If you had a loop while (i_count $<= 10$) you would test with i_count $= 9, 10, 11$.

To test well, you must know what the software is supposed to do. If you are testing a sorting routine, you have to know the minimum and maximum record lengths of the input data, and the minimum and maximum numbers of records allowed. Without this knowledge you can't determine the equivalence groups and you can't do all the boundary condition testing that you should.

What are the troublesome values?

These are values and conditions that are likely to produce more than their fair share of errors. These include cases like zero values, negative values, end-of-file conditions, zero occurrences of things, one occurrence of something, zero-filled records, records with no data, etc. This is one area where you can really use your imagination to think of strange cases that the software might not handle. Without imagination and experience you would never think to test the sorting routine with records that are already in sorted order, or records that all contain identical data.

Are there any other places to concentrate?

Yes. There are a couple of ways of measuring the code that will help you decide where to put the most focus.

- ○ Program complexity. The more complex a program, the more likely it is to have bugs. There are different ways of measuring complexity, one of which is to simply count the number of compares the code does.

- ○ Error proneness. Over time, have there been more bugs in this module than you'd expect? If so, it's a candidate for additional testing.

If you are testing your own software, how can you be expected to think of test cases that you didn't think of when writing the code?

Test plan and test case reviews will help by suggesting other ideas, but generally, thinking of test case ideas comes with experience and discipline. You have to observe and learn from previous errors so that you can both avoid the errors next time, and devise test cases to test the conditions that you have learned are most likely to produce errors.

Any suggestions here?

Every time I find a bug in code I've written, I write down the bug, then figure out the general case for which this bug is a specific example. I try to understand how I could have avoided the error and how I could have tested for it.

For example, I wrote some software that processed data buffers that were sent to it. Most buffers had a fixed size, but some buffers were variable-length and contained a word giving the byte length of the buffer. Sometimes the buffers were received as single buffers, but sometimes they came in as part of a ''super buffer'' consisting of up to 30 single buffers. In this case I worked through the buffers one at a time, incrementing a pointer into the super buffer by the size of the buffer I had just processed. One day a new type of variable-length buffer was sent to my software, and the programmer had forgotten to fill in the buffer size. I happily added the uninitialized value in the relevant word and ended up with an access violation caused by a pointer that was out of range.

The particular class of problem I generalized to was the problem of adding a value to a pointer. The solution I identified was to always make sure that the value I add to a pointer is meaningful. I try to make sure that I write test cases that contain inappropriate values to add to pointers. Of course, I may forget to do this on occasion, but the act of going through this exercise makes it more likely that I won't make the same mistake again.

Once you have accumulated data on a variety of bugs, you may find patterns emerging. If you find that you often use variables before initializing them, you may decide to always initialize variables when you declare them. Or, if you write in C, you may decide to always use lint.

So you can learn from your mistakes.

I hope so! There's always something to be learned when you find a bug in code that you thought was working. And extending this idea further:

- ○ When the test organization finds bugs during testing, someone should be asking:
  - Why didn't the developer find the bug?
  - What will the developer do differently to avoid making this error the next time?
  - Over time, are there any patterns in the type of bug created but not found by particular developers?
- ○ When bugs are found in the field, someone should be asking:
  - As above.
  - Why didn't the test organization find the bug?
  - What will the test organization do to make sure they find this type of bug in the future?

Even with all this, I'm still not sure that developers are the ones to test their own code.

I agree, there can still be problems when developers test their own code. In this chapter I'm describing ways to do better testing, but it's difficult to force developers to use them. In my experience, some developers are simply just not very good at testing, others don't care very much, while others feel under so much pressure to get code out that they do superficial testing. I've also worked with people who are very good at testing and very dedicated to good testing. But given that you want to get a good product out, you probably shouldn't rely only on the aptitudes and attitudes that individual developers bring to testing. It would be nice if the structure helped ensure a good product. For example, I like to include some dedicated test engineers in the development organization. The number of testers needed depends on the number of people developing software.

Doesn't this just increase the cost of developing the software?

No, because someone has to test the software anyway, whether it's the developer or someone else, and the longer it takes to find the errors, the more expensive it is to fix them. It's hard to have skills in everything, and developers generally have more interest in learning new development technologies than new test techniques. You'll get more effective testing if you involve someone who is dedicated to testing, understands testing, and is good at testing.

What is the job description of someone doing testing in the development organization?

The job description I have is probably more than one person can do effectively, and I have different people who specialize in different aspects of it. What I want the test person or people to do is:

- Be involved in technical reviews to make sure that requirements and design are testable.
- Be involved in technical reviews to make sure that designs satisfy requirements.
- Create test plans from designs.
- Maintain test plan and test case standards.
- Review developer test cases with developers.
- Assist developers in testing software, if requested.
- Write test drivers and test cases for random testing of functions or objects or testing particularly complex software.
- Assist with integration/system testing.
- Make sure test plans, test cases, test drivers, etc., conform to standards, and are checked in and maintained with the code.
- Run regression test suites after every software build to make sure that the build seems okay.
- Provide test training and guidance to developers as requested.
- Contribute to automated generation of test cases and regression testing.

People doing testing in the development organization must be good developers in their own rights. And just as better developers create better software, better developers generally do better testing. Test engineers must have the respect of the developers, and they must be made to feel they are just as important as the developers. The titles should be the same, and the salaries should be the same (perhaps higher for test people).

How do you know who will make a good tester?

If you are using people already in the development organization, look at how they design. Are they good at coming up with new ideas and new designs, or are they good at pointing out the flaws in someone else's design. Both are useful skills, but people good at pointing out flaws will usually make the better testers.

Doesn't this absolve the developers from the responsibility to test their software?

No. The test engineers will not be doing all the testing. They may be creating test plans from the design, but the developers themselves should be creating and executing the tests. The test engineers will be looking at code and testing some percentage of it. The software they select may be based on a complexity analysis, the importance of that piece of software, the error-producing history of particular developers, or perhaps may be selected randomly. Developers must test the software first and will often ask for assistance in figuring out how to do better testing, rather than have bugs found in the software after they've finished testing it.

How do you know when you've done enough testing?

If you're the developer, you've probably done enough testing when you've tested every different condition in the code using all the equivalence groups, all the boundary values, and all the troublesome values you can think of, and when the program appears to be reliable using both test data and real data.

Most test organizations don't work in this way. They typically treat the program as a black box, feeding input in and seeing what happens. So it's harder to know how much is enough. In the end, most groups stop testing when the number of bugs found drops down to zero or slightly above. There are a couple of more formal ways to get information you need:

1. Plot the number of bugs found over time. The curve should drop rapidly, then ease off.
2. Seed the code with bugs. If the bugs are well-chosen and sufficiently subtle, the number of seeded bugs found can predict the likely number of real bugs in the code.

$$\frac{\text{Number of real bugs in code}}{\text{Number of seeded bugs in code}} = \frac{\text{Number of real bugs found}}{\text{Number of seeded bugs found}}$$

So, the number of real bugs left =

$$\left(\frac{\text{\# of real bugs found}}{\text{\# of seeded bugs found}} \times \text{\# of seeded bugs in code}\right) - \text{\# of real bugs found}$$

When you've found 50 percent of the seeded bugs, you've probably found about 50 percent of the real bugs. When you've found 99 percent of the seeded bugs, you've probably found about 99 percent of the real bugs. But this depends on whether the seeded bugs are subtle enough.

Tell me about reusable test cases.

Reusable test cases allow you to redo boring test runs easily, which both improves the quality of the product and gives you more time to create more interesting and sophisticated tests. Most test organizations tend to employ people to sit at keyboards and test the software. This approach suffers from the disadvantages that it takes a lot longer to hit keys than to run a test case, and it's almost impossible to guarantee that the same test is run twice. Having a set of test cases to verify that nothing has broken is called *regression testing*. Now, regression testing can never take away the need for human ingenuity when testing, but it does allow you to verify that something that used to work still appears to work.

When fixing a bug, there is a 20-to-50-percent chance of introducing another bug. Regression testing helps find that other bug while the cost of finding it is still low.

Whenever you design a test, keep the test so that it can be used again later. There's no point in writing throwaway tests when, with just a little extra effort the same test can be used again and again. If possible, the test data should reside in a file rather than in a driver program, because it makes the addition of new data much easier. Every bug you find gives you a new test situation you can add to the file.

If you have a driver that tests a function, give the driver a standard name that includes the function name; e.g., the function is dc_if_capture_data(). The test program name might be test_dc_if_capture_data.c. Even if the test program has to change, it's quicker to do that than write a new one from scratch. If you have a library, keep the tests in the library so that people modifying the function can test with the test driver.

Another approach that works well when a function can be tested in isolation, or when a family of functions live in the same file, is for the file to contain the test driver. You can do this by having conditional compile statements around the main routine:

```
#if defined (TESTMAIN)

main()
{
    /* Code to test the function */
    ...
}

#endif     /* TESTMAIN */
```

You could then compile the source file with TESTMAIN defined, and run the program that is created. When you want only the function, you leave TESTMAIN undefined. This way, you keep the testing program with the function or functions that it's testing.

On some systems it can take an incredibly long time to set up and run a test.

There are a few things you can do to help speed things up:

- Restart capability. Build in an ability to restart the software from any point. This is often tied in with a checkpoint capability—the ability to save the context so that you can restart from that point whenever you want.

- On a system where there are several modules that send messages or information to each other, build in a way to run each one in isolation, and get its data from a file instead of another process.

- Have a way for a module to write data it receives to a file and mark the end of each buffer. You can write the program to get data from the file. To size down the test, you can edit the data file or have the program skip a predetermined number of data buffers.

- Have the program display or write a message about the number of the message or transaction received: each one, every 10, every 100, every 1000. Give it the ability to turn on this display after a certain number of transactions. This is useful when an error occurs after several hours and you want to isolate the particular transaction causing the problem.

How do you design testing into the system?

The test design is one of the key parts of the design, both because testing is so important and because it's difficult to retrofit a good test scheme into a system. It's important to have an underlying mechanism that allows you to play through test cases and to give you information on whether the results were different from last time.

In *The Mythical Man-Month*, Fred Brooks says that it's not uncommon for there to be half as much code in the "scaffolding" as in the final product. By scaffolding, he means test drivers, etc. You've got three basic choices: you can test in a piecemeal fashion with no drivers, but you'll take more time in the long run, regenerating tests and finding bugs later on; you can build throw-away scaffolding; or you can build the test environment into the product. The latter is far and away the best system, especially because you can use many of the tools and techniques, improved through experiences, on the next project.

There are various "test managers" on the market that will check results against previously stored results, and there are products available that allow you to capture and replay keystrokes and mousestrokes; it's worth looking into these.

But let's look at how you might design a test environment. We'll look first at a character-screen-oriented program.

The test mechanism has to be designed in from the start. One obvious way is to have a variable (let's assume it's a global called tst_B_file_input) that is TRUE if input comes from a file of stored keystrokes and FALSE if input comes from the keyboard. The function that actually reads the keyboard or mouse input would now do exactly that if tst_B_file_input is FALSE, and would get its input from a file if the variable is TRUE. Regardless of whether the input came from a file or the user, it would return the appropriate codes to the caller.

```
if_read_input (...)
{
    if (tst_B_file_input) {
        read next thing from file
        return (...);
    }

    /* The input is from the keystroke, so do the normal things */
    ...

    return (...);
}
```

There would probably be a translation mechanism so that in the file you could write CTRL-A and the translation would produce the same codes as if the user had pressed Ctrl-A at the keyboard. An example of a file content definition might be:

All typing characters (A-Z, a-z, 0-9, plus all symbols such as ! @ + =, except {) could be typed as is and would pass through.

All special symbols and things to be translated would appear within curly brackets { }; e.g., {CTRL-A} {RET} {DOWN} {INSERT}

{ would be coded as {{}

Anything after { } would be a comment.

Would a scheme like this work for windows-oriented software?

How you would do it depends on how the software is written. There are two basic ways of doing windows-oriented programs:

Event-driven programs with a large switch/case block. If your code is written in this fashion, you probably call a get_event function to get the next event. You could modify that function if you have the source code, you could add another function layer above it that either calls the get_event function or reads the data file, or you could have your program code either call the get_event function or read the data file.

Programs that rely on callback procedures.   Many X-windows programs use this method. You never see the event—it's handled at a lower level, and that lower level simply calls functions that you've specified, depending on what the event was. To add the ability to read from a data file, you'd need either to modify the source code of the window-managing software, write a layer between the operating system and the window software, or to buy a commercial keystroke/mousestroke capture/replay package.

How would you know if the program is doing the right thing when the file-driven test case is running?

Let's start with a simple approach and build up. We could define two commands for the file as follows:

{ PRINT ''created new correction transaction'' }   would instruct the software to write the message in quotes to a log file.

{ BREAKPOINT }   would instruct the software to execute a function called tst_vf_breakpoint(). If you have a situation where an error occurs between two particular writes to the logging file, you could insert { BREAKPOINT } in the data file at the appropriate place and put a breakpoint on tst_vf_break-point(). When you hit the breakpoint, you could start debugging.

Okay, we now have a way to track down crashes. What about tracking down errors that don't cause a crash?

Let's look at the situation where one test run stores a record in the database, but the next time we get an error message. In both cases the program continues. How to discover the difference?

```
i_status = dc_if_write_record();
trc_vf_trace("status %d on call to dc_if_write_record", i_status);
if (i_status != SYS_SUCCESS)
    . . .
```

trc_vf_trace writes to a log file. Two test runs should write exactly the same data to the log file, so doing a comparison (difference) of the files would tell you where the results diverged. You could extend this even further to write out other values you get. I've devoted a whole chapter to tracing because it's useful for both testing and debugging.

What about if your software is not interactive—if it processes a stream of data?

The basic difference will be in the data you put in the file. If it is purely ASCII, it's pretty straightforward. If it's binary data, you have three choices. You can write a data editor that knows the format of the data and allows you to create and edit a file of binary data. Or you can write a general data editor that parses the data structure definition and displays and stores the binary data based on the data structures. Or you can put the data in an ASCII text file and write a translation program to convert it into the data you need.

The third approach is slightly more primitive but at the same time very flexible. I've included an example of such a general translation program in an Appendix.

In summary, having the test environment designed into the software saves so much time and expense while ensuring a quality product that it's difficult to understand why it's not a universal practice. The bulk of the conceptual work and tool creation is done the first time and on all subsequent projects it's just a matter of refinement and extension as you learn from each project.

Most software work involves maintenance, not creating new software. Are there any special techniques for testing changes to existing code?

If you are modifying existing software that doesn't have built-in testing, it's still a good idea to have a test driver, but it may not be feasible if you are just making small changes to a lot of functions. In either case you should step through the changes with the debugger, seeing what happens with good data and with bad data. If you have regression testing set up, you can add test cases to the regression test data to help check out your changes.

If you are in a situation where there is no regression testing and no underlying test mechanism, you'll have to decide whether it's worth the effort to retrofit a test mechanism. The input from a file is fairly straightforward; what takes the time is creating sufficient calls to the tracing functions to make creating a test mechanism worthwhile. If you'll be living with the software for a few years, it's probably worth implementing a test tracing system, then over time putting in the tracing calls and creating the test data files.

Do you have examples of testing functions?

I've included functions to save keystrokes, get keystrokes from a file, get a binary buffer from a text file, and the various support routines for these. Let's start with a function that saves keystrokes as you type. It needs to be called at the point when the program gets the keystrokes, and should only be called if you have chosen to save keystrokes.

```
FUNCTION int    tst_if_save_key (void *vpr_buff, int ir_translate)
{
    int         i_stat;
    int         i_len;
    static int  i_line_len = 0;
    char        ca_string[TST_LINE_LEN];
    BOOLEAN     B_translated;

    if (Fp_Save_file == NULL || vpr_buff == NULL)
        return (SYS_NULLPTR);

    /* Translate the data to save file format.  */
    i_stat = tstint_if_translate_to (vpr_buff, ca_string, ir_translate);
    if (i_stat == SYS_SUCCESS) {
        B_translated = TRUE;
        i_len        = (int) strlen(ca_string);
    }
    else  {
        B_translated = FALSE;
        i_len        = 1;
    }

    /* Put in a newline if the line would be too long */
    if (i_line_len + i_len > 79)  {
        fprintf (Fp_Save_file, "\n");
        fflush (Fp_Save_file);
        i_line_len = 0;
    }

    /* Now write the data out */
    if (B_translated)
        fprintf (Fp_Save_file, ca_string);
    else
        fprintf (Fp_Save_file, "%c", *((char *)vpr_buff));

    /* And increment our line length */
    i_line_len += i_len;

    return (SYS_SUCCESS);
}
```

Now here is the corresponding routine to get the keystroke from the file. It's designed to handle the following special "tokens," all of which are surrounded by curly brackets { }.

{ }	Everything after this is a comment
{BREAKPOINT}	Call function tst_vf_breakpoint. This is useful to get the software to break after a particular point in the execution. Just insert {BREAKPOINT} in the file at the appropriate point and put a breakpoint on tst_vf_breakpoint.
{DEBUGOFF}	Switch debug printing off.
{DEBUGON}	Switch debug printing on. With debug on, the program prints out each internal token, each potential keystroke token, and each passthrough character.
{LOAD xxxx}	Load keystroke file xxxx and use it for test input. This is useful when you want to chain together a series of keystroke files. The last token in a file will be {LOAD xxxx}, where xxxx is the name of the next keystroke file.

{PAUSE}	Pauses until the user presses Return. No prompt or message is given.
{PRINT xxxxxx}	The software will call trc_vf_trace and print the entire data element. It leaves the {PRINT } in the line to help find it in the output file.
{WAIT x.yy}	Wait x.yy seconds before returning the next keystroke. After the keystroke is returned, the wait variable is reset.
{WAITALL x.yy}	Wait x.yy seconds before returning each keystroke. You can enter values to the nearest 1/100th of a second.
{WAITCHAR x.yy}	Wait x.yy seconds before returning a character keystroke. You can enter values to the nearest 1/100th of a second. This takes precedence over WAITALL for character values.
{WAITTOKEN x.yy}	Wait x.yy seconds before returning a token {..} keystroke. You can enter values to the nearest 1/100th of a second. This takes prece-dence over WAITALL for token values.

```
FUNCTION int    tst_if_get_key (void *vwp_fill_buff, int ir_translate)
{
    int         i_stat;
    static char ca_filebuff[TSTINT_MAX_READ_BUFFER];

    if (Fp_Key_file == NULL || vwp_fill_buff == NULL)
        return (SYS_NULLPTR);

    /* Get the next data element from the file and return if we get an
       end of file or an error status.   */

    i_stat = tstint_if_next_data(Fp_Key_file, ca_filebuff);
    if (i_stat == TST_ENDOFFILE)  {
        (void)tst_if_close_key_file();
        return (i_stat);
    }
    else if (i_stat != SYS_SUCCESS)
        return (i_stat);

    /* Do we have a "token" */
    if (ca_filebuff[0] == '{')  {
        /* Translate the data "token" from file format into binary bytes */
        i_stat = tstint_if_translate_from (ca_filebuff,
                                       vwp_fill_buff, ir_translate);
        if (i_stat != SYS_SUCCESS)
            return (i_stat);

        /* Now wait the appropriate delay */
        if (tstint_f_wait != (-1.0))  {
            /*  Next character only - 0 is valid wait  */
            (void) sys_wait(&tstint_f_wait);
            tstint_f_wait = -1.0;
        }
        else if (tstint_f_wait_token != 0.0)
            (void) sys_wait(&tstint_f_wait_token);
        else if (tstint_f_wait_all != 0.0)
            (void) sys_wait(&tstint_f_wait_all);
    }
    else  {       /* No token, just a data byte */
        if (ir_translate == TST_XX_TRANSLATE)
```

```
            *((int *)vwp_fill_buff) = (int)ca_filebuff[0];

        /* Now wait the appropriate delay */
        if (tstint_f_wait != (-1.0)) {
            /*  Next character only - 0 is valid wait  */
            (void) sys_wait(&tstint_f_wait);
            tstint_f_wait = -1.0;
        }
        else if (tstint_f_wait_char != 0.0)
            (void) sys_wait(&tstint_f_wait_char);
        else if (tstint_f_wait_all != 0.0)
            (void) sys_wait(&tstint_f_wait_all);
    }
    return (SYS_SUCCESS);
}
```

Here are the various internal support functions for the keystroke read-and-save routines.

```
/* This structure is used to translate between text and keystroke bytes.
   If you want to add another, simply add the data type after i_xx_key.
   This is a general-purpose structure used for two-way translation for
   all keystroke models. xx is just a placeholder for a name that is more
   descriptive of your particular model.  */

struct tst_translate
{
    char    ca_text[16];
    int     i_xx_key;
};

static struct tst_translate s_translations[] =
{
        "{F1}",          KEY_F1,
        "{F2}",          KEY_F2,
        ...              ...
        "{RET}",         KEY_RETURN,
        "{BACKSPACE}",   KEY_BACKSPACE,
        "{TAB}",         KEY_TAB,
        "{ESC}",         KEY_ESC,
        "{UP}",          KEY_UP,
        "{DOWN}",        KEY_DN,
        "{LEFT}",        KEY_LEFT,
        "{RIGHT}",       KEY_RIGHT,
        ...              ...
        "{CTRL-A}",      KEY_CTRL_A,
        "{CTRL-B}",      KEY_CTRL_B,
        "{CTRL-C}",      KEY_CTRL_C,
        ...              ...
};
```

This function translates from a token into a binary keystroke. The keystroke can be any number of bytes long; the exact number of bytes will depend on the particular translation.

```
FUNCTION int  tstint_if_translate_from (char *capr_str, void *vwp_fill_buff,
                                        int ir_translate)
{
    int   i;

    /* Compare our token with the various allowable tokens */
    for (i=0; i< (int)(sizeof(s_translations)/sizeof(struct tst_translate)); i++)  {
        if (strcmp(s_translations[i].ca_text, capr_str) == 0)  {
            if (ir_translate == TST_XX_TRANSLATE)  {
                memcpy (vwp_fill_buff, &s_translations[i].i_xx_key, 4);
                return (SYS_SUCCESS);
            }
        }
    }
    return (TST_INVALVAL);
}
```

This function translates from the keystroke to a token.

```
FUNCTION int  tstint_if_translate_to (void *vpr_buff, char *cawp_string,
                                      int ir_translate)
{
    int   i;

    /* Compare our token with the various allowable tokens */
    for (i=0; i< (int)(sizeof(s_translations)/sizeof(struct tst_translate)); i++)  {
        if (ir_translate == TST_XX_TRANSLATE)  {
            if (s_translations[i].i_xx_key == *((int *)vpr_buff))  {
                strcpy(cawp_string, s_translations[i].ca_text);
                return (SYS_SUCCESS);
            }
        }
    }
    return (TST_INVALVAL);
}
```

Here is where we get the next piece of data from the keystroke file, whether it is a single character or a token.

```
FUNCTION int tstint_if_next_data (FILE *Fpr_file, char *cawp_out_buff)
{
    int         i_stat;
    static char ca_inbuff[TSTINT_MAX_READ_BUFFER] = {'\0'};
    char        ca_input[TST_LINE_LEN];
    static char *cp_in = ca_inbuff;
    char        *cp_out;
    char        *cp_temp;

    /* Loop until we have valid data */
    for (;;)  {
        /* If we have a null string, loop until we have a real string or
           have reached the end of file */
        while (*cp_in == '\0')  {        /* At end of buffer */
            i_stat = if_get_next_buffer (Fpr_file, ca_inbuff);
            if (i_stat != SYS_SUCCESS)  {
                *cp_in = '\0';                /* Set it up for next time. */
```

```
            return (i_stat);
        }
        cp_in = ca_inbuff;
};

/* Set our pointer to the start of the output buffer */
cp_out = cawp_out_buff;

/* If we don't have a "token," just return the character */
if (*cp_in != '{') {
        /* The character is not a data element start character */
        *cp_out = *cp_in;
        cp_in++;            /* Increment pointer for next time in */
        return (SYS_SUCCESS);
}

/* We have a token.  It starts with { so go through the input,
   copying the characters into the output buffer, until we find
   the }.  Note that when we are done, cp_in will be incremented
   past this token, ready for the next call to this function.  */

while ((*cp_out = *cp_in++) != '}') {
        if (*cp_out == '\0') {  /* End of line without a terminator */
            *cp_in = '\0';              /* Set it up for next time in */
            return (TST_INVALDATA);
        }
        cp_out++;
}
*(++cp_out) = '\0';         /* Null terminate */

/* CHECK FOR SPECIAL TOKENS THAT HAVE INTERNAL MEANINGS */
/*  If we have a comment line, we want to ignore the rest of the line,
        so we set *cp_in to 0 so that we get a new buffer */
if (strcmp(cawp_out_buff,"{}") == 0)
        *cp_in = '\0';
else if (strcmp(cawp_out_buff, "{PAUSE}") == 0)
        (void) gets(ca_input);
else if (strncmp(cawp_out_buff,"{LOAD", 5) == 0) {
        /*  If we have to load a new file, we want to read in a new buffer,
            so we set *cp_in to 0 so that we get a new buffer.  However,
            if we can't load the file, we'll just continue from where we are
            now.  Note that we'll stop pretty soon because the open first
            closes any existing keystoke files and sets file input off.
            Replace trailing } with a \0 then try and open file. */
        if ((cp_temp = strchr(&cawp_out_buff[5], '}')) != NULL) {
            *cp_temp = '\0';
            i_stat = tst_if_open_key_file (&cawp_out_buff[5]);
            if (i_stat == SYS_SUCCESS)
                *cp_in = '\0';
        }
}
else if (strcmp(cawp_out_buff,"{BREAKPOINT}") == 0)
        /* If we have {BREAKPOINT} we do a call to tst_vf_breakpoint() so that
            you can set a breakpoint there.  Then we get the next data element. */
        tst_vf_breakpoint();
else if (strncmp(cawp_out_buff,"{PRINT", 6) == 0)
        /* If we have {PRINT we print out the entire data element to the tracing
            file, then we get the next data element. */
```

```
              trc_vf_trace (NULL, "%s\n", cawp_out_buff);

      /* If we have (WAITxxx we set up a wait variable.  This causes
         a delay between all subsequent keystrokes.  There are 4 options:
         WAIT #.#          Wait #.# seconds before the next keystroke.
         WAITALL #.#       Wait #.# seconds between ALL keystrokes.
         WAITCHAR #.#      Wait #.# seconds between character keystrokes.
         WAITTOKEN #.#     Wait #.# seconds between Token (...) keystrokes.
      */
      else if (strncmp(cawp_out_buff, "(WAIT ", 6) == 0)
          tstint_f_wait = (float)atof(&cawp_out_buff[6]);
      else if (strncmp(cawp_out_buff, "(WAITALL", 8) == 0)
          tstint_f_wait_all = (float)atof(&cawp_out_buff[8]);
      else if (strncmp(cawp_out_buff, "(WAITCHAR", 9) == 0)
          tstint_f_wait_char = (float)atof(&cawp_out_buff[9]);
      else if (strncmp(cawp_out_buff, "(WAITTOKEN", 10) == 0)
          tstint_f_wait_token = (float)atof(&cawp_out_buff[10]);
      else    /* We don't need to stay in the loop, so let's break out */
          break;
   }         /* End for loop */
   return (SYS_SUCCESS);
}


FUNCTION static int if_get_next_buffer (FILE *Fpr_file, char *cawp_buff)
{
   char *cp_char;
   /* Get next buffer */
   if (fgets(cawp_buff, TSTINT_MAX_READ_BUFFER, Fpr_file) == NULL)
      return (TST_ENDOFFILE);        /* End of file */

   /* replace any trailing \n with a NULL */
   if ((cp_char = strchr(cawp_buff, '\n')) != NULL)
      *cp_char = '\0';

   return (SYS_SUCCESS);
}
```

Well, that's it for the keystroke routines. If you start with something simple but useful, you can extend it as needed and bring it from project to project. The routines shown here provide some basic functionality. Obvious extensions include the ability to:

- ○ Perform loops.
- ○ Do ''if'' tests.
- ○ Increment and print counter.
- ○ Allow the user to interactively turn file read mode on or off and to specify what keystroke file to read from.
- ○ Call another keystroke routine, returning to where you are.
- ○ Have a keystroke that puts you into ''store comments'' mode, so you can make more sense of a keystroke file when you edit it.
- ○ Single-step through the keystroke file.

- ○ Pause the keystroke playback by pressing a specified key.
- ○ Press a specified key and have the software display the keystroke file line number and line position of the token or character at the current position.

Let's now look at a function that takes a text file and translates its contents to a binary buffer for use within a program. Before showing the code, let's see what are valid entries in the file.

!	An exclamation point in the first position of a line means the line is a comment line.
`PRINT`	Print the rest of the line.
`ENDREC`	If a data element is exactly the text ENDREC, we send the data so far to the calling function. We do not add any bytes to indicate the end of a record. It is there solely as a way to visually separate chunks of data in the file, and to keep the data in units of a manageable size.
`DEBUGON`	Switch to debug reporting mode and report each data element.
`DEBUGOFF`	Switch debug reporting mode off.
`SEPARATOR=`	Specify the character that separates the control information from the real data. It defaults to colon: I:333 SEPARATOR = * I*333
`SPACE=`	Specify the character that should be replaced with a space. Spaces are delimiters, so to get spaces in text-type fields, you must replace the spaces with the embedded space character. The default is to not allow embedded spaces: SPACES = ^ Now^is^the^time
`I:`	Integer field follows: I:234455
`S:`	Short integer (2 bytes) field follows: S:26948
`L:`	Long integer (4 bytes) field follows: L:5698823
`C:`	Character field. There are several options. If the first character after the delimiter is a digit, the whole thing is assumed to be a one byte integer: C:98 If the first character is NOT a digit, we have a sequence of characters, e.g., C:YES If we have a character string, there are some options to embed non-ASCII characters:

\t	Tab
\n	Newline
\b	Backspace
\0	Null
\###	Octal number to be translated to one-byte integer. Note: If there are less than three digits following the backslash, we assume that it is literal characters, e.g., \03A is translated to four bytes (hex 5C303341). Note: To embed a space in a sequence of chars, use \040, the hex value of a char, e.g., Now\040is\040the\040time.

`T:`	Text string field. Text strings are assumed to be NULL filled to the specified length unless one of the options below is specified. The options can appear in any order before the separator or number.

S	Space fill
N	Null terminate

If the next character after any possible options is a digit, this is a fixed-length string of length specified in the number given. If there is no number, the output data should be exactly the same length as the string (plus a possible NULL terminator).

T:hello	is a 5-character string
TS:hello	is a 5-character string (the S is superfluous)
TN:hello	s a 6-character string (it has a NULL terminator)
TSN10:hello	is a 10-character string with 4 trailing blanks and a NULL terminator

TS10:hello	is a 10-character string with 5 trailing blanks
T10:hello	is a 10-character string with 5 trailing NULLs

Examples:

```
! Set up the defaults
DEBUGON SPACE=^
PRINT Here's some integers and character sequences
I:23444 I:492344 S:998923 C:HELLO C:99 C:\t\t\tnow\040is\040the\040time S:333
S:9343 S:9234 C:122 C:01 C:\001HELLO ENDREC DEBUGOFF
PRINT Now we'll print some text strings.
T10:hello DEBUGON TS20:fill^with^spaces
```

```c
FUNCTION int  tst_if_buffer (char *cawp_fill_buff, int *iwp_bytes,
                             int ir_max_buff)
{
    int    i_stat;
    int    i_buffer_size = 0;        /* Number of bytes in buffer */
    int    i_bytes;                  /* Number of bytes in data element */
    char   *cp_buff;
    char   ca_inbuff[TSTINT_MAX_READ_BUFFER];

    unsigned char  cua_data[TSTINT_MAX_READ_BUFFER];

    if (Fp_Buffer_file == NULL || cawp_fill_buff == NULL)
        return (SYS_NULLPTR);

    /* Set our pointer to the start of the buffer */
    cp_buff = cawp_fill_buff;

    /* Stay in a loop until we reach the end of the file.  Get the next data
       element from the file */
    while ((i_stat=if_get_next_data(Fp_Buffer_file, ca_inbuff)) != TST_ENDOFFILE) {
        if (i_stat == TST_ENDOFREC) {
            /* We're at the end of the record so return the number of bytes we've
               put in the buffer */
            *iwp_bytes = i_buffer_size;
            return (SYS_SUCCESS);
        }
        /* Translate the data element into binary bytes */
        i_stat = if_translate_all_data(ca_inbuff, cua_data, &i_bytes);
        if (i_stat != SYS_SUCCESS)
            return (i_stat);

        /* If we don't have room in the buffer, return an error status */
        if (cp_buff - cawp_fill_buff + i_bytes > ir_max_buff)
            return (TST_OVERFLOW);

        /* Add the binary bytes to the buffer */
        memcpy (cp_buff, cua_data, (unsigned int)i_bytes);

        /* Increment our buffer pointer .... and the count of bytes we've put in
           the buffer */
        cp_buff         += i_bytes;
        i_buffer_size   += i_bytes
    }      /* end while */
```

```
        /* End of file */
        if (i_buffer_size == 0)
            return (TST_ENDOFFILE);
        else {
            *iwp_bytes = i_buffer_size;
            return (SYS_SUCCESS);
        }
    }
```

The next functions get the next piece of data from the file and check to see if it is a special token.

```
FUNCTION static int if_get_next_buffer (FILE *Fpr_file, char *cawp_inbuff)
{
    char *cp_char;

    /* Loop until we get a valid data element */
    while (fgets(cawp_inbuff, TSTINT_MAX_READ_BUFFER, Fpr_file) != NULL)
    {
        if (cawp_inbuff[0] == '!')              /* Comment line */
            continue;
        else if (cawp_inbuff[0] == '\0')        /* Blank line */
            continue;
        else if (strncmp (cawp_inbuff, "PRINT", strlen("PRINT")) == 0) {
            /* Line to print.  Note there's already a \n at the end */
            printf (&cawp_inbuff[strlen("PRINT") + 1]);
            continue;
        }
        else {
            /* replace any trailing \n with a NULL */
            if ((cp_char = strchr(cawp_inbuff, '\n')) != NULL)
                *cp_char = '\0';
            return (SYS_SUCCESS);
        }
    }
    return (TST_ENDOFFILE);
}




FUNCTION static int if_get_next_data (FILE *Fpr_file, char *cawp_outbuff)
{
    int            i_stat;
    static char    ca_filebuff[TSTINT_MAX_READ_BUFFER];
    static char    *cp_str;
    static BOOLEAN B_need_new_buffer = TRUE;

    /* Loop until we get a valid data element */
    for (;;) {
        if (B_need_new_buffer) {
            if (if_get_next_buffer (Fpr_file, ca_filebuff) == TST_ENDOFFILE)
                return (TST_ENDOFFILE);

            B_need_new_buffer = FALSE;

            /* Get first data element from the buffer */
            cp_str = strtok(ca_filebuff," \t");
```

```
        }
        else {
            /* In an existing buffer from the file so get the next data element */
            cp_str = strtok(NULL," \t");
        }

        /* If we have something, check the token type. If it's internal, we repeat
           the loop, otherwise we copy the text into the output buffer and return */
        if (cp_str == NULL)
            B_need_new_buffer = TRUE;
        else {
            i_stat = if_token_check (cp_str);
            if (i_stat == TSTINT_NEED_NEW_BUFFER)
                B_need_new_buffer = TRUE;
            else if (i_stat == TSTINT_END_OF_RECORD)
                return (TST_ENDOFREC);
            else if (i_stat == TSTINT_NORMAL_TOKEN)  {
                strcpy (cawp_outbuff, cp_str);
                break;
            }
        }
    }          /* end for (;;) */
    return (SYS_SUCCESS);
}
```

This is where we check to see if we have a token.

```
FUNCTION static int if_token_check (char *capr_token)
{
    int    i_token_type;

    if (strcmp(capr_token, "DEBUGON") == 0) {
        B_Print = TRUE;
        i_token_type = TSTINT_INTERNAL_TOKEN;
    }
    else if (strcmp(capr_token, "DEBUGOFF") == 0) {
        B_Print = FALSE;
        i_token_type = TSTINT_INTERNAL_TOKEN;
    }
    else if (strcmp(capr_token, "ENDREC") == 0)  {
        i_token_type = TSTINT_END_OF_RECORD;
    }
    else if (strncmp(capr_token, "SPACE=", strlen("SPACE=")) == 0) {
        capr_token      += strlen("SPACE=");
        c_Embedded_space = *capr_token;
        i_token_type     = TSTINT_INTERNAL_TOKEN;
    }
    else if (strncmp(capr_token, "SEPARATOR=", strlen("SEPARATOR=")) == 0) {
        capr_token  += strlen("SEPARATOR=");
        c_Separator  = *capr_token;
        i_token_type = TSTINT_INTERNAL_TOKEN;
    }
    else
        i_token_type = TSTINT_NORMAL_TOKEN;

    return (i_token_type);
}
```

This is where we translate the text string into binary data.

```
FUNCTION static int  if_translate_all_data (char *capm_str, void *vwp_data,
                                            int *iwp_bytes)
{
    int i_stat;

    if (capm_str == NULL || vwp_data == NULL || iwp_bytes == NULL)
        return (SYS_NULLPTR);
    switch (*capm_str)
    {
        case 'C':               /* Char */
        case 'c':
            i_stat = if_translate_char (capm_str, vwp_data, iwp_bytes);
            break;
        case 'I':               /* Integer */
        case 'i':
            i_stat = if_translate_int (capm_str, vwp_data, iwp_bytes);
            break;
        case 'L':               /* Long integer */
        case 'l':
            i_stat = if_translate_long (capm_str, vwp_data, iwp_bytes);
            break;
        case 'S':               /* Short integer */
        case 's':
            i_stat = if_translate_short (capm_str, vwp_data, iwp_bytes);
            break;
        case 'T':               /* Text string */
        case 't':
            i_stat = if_translate_text (capm_str, vwp_data, iwp_bytes);
            break;
        default:
            i_stat = TST_INVALDATA;
            break;
    }
    if (i_stat == TST_INVALDATA)
        printf ("Found invalid data element %s\n", capm_str);

    return (i_stat);
}


FUNCTION static int  if_translate_char (char *capm_str, void *vwp_data,
                                        int *iwp_bytes)
{
    char        *cp_data;
    char        ca_temp[10];
    char        *cp_end;
    int         i_temp;
    int         i;
    BOOLEAN     B_number;

    cp_data = vwp_data;         /* Set pointer to start of output string */

    /* The first character is 'C'.  Check that the next character is a
       separator character */
    capm_str++;
```

```
          if (*capm_str != c_Separator)
              return (TST_INVALDATA);

          capm_str++;        /* The next character is the first real character.*/

          if (isdigit(*capm_str) || *capm_str == '-')               /* Number    */
              B_number = TRUE;
          else
              B_number = FALSE;

          while (*capm_str != '\0')  {
              if (B_number) {                    /* Numeric value of single char */
                  i_temp = atoi(capm_str);
                  *cp_data++ = (char)i_temp;
                  /* Increment the pointer enough so we exit the loop */
                  capm_str += strlen(capm_str);
              }
              else if (*capm_str == '\\') {                /* Backslash    */
                  if (isdigit(capm_str[1]) &&  isdigit(capm_str[2]) &&
                      isdigit(capm_str[3])) {               /* Octal number */
                      strncpy(ca_temp,&capm_str[1],3);
                      *cp_data++ = (char)strtol(ca_temp, &cp_end, 8);
                      capm_str += 4;
                  }
                  else if (capm_str[1] == '0') {            /* Null         */
                      *cp_data++ = '\0';
                      capm_str += 2;
                  }
                  else if (capm_str[1] == 'b') {            /* Backspace    */
                      *cp_data++ = '\b';
                      capm_str += 2;
                  }
                  else if (capm_str[1] == 'n') {            /* Newline      */
                      *cp_data++ = '\n';
                      capm_str += 2;
                  }
                  else if (capm_str[1] == 't') {            /* Tab          */
                      *cp_data++ = '\t';
                      capm_str += 2;
                  }
                  else {
                      *cp_data++ = *capm_str++;      /* The backslash is a character  */
                  }
              }
              else if (isprint(*capm_str)) {          /* Printable character */
                  *cp_data++ = *capm_str++;
              }
          }

          /* Set up the data to send back */
          *iwp_bytes = cp_data - (char *)vwp_data;

          if (B_Print) {
              printf ("Chars in hex=");
              for (i=0; i< *iwp_bytes; i++) {
                  printf ("%02x ",*(char *)vwp_data);
                  vwp_data = (void *)((char *)vwp_data + 1);
              }
```

```
            printf ("\n");
        }
        return (SYS_SUCCESS);
    }




FUNCTION static int  if_translate_int (char *capm_str, void *vwp_data,
                                       int *iwp_bytes)
{
    /* The first character is 'I'.  Check that the next character is a
       separator character */
    capm_str++;
    if (*capm_str != c_Separator)
        return (TST_INVALDATA);

    capm_str++;       /* The next character is the first real character.  */
    *(int *)vwp_data = atoi(capm_str);

    if (B_Print)
        printf ("Int=%d dec, %02x hex\n",*(int *)vwp_data, *(int *)vwp_data);

    *iwp_bytes = sizeof(int);
    return (SYS_SUCCESS);
}
```

We have similar functions for translating longs and shorts.

```
FUNCTION static int  if_translate_text (char *capm_str, void *vwp_data,
                                        int *iwp_bytes)
{
    char       *cp_text;
    char       c_fill_char;
    char       ca_text[TSTINT_MAX_READ_BUFFER];
    int        i;
    int        i_size;
    int        i_length;
    BOOLEAN    B_null_terminator;

    capm_str++;                       /* Get the type of string       */
    c_fill_char = '\0';               /* NULL fill by default         */
    B_null_terminator = FALSE;        /* No null terminator by default */

    /* Figure out whether to space fill and whether to NULL terminate */
    while (*capm_str != c_Separator && (! isdigit(*capm_str))) {
        if (*capm_str == 'S' || *capm_str == 's')       /* Space fill      */
            c_fill_char = ' ';
        else if (*capm_str == 'N' || *capm_str == 'n')  /* Null terminator */
            B_null_terminator = TRUE;

        capm_str++;
    }

    if (*capm_str == '\0') {
    /* Got to end of data without seeing either a number or a separator */
    return (TST_INVALDATA);
    }
    else if (*capm_str == c_Separator) {
        /* No number, so the string is the length of the text */
```

```
            capm_str++;
            strcpy (ca_text, capm_str);
            if (B_null_terminator)
                i_size = (int)strlen(ca_text) + 1;
            else
                i_size = (int)strlen(ca_text);
        }
        else {                              /* Fixed-length string */
            i_length = atoi(capm_str);
            if (i_length == 0)
                return (TST_INVALDATA);

            while (isdigit(*capm_str))
                capm_str++;                 /* Get first non-digit character */

            if (*capm_str != c_Separator)
                return (TST_INVALDATA);

            capm_str++;                     /* Go past separator */

            if ((strlen(capm_str) + 1 * (B_null_terminator)) > (unsigned int)i_length)
                return (TST_INVALDATA);

            strcpy (ca_text, capm_str);
            cp_text = ca_text + strlen(ca_text);
            for (i= (int)strlen(ca_text) + 1; i<=i_length; i++)  {
                if (i==i_length && B_null_terminator)
                    *cp_text = '\0';
                else
                    *cp_text++ = c_fill_char;
            }
            i_size = i_length;
        }

    /* Replace embedded space tokens with spaces */
    if (c_Embedded_space != '\0')  {
        for (i=0, cp_text=ca_text; i<i_size; i++, cp_text++)  {
            if (*cp_text == c_Embedded_space)
                *cp_text = ' ';
        }
    }
    memcpy (vwp_data, ca_text, (unsigned int)i_size);

    if (B_Print)
        printf ("Text=%.*s\n",i_size,(char *)vwp_data);

    *iwp_bytes = i_size;
    return (SYS_SUCCESS);
}
```

Further Reading

Beizer, Boris. 1983. *Software System Testing and Quality Assurance*. New York: Van Nostrand Reinhold.

Beizer, Boris. 1990. *Software Testing Techiques (2nd Edition)*. New York: Van Nostrand Reinhold.

Hetzel, Bill. 1988. *The Complete Guide to Software Testing*. Wellesley, MA: QED Information Sciences.

Meyers, Glenford. 1979. *The Art of Software Testing*. New York: Wiley.

Summary

Testing is the process of trying to show that the software *doesn't* work. Testing is difficult and creative work, and surprisingly little emphasis is placed on it, considering the time and cost involved in testing the software and fixing any errors found. The time and cost can be reduced by reducing the number of errors created in the software, but for the foreseeable future, some testing will always be required. In this chapter we discussed the following, and showed various practical techniques.

- Develop good test methods.
- Develop good test cases.
- Develop reusable test cases.
- Design testing into the system.

We then showed program listings for a testing system that would save and replay keystrokes, and for a system that would feed in buffers of binary data that had been stored in a regular text file.

25

Debugging

What is the difference between testing and debugging?

Testing is the process of trying to break the software. Debugging is the process of finding and fixing the code in error after the software breaks.

How should a person debug software?

The first step to debugging well is to write well-modularized, well-structured code, with well-defined interfaces. If an error occurs, there will be only a few places where it could have been caused. You'll have a good idea of where an error occurred without even running the program.

Now come back to reality. Most of us have to deal with code we don't know, code that is badly written, and code that has very loose interfaces with other modules.

Debugging can be split into two fundamental parts: getting the data you need, and using intuition and logic to figure out what caused the error. People often focus on the data-gathering part and jump into the debugger without trying to solve the problem by thinking it through. A lot more problems can be solved without the use of the computer than people tend to believe. And it's a skill worth developing because often it's very difficult to gather more data; for example, the computer may be at a customer site and there are no dial-in modems.

Being able to debug a problem using thought power is especially useful in the case of the bug that you can't reproduce, either because you can't recreate the conditions under which it occurred, or because it seems to have mysteriously disappeared (bugs that mysteriously disappear are likely to mysteriously reappear).

Okay, how can you solve debugging problems by thought power?

You have two powerful tools: intuition and logic. The general method is to gather and study enough data to come up with a theory or hypothesis. Once you have the theory, you use logic to determine if the theory satisfies the symptoms.

Debugging is like the process of scientific advance. Someone comes up with a theory. It's totally irrelevant to the process where the theory came from—perhaps it was an inspired thought, perhaps it came in a dream or even from being hit on the head. Now logic comes into play and the process of trying to disprove the theory starts. Does the theory satisfy all known facts? Can you think of any experiments that might disprove the theory? Does the theory predict anything that you can check?

So it is with debugging. Once you've come up with a theory, you have to go through the process of seeing if it satisfies the facts that you know. Does the theory contradict anything you know to be true? Are there unexplained problems or symptoms that the theory doesn't explain? If the theory doesn't explain all of the symptoms, it's either wrong, or incomplete, or there are other errors.

It's easy to jump to conclusions—we want to solve the problem so we want to believe that we've found the solution. Most programmers have had the experience of finding an answer that almost explains the symptoms, but that fails to explain one little thing. We make the appropriate fix and cross our fingers that it has corrected everything. It never has, of course. The theory has to explain *all* the symptoms—if it doesn't, find a new theory. It's a lot quicker than making changes, recompiling, relinking, and testing only to find out there are still bugs. When you have a theory that satisfies all the facts, test it in practice.

Could a theory be correct but incomplete?

No question about it. Like a scientific theory, your theory may explain all the known facts, but be incomplete. For example, a function expects and handles input of positive integers. You have a theory that the problem you see is caused because the code gets passed a value of zero. This theory explains all the facts and turns out to be correct. However, the code may also fail if passed a negative integer. The debugging is done, and the theory is correct but incomplete. We're now outside the realm of debugging, and into the realm of testing. You need a good test case that tests the various equivalence groups. There's a lot more about test case design in Chapter 24, "Testing."

How do you come up with a theory? This seems like the hard part.

Just like with scientific theories, there's no guaranteed way to come up with a theory. But like scientific theories, there are things that will help: have a strong knowledge of the background data and organize your information. While the source of the inspiration is irrelevant, it is true that someone is *more likely* to come up with a good theory if he or she has spent time studying and thinking about the available information. Once you have the background knowledge and have organized your information, you're more likely to see relationships, which allows you to come up with theories. Pattern recognition is one of those critical parts of the human experience—it's what allows us to solve new problems based on prior knowledge and prior situations.

How do you organize your information?

When you're trying to organize things, it's always useful to write things down because writing forces you to clarify your thinking. Rather than just write things down haphazardly, try using one of the following forms.

	..the symptoms are	..the program runs correctly
What		
Where		
When		

Or:

What the symptoms are.
What the program does correctly.
Where the symptoms occur.
Where the program runs correctly.
When the symptoms occur.
When the program runs correctly.

Obviously you'll need a physically different form, but aim to write down these bits of information. What are the symptoms of the problem, and under what circumstances does the program run correctly.

Information given by the "under what circumstances does the program run correctly" category is just as important as information in the "symptoms are" category. Giving a non-trivial answer to how and when the program runs correctly often requires considerable thought, and the contradictions between situations that exhibit the symptoms and situations that don't can lead quickly to a theory and solution to the problem.

Another way to organize your thoughts is to explain the problem to someone else, especially someone with more experience in that area. When you play with an idea in your mind, you tend to believe that you have a good grasp on it, that it's well-organized and well-thought-through. Unfortunately, this is usually an illusion. If you try to explain your ideas to someone else you realize very soon that your ideas are less clear and less coherent than you thought. To explain something, you have to organize your knowledge and your thinking, and in doing so you often see things that you missed before. Many a problem has been solved by explaining it to someone else, even if the other person doesn't have a clue what you are talking about. If the other person does know what you are talking about, he can ask questions that force you to think more deeply about various aspects of the problem and the software.

Once you have sorted out your thoughts and the data to the extent that you can categorize what you know, you'll probably start seeing patterns. Once you see a pattern, it should lead to a theory.

Some people say that when you find the bug, it jumps out and hits you.

There's a lot of truth in that—it's sometimes known as the Eureka principle. When you find the bug, it's usually very obvious that it's the bug (it's also often such a simple bug that you wonder why it took so long to find). If you aren't sure that you've discovered the bug, you probably haven't.

If you think something is the possible cause of the bug, but it doesn't make you hit yourself on the forehead and say "Of course!" make a note of where you think the bug is, and why, and spend some more time looking for, and noting, other possible causes. If you still don't find one that jumps out at you, you still have at least one theory to explore further.

What if you can't think of any theories?

You can always come up with some theories. One approach is to write down every possible cause you can think of. You now have a whole bunch of theories. Go through each one in turn, examine it, and look for contradictions between the theory and the available data.

Sometimes you will know exactly the line of code that causes the symptoms, but the difficulty may be in discovering why that line of code was executed or why particular values existed when the line was executed. Backtrack through the code until you find the places where the variables in question were set. Keep backtracking and asking yourself why things are getting set, until you have a theory about the original cause of the problem.

Once you have some theories, eliminate them one by one until you're left with only one that satisfies the conditions.

What if you eliminate them all?

If you eliminate them all, you need some new ideas. Your best chance is to gather more information so that you have an opportunity to come up with more theories.

Does it help to work with someone else?

As I mentioned above, explaining the problem to someone else can help you solve the problem. Some experiments suggest that the most productive and cost-effective way to debug difficult errors is to have two people working on the problem separately, then getting together to pool their ideas and knowledge.

One problem I often have is that a user-reported bug often turns out to be an operator error.

It's tough because if you don't believe there's a bug, it's terribly difficult to do the mental jumps necessary. In a sense though, the code *is* badly designed or badly written if a person can do something wrong, or if the result doesn't make it clear what the person did to get that result. In situations like this, you need to go through each step made by that person to see if any of the steps were wrong.

It gets insidious when the users have done all the right steps, but get different results than you do. Then it's easy to believe that they just misread the results, or didn't understand what they were seeing. There are no easy answers except to give everyone the benefit of the doubt and believe that they saw what they said they saw. If it turns out that someone was wrong, and this pattern occurs several times, that person becomes like the boy who cried wolf. After a while no one takes him seriously, and you may miss a real bug.

How do you go about getting more information?

You need to distinguish between situations where it's easy to gather information, and situations where it's difficult. Some problems lend themselves to recreation. If a user can enter a certain sequence of keystrokes and reliably get the error, you can probably reproduce it yourself and use the debugger or test cases to get more information. On the other hand, if you wrote software for a guided missile, you're not going to be able to sit in the missile with a debugger while it goes about its tasks. You need a completely different mechanism for getting the data you'll need. For the sake of terminology, let's use the word *local* to describe a system where you can reproduce situations, and *remote* to describe a system where you can't, either because there's no way to reproduce a live run or because a live system is larger and more complex than you can create.

If you want to get information from a remote system, you must design and code it to give you information. You can sprinkle log statements liberally through the code to log all the key values and actions taken and provide a way to turn the logging on or off. Or if you have an error that occurs only seldom, you can log these values and actions into a circular linked list in memory, keeping only the last 200 or thousand or so pieces of data. Once you've detected the error, you can dump the linked list and analyze it. The whole subject of logging or tracing information is so important that I've devoted a whole chapter to it (Chapter 26, "Tracing").

What about debugging on local systems. This must be much easier.

Getting information from local systems is, by definition, much easier. You can use the tracing mechanisms I describe in the chapter on tracing, you can create more test cases and examine the results, and you can use the debugger. One caution before we talk more about the debugger: it's useful for both testing and debugging, but don't rely on it exclusively. You may need to debug remote systems sometime. Equally, you may need to "prove" that your code works. If you don't have test cases that exercise the code without failing, you'll never be able to convince anyone that your code has been tested marginally, let alone thoroughly.

Some people advocate the non-use of a debugger on the grounds that it stops you using your mind. There's some truth to that because you can usually solve a lot of problems without a debugger, but sometimes it can be so simple to step through a program with the debugger to see where things are going wrong. The more complex the system, however, the more intelligence should factor into it. If it takes an hour to set up a test and then get into the debugger, you may well be able to solve the problem more quickly with logic and intuition. But if you don't know the code very well, your best bet will probably be to use the debugger.

Unless you have an idea where to focus your search, probably the best approach with the debugger is to step over functions and examine variables before and after, trying to narrow down the place where the bug occurs. (This contrasts with using the debugger to step through every line on the first run of new code to see what it's doing and get insight into things you're doing wrong or could do better.) Using a debugger to narrow the scope can overcome certain mental barriers where you firmly believe that a particular function is bomb-proof. The debugger can provide hard proof that the error is happening there, contrary to your mind-set.

What if you don't have a debugger?

Then you are lacking one of the basic tools for creating quality software and should seriously consider getting a development environment that gives you a good source code debugger. While there are other techniques for debugging, having a good debugger available is invaluable, especially when dealing with other people's poorly written code. If you don't have one, you can use the techniques described in the chapter on tracing, you can write well-structured, well-modularized code, or you can look for a better job. There's more information about what to look for in a debugger in Chapter 6, ''Software Tools.''

Are there any general rules or guidelines about where to look for bugs?

Intermittent, non-reproducible bugs are often memory-dependent or timing-dependent. Memory-dependent bugs are often caused by uninitialized variables, by indexing out of bounds, or by going past the boundaries of allocated memory. If you are using C, lint will pick up uninitialized variables.

Bugs that occur when the program is running normally, but can't be reproduced when using the debugger tend to be memory-dependent or timing-dependent. Memory-dependent bugs are often caused by uninitialized variables. If you are using C, lint will pick up uninitialized variables.

Access violations/exception conditions. Possible causes are: uninitialized variables (lint will pick up uninitialized variables in C); array indexes going out of bounds; pointers being incremented out of bounds; or mismatched function arguments. Some operating systems will give a traceback list of functions that were on the stack when the exception happened, showing the functions down to the line. If you don't have that, it's fairly straightforward (if you know something about the underlying computer architecture) to write software to trap the various exception conditions, and to unwind the stack, reporting as it goes. Even if it only reports memory locations, you can make a correspondence with the function name by looking at the link map or by going into the debugger and examining the specified location.

In addition, bugs are more likely to occur in code that is complex or error-prone. If you can isolate the problem down to a certain level, look next at code that is particularly complex or has a history of having bugs.

Some people keep a log of debug sessions. Is that useful?

Keeping a log can be very useful. Typical things to record in your debugging log are:

- The date
- The time

- ◦ The symptoms
- ◦ The table shown earlier
- ◦ Your theories and ideas
- ◦ How the theories stood up to the facts
- ◦ Why you thought the bug might have been in a particular place
- ◦ Details of tests you ran and their results

Keeping this information does three things for you. First, it gives you more opportunity to think about and remember bugs and how you found them; it makes them stick in the mind, and makes it easier to recognize patterns. Second, when faced with a particularly nasty bug, you can often go back through the log and find ideas or information that will help you find the bug. Third, if you record all the places you thought the bug might be, and why, you have a list of routines or algorithms that you found unclear or confusing. These routines are all candidates to be rewritten or at least documented.

What do you do about rewriting or documenting them?

If you had to spend the time to understand a piece of code, that effort shouldn't go to waste. Sometime in the future someone may have to go through the same effort again, and that someone might be you. If the code is very confusing, it might well be wrong. Certainly if it's confusing, making enhancements to it will be fraught with danger. If you know what it's supposed to do, consider rewriting it. If you don't want to rewrite it, or it's correct but difficult to understand, you might just document it, with diagrams if necessary.

If you rewrite the code, have it reviewed, and create good test cases. There's nothing worse than "improving" something that works, only to find that the "improvement" broke the code. Towards the end of a release cycle, it's generally not worth the risk of making unnecessary changes, so make an electronic copy of the changes or documentation so you can implement them early in the next release cycle.

Are there any rules for fixing a bug once you've found it?

There are several things to consider. Errors tend to cluster together, so if you found one bug, there may well be another. Look for other possible bugs in the general area of your fix.

Make sure the fix actually fixes the error, not just some of the symptoms. As we said earlier it's easy to latch onto a "fix" that doesn't satisfy all the symptoms.

All too often a change to the software breaks something else. You must understand all the implications of the fix—i.e., what effect it will have elsewhere in the software. As the size of the program or software system increases, so does the probability of the fix breaking something else. Making a fix should put you into design mode, especially with large or complex systems. Have someone review the fix, both the design and the code.

Test the fix with a good set of test cases that cover all the equivalence groups and boundary conditions. It's too easy to assume that a fix will work. Many times it does, but often it doesn't. As the size of the program or software system increases, the likelihood drops that the fix is correct.

Presumably you can learn from the bug fix?

If you don't, you should be asking yourself why not! Analyzing bugs can be extremely rewarding in terms of reducing the number of mistakes made in the future and reducing the time taken to find future bugs. Unfortunately, doing the analysis is time-consuming, but it's worth the effort—at least for the more interesting or obscure bugs. Questions to ask include:

- *What was done wrong?* Bad parameters not being detected? Return values not checked? Variables not initialized? Incorrect algorithm? Incorrect use of variable addresses? Pointers being incremented incorrectly? Error conditions not being trapped? Incorrect use of the programming language? Code being commented out by mistake? Incomplete requirements?

- *What caused the error to occur?* Lack of knowledge about the programming language? Lack of knowledge about what had to be done? Not using tools such as lint? Code too complex to understand? A design that didn't consider all the possible conditions? Lack of understanding of requirements? False assumptions? Not following a procedure?

- *In what part of the process did it originate?* Was the error purely a coding error: i.e., miscoding something that was correctly understood? Was it an algorithmic error? Was it caused by a design error? A requirements error? A compiler or optimizer error?

- *Why wasn't the error found sooner?* Why wasn't it found in the appropriate review: code review, design review, requirements review? If the error was found after the testing phase, why wasn't it detected during the test phase? Why did the test plan review not detect the lack of a test to cover this error?

- *How could the error have been prevented?* Most important is to translate the knowledge obtained from finding the error into actions that will prevent future errors.

- *How was the error found?* Was it detected by a test case? What was being tested? Why was the test successful? Did you forget some test cases initially? What can you learn for future test case design?

- ○ *Who made the error?* If the same person or people make most of the mistakes or most of a certain type of mistake, perhaps some training is required.

Further Reading

Smith, Truck. 1984. *Secrets of Software Debugging*. Blue Ridge Summit, PA: Tab Books.

Ward, Robert. 1989. *A Programmer's Introduction to Debugging C*. Lawrence, KS: R&D Publications.

Summary

The best way to debug is to write well-modularized, well-structured code with well-defined interfaces. If that fails, debugging involves getting enough information to develop a theory, then testing out the theory. The cause of a bug will usually jump right out at you. If it doesn't, you may not have found the real cause.

Ways to organize your information and thoughts include writing on a form and explaining your ideas to someone else. An effective way of debugging difficult problems is to have two people working independently on the problem, then getting together to discuss their ideas and information.

Keep a debugging log while debugging, and record what you did and what you learned. Keeping a log will help you if you are facing a similar problem in the future (of course, it will be someone else who created the bug because you will have learned from the last bug how to avoid creating this type of error).

26

Tracing

What do you mean by tracing?

I mean recording what is going on in the program, what functions it is entering and leaving, the values of parameters, return values, and the values of key variables within the functions.

As we talked about in the chapters on Testing and Debugging, there are several uses for tracing how a program is behaving. If you don't have a debugger, or the program is running where there is no debugger, it may be the only way to see what is happening internally. It can be the best way to get a feel for the functions being called, and how often they are called. And tracing can help with testing by giving you a comparison between two different runs of the software. There are many different ways to trace, some of which are:

- Tracing to a log file
- Tracing to a circular buffer or circular list
- Tracing by specific functions
- Tracing by levels
- Tracing function parameters
- Tracing input data
- Tracing by milepost

In what follows, I'll give lots of examples, but to save space I won't always include everything necessary. For example, I may not declare variables or show #defines, or I'll hide functionality in a function call for which I don't show the code. And despite my belief in the value of function header documentation, I have left it all out to save space. Let's start with a simple function that records trace information in a log file.

```
FUNCTION void trc_vf_trace (char *capr_format, ...)
{
    va_list    xp_arg;

    if (trc_B_tracing_on)
    {
        /* If we don't have a file to print to, let's use stderr */
        if (Fp_Trace_file == NULL)
            Fp_Trace_file = stderr;

        /* Now print the variable argument list to the trace file */
        va_start (xp_arg, capr_format);
        (void) vfprintf (Fp_Trace_file, capr_format, xp_arg);
        va_end (xp_arg);
    }
}
```

What is "circular list" tracing?

If you have a situation in which every few days or every few weeks a variable gets corrupted, but you can't figure out why, you might want to continually trace the most recent few hundred key values or events. You don't want to create a monster disk file, so there are two main ways of tracing the values. The first way is to have a large ring buffer in which you write key values. When you get to the end of the buffer, you start writing again at the beginning, overwriting values that were previously stored there. It's called a ring buffer because conceptually there's no beginning and no end to it.

The other way is to have a circular linked list with however many entries you need. You'd keep adding entries until you have the maximum number of entries that you allow, then each time you add an entry to the end of the list, you free up the entry at the beginning. If you want to save processing time, you could make the linked list entries all the same size, and when you have allocated the maximum allowed entries, you'd simply relink the first entry to make it the last entry, and write your new information into that entry.

Either way, you'd also need to write a routine that will dump the ring buffer or linked list at the point you know your data is corrupted. Here's an example of how you might modify the tracing function to incorporate a circular linked list. I've hidden the circular linked list information in function calls to a linked list manager, which is another of those reusable software facilities you should have.

```
FUNCTION void trc_vf_trace (char *capr_format, ...)
{
    char       *cp_string;
    char       ca_print_string[TRC_MAX_PRINT_SIZE];
    va_list    xp_arg;
```

```
if (trc_B_circular_tracing_on)
{
    /* Check that we have a circular list header.  If not,
       we'll create one with a default number of entries. */
    if (trc_vp_circular_list_hdr == NULL)
    {
        if ((trc_vp_circular_list_hdr =
            dll_vpf_create_circular(TRC_DEFAULT_LIST_ENTRIES)) == NULL)
        {
            /* Failed to create the circular list, so cancel circular
               list tracing.  Turn regular tracing on. */
            trc_B_circular_tracing_on = FALSE;
            trc_B_tracing_on          = TRUE;
        }
    }
    if (trc_vp_circular_list_hdr != NULL)
    {
        /* Print our message into a large string, then create a circular list
           entry to hold the string, then copy the string into the circular
           list entry.  If you wanted more speed, you could assume a maximum
           size for the string, create a list entry that size, then print the
           message directly into the list entry. */
        va_start (xp_arg, capr_format);
        (void) vsprintf (ca_print_string, capr_format, xp_arg);
        va_end (xp_arg);
        cp_string = dll_vpf_add (trc_vp_circular_list_hdr,
                                 strlen(ca_print_string) + 1);
        strcpy (cp_string, ca_print_string);
    }
}
if (trc_B_tracing_on)
{
    ....
}
```

You could eliminate much of the circular list tracing code by having a trace initialization function that creates list headers if necessary and turns on the appropriate flags.

If you plan to do most of your tracing into a fixed-size ring buffer, you will probably want to save space by eliminating any non-vital information. You'll need to record the program location, plus the key values, but you don't need the variable names. Looking at the program listing should tell you what variables you have recorded. One way to record the program location is to have a unique number for each place where data is being traced (2 bytes if there are less than 65,535 different places, 4 bytes otherwise). Don't try and build intelligence into the number; sooner or later all intelligence schemes break down. Instead, keep a file that can be checked out from the source code library, and which contains a list of all the numbers used, with the name of the source file where they are used. To make it usable, the numbers should be sequential, and whenever someone needs a new location number, they add the next sequential number to the bottom of the list, and add the source file name. For example,

3274   dc_read_file.c
3275   prc_compute_totals.c

Another option would be to use a four-character key. For example,

AMDF   dc_read_file.c
AMDG   prc_compute_totals.c

After recording the key, record the data. Again, there are various options: you could store the data out in ASCII format, which would make it easy to simply dump the buffer and look at the information, or you could store the data in binary format, and preface each piece of data with a coding of what the data is, so that the software to dump the data knows how to interpret the next so-many bytes. For example, you might have the following codings: c = char, d = double, f = float, i = int, l = long, s = short, c = char, t### = string (text) of size ###, x### = structure of size ###.

Finally, you need to keep a pointer to the position in the ring buffer where you will start the next write. To do this, you need to know how many bytes you are writing, and you may want to also record this count in the buffer after the data (the software to interpret the buffer will probably want to work backwards from the current location, and it helps to know how far back to go to the start of each packet of data).

What is function-specific tracing?

Function-specific tracing allows you to only print trace information if you are in particular functions. If you know that a problem is happening in one of a few specific functions, why bother logging everything? Let's expand what we have to include function-specific tracing. We'll take the easy way of passing the function name as the first parameter.

```
FUNCTION void trc_vf_trace (char *capr_function,           /* Calling function */
                    char *capr_format, ...)          /* Format string .. */
{
    char        *cp_function;
    va_list     xp_arg;

    if (trc_B_function_tracing_on)
    {
        /*  We are using a doubly linked list of function names. This gives us an
            unlimited number of functions.  If you want greater speed but less
            flexibility, you could use an array of function names instead. */

        cp_function = dll_vpf_get_first(trc_vp_function_list_hdr);
        while (cp_function != NULL)
        {
            if (strcmp (cp_function, capr_function) == 0)
            {   /* We are in one of the functions the user selected */
                break;
```

```
            }
        cp_function = dll_vpf_get_next(cp_function);
    }
    /* If we are here with a NULL function name, we are not in a function
       we want to trace.  */
    if (cp_function == NULL)
        return;
    }
    if (trc_B_circular_tracing_on)
    {
        ...
}
```

What about tracing by levels?

Tracing by levels gives you the ability to log different amounts of information, depending on how much detail you want to see. Each piece of information you log has a number associated with it, and you log that information only if you are tracing at that level or higher. A high-level number is associated with a high level of detail.

For example, level 1 tracing might trace entry to and exit from functions, with return values and parameter values. Level 2 might add information about what functions are being called, with what parameters, and what values were returned. Level 3 might add values from the major computations in the function. Level 4 might add values from minor computations in the function, and so on.

Now let's expand our tracing function to include tracing by levels. We'll trace by function and by level. In this example, we'll store the function names in an array. This gives slightly greater performance than keeping them in a linked list, but limits you to a predefined number of function names.

In this code, the software passes a level number to the tracing function. We have a general, background trace level, and a specific level for each function. If the general trace level is higher than or equal to the one for this call, the data will be traced, regardless of whether or not we are in a specified function. To trace data *only* if we are in one of the user-specified functions, the general trace level would be set to zero.

To trace all levels, you'd set the general trace level to some high number, such as 99999. If you didn't want to be restricted in this way, you could modify the algorithm to make zero mean all levels, but you'd have be careful because, if you are tracing by function, zero will have a different meaning in a traced function and a non-traced function.

```
FUNCTION void trc_vf_trace (int ir_level_to_print_at, char *capr_function,
                            char *capr_format)
{
    int        i;
    BOOLEAN    B_trace = FALSE;
    va_list    xp_arg;

    if (trc_i_trace_level >= ir_level_to_print_at)
```

```
    {
        /* Level high enough to print */
        B_trace = TRUE;
    }
    else
    {
        /* See if we have any functions with specific levels */
        for (i=0; i < MAX_TRACE_FUNCTIONS; i++)
        {
            if (trc_sa_functions[i].ca_fname == '\0')         /* No more functions */
                break;
            else
            {
                /* Still have functions to check */
                if (strcmp (trc_sa_functions[i].ca_fname, capr_function) == 0)
                {
                    /* We are in one of the functions the user selected */
                    if (trc_sa_functions[i].i_level >= ir_level_to_print_at)
                    {
                        /* The level is high enough */
                        B_trace = TRUE;
                        break;
                    }
                }
            }
        }
    }
    if (! B_trace)
        return;

    if (trc_B_circular_tracing_on)
    {
        ...
}
```

What is milepost tracing?

Suppose you have a problem that only occurs after a particular function has been executed a couple of thousand times. You want a way to turn on tracing, whether function level or overall tracing, after that function has been called two thousand times. Whether you are using the linked list or the array method of storing function names, you'd have a structure that contained the function name, the trace level, the number of iterations to wait before turning on tracing, and the current iteration. Since the tracing function knows the name of the function, it can increment the counter associated with the function. However, the implementation is up to you!

Going back to function-level tracing—how would you trace everything that happens in a particular function, including things that happen in functions called by this one?

I'm going to describe a tracing system that I use a lot. It doesn't use circular tracing or tracing by level, but it does provide the ability to trace not only by function, but by function-tree (everything that happens in this function and the tree of functions it calls). This system has specific function calls for entering and exiting a function so that it can keep a stack of function names. Because I add function names to the stack and remove them, I also have an option that simply tells the software to report any inconsistencies between adding and removing functions.

```c
struct trc_function
{
    char    c_type;
    char    ca_function[TRC_FUNC_NAME_LEN + 1];
};

FUNCTION void trc_vf_trace (char *capr_format, ...)
{
    va_list              xp_arg;
    struct trc_function  *sp_func;

    /* Don't do anything if we're just reporting errors or we're not tracing. */
    if (trc_B_show_errors || ! trc_B_tracing_on)
        return;

    if (trc_B_function_tracing_on)
    {
        /* Using a doubly linked list to store the function names to trace.  */
        sp_func = dll_vpf_get_first(trc_vp_func_list_hdr);
        while (sp_func != NULL)
        {
            /* Compare the user-specified function with the function we are in, as
               shown in the current function in our stack of function names.  */
            if (strcmp (sp_func->ca_function,
                        trc_caa_func_stack[trc_i_stack_index]) == 0)
            {
                /* We are in one of the functions the user selected */
                break;
            }
            sp_func = dll_vpf_get_next(sp_func);
        }
        /* If we are here with a NULL function name, we are not in a function we
           want to trace */
        if (sp_func == NULL)
            return;
    }

    /* If we don't have a file to print to, let's use stderr */
    if (trc_Fp_log_file == NULL)
        trc_Fp_log_file = stderr;

    /* Now print the variable argument list to the tracing file */
```

```
    va_start (xp_arg, capr_format);
    (void) vfprintf (trc_Fp_log_file, capr_format, xp_arg);
    va_end (xp_arg);

    return;
}
```

Now let's see the function that is called when we enter a function. The main thing we do is to store the function on the stack of function names, and compare it with our list of functions to see if we want to log anything or set things up for function tree logging.

```
FUNCTION void trc_vf_enter (char *capr_function)
{
    BOOLEAN              B_log_func_name = FALSE;
    BOOLEAN              B_tree_function;
    struct trc_function  *sp_func;

    /* Return if we're not tracing */
    if (! trc_B_tracing_on)
        return;

    /* Make sure we have a file to print to */
    if (trc_Fp_log_file == NULL)
        trc_Fp_log_file = stderr;

    /* Increment our array index.  The initial value is -1   */
    trc_i_stack_index++;

    /* Check that we don't have too big a function stack */
    if (trc_i_stack_index == TRC_FUNC_STACK_SIZE)
    {
        /* Log an error and return... */
    }

    /* Add the function to our stack.  */
    strcpy(trc_caa_func_stack[trc_i_stack_index], capr_function);

    /* If we are doing function-level tracing, see if this function is one
       that we want to trace or do function-tree tracing on. */
    if (trc_B_function_tracing_on)
    {
        sp_func = dll_vpf_get_first(trc_vp_func_list_hdr);
        while (sp_func != NULL)
        {
            /* Compare the user-specified function with the function we are in, as
               shown in the current function in our stack of function names.   */
            B_tree_function = (sp_func->c_type == 'T');
            if (strcmp (sp_func->ca_function,
                    trc_caa_func_stack[trc_i_stack_index]) == 0)
            {
                B_log_func_name = TRUE;
                if (B_tree_function)
                {
                    /*  We are in one of the functions the user selected and are
                        doing function-tree tracing on it.  We store the function
                        name then turn function-level tracing off because we now want
                        to trace everything until we see the exit for this function.
```

```
                              Function level tracing is turned on again in trc_vf_exit.  */
                         strcpy (trc_ca_tree_function, sp_func->ca_function);
                         trc_B_function_tracing_on = FALSE;
                    }
                break;
            }
            sp_func = dll_vpf_get_next(sp_func);
        }
    }
    else        /* Not doing function level tracing */
        B_log_func_name = TRUE;

    /* Now log the entry to the function, if appropriate */

    if (B_log_func_name && ! trc_B_show_errors)
        (void) fprintf (trc_Fp_log_file,
                            "+++ Entered function: %s\n", capr_function);

    return;
}
```

And here's the corresponding exit function.

```
FUNCTION void trc_vf_exit (char *capr_function)
{
    BOOLEAN             B_found_func    = FALSE;
    BOOLEAN             B_log_func_name = FALSE;
    int                 i;
    struct trc_function *sp_func;

    /* Return if we're not tracing */
    if (! trc_B_tracing_on)
        return;

    /* Make sure we have a file to print to */
    if (trc_Fp_log_file == NULL)
    trc_Fp_log_file = stderr;

    /* Check that we have something on the function stack */
    if (trc_i_stack_index < 0)
    {
        (void) fprintf (trc_Fp_log_file,
                        "*** Error.  Exiting %s but have nothing on stack\n",
                        capr_function);
        return;
    }

    /* Remove the function from the stack.  Check that it's the last one on the
       stack.  If not, log an error, then work backwards looking for it, logging
       errors as we go.  If we find it, we pop the stack up to that point.  */
    if (strcmp (capr_function,
                trc_caa_func_stack[trc_i_stack_index]) == 0)
        B_found_func = TRUE;
    else
    {
        (void) fprintf (trc_Fp_log_file,
                        "*** Error.  Exiting %s, but last function on stack is %s\n",
                        capr_function, trc_caa_func_stack[trc_i_stack_index]);
```

```
        /* It's not the last function on the stack so go up the stack
           looking for it. */
        for ( i = trc_i_stack_index - 1; i >= 0; i-- )
        {
            if (strcmp (capr_function, trc_caa_func_stack[i]) == 0)
            {
                trc_i_stack_index = i;
                B_found_func      = TRUE;
                break;
            }
            else
            {
                (void) fprintf (trc_Fp_log_file,
                            "*** Error.  Function %d on stack is %s\n",
                            i, trc_caa_func_stack[i]);
            }
        }
    }

/* If we are doing function-level tracing, see if this function is one
   that we want to do tracing on. */
if (trc_B_function_tracing_on)
{
    sp_func = dll_vpf_get_first(trc_vp_func_list_hdr);
    while (sp_func != NULL)
    {
        /* Compare the user-specified function with the function we are in, as
           shown in the current function in our stack of function names.  */
        if (strcmp (sp_func->ca_function,
                    trc_caa_func_stack[trc_i_stack_index]) == 0)
        {
            B_log_func_name = TRUE;
            break;
        }
        sp_func = dll_vpf_get_next(sp_func);
    }
}
else        /* Not tracing by function */
    B_log_func_name = TRUE;

/* Decrement the stack index if we found the function we're exiting. */
if (B_found_func == TRUE)
    trc_i_stack_index--;

/* If this function is the function that started function-tree tracing,
   turn function level tracing back on and clear out the stored name
   of the function-tree function.  */
if (strcmp(trc_ca_tree_function, capr_function) == 0)
{
    trc_ca_tree_function[0]    = '\0';
    trc_B_function_tracing_on  = TRUE;
}

/* Now log the exit from the function, if appropriate */
if (B_log_func_name && ! trc_B_show_errors)
    (void) fprintf (trc_Fp_log_file,
                    "--- Exited  function: %s\n", capr_function);
```

```
        return;
    }
```

What about parameter tracing?

Let's extend trc_vf_enter to also print out parameters passed to the function (you should also print global variables used since they are effectively input and output parameters). We have a special flag that is set to TRUE if we want to trace the parameters. Note that it's up to you to pass the parameters as part of the variable argument list.

```
FUNCTION void trc_vf_enter (char *capr_function, char *capr_format, ...)
{
    BOOLEAN              B_log_func_name = FALSE;
    BOOLEAN              B_tree_function;
    struct trc_function  *sp_func;
    va_list              xp_arg;

    /* Return if we're not tracing */
    if (! trc_B_tracing_on && ! trc_B_show_parameters)
        return;

    ....

    /* Now log the entry to the function, if appropriate */
    if (B_log_func_name && ! trc_B_show_errors)
    {
        (void) fprintf (trc_Fp_log_file,
                        "+++ Entered function: %s\n", capr_function);
        if (trc_B_show_parameters && capr_format != NULL)
        {
            va_start (xp_arg, capr_format);
            (void) vfprintf (trc_Fp_log_file, capr_format, xp_arg);
            va_end (xp_arg);
        }
    }
    return;
}
```

If you have no parameters, pass either an empty string (`""`) or a NULL as the second parameter. We would also modify trc_vf_exit to use variable-list arguments, and we'd print out the output parameters, the global variables changed, and the return status.

Let's extend the idea and also look at tracing for regression testing. Whatever method we choose, it must be such that new enhancements and new releases don't break all the tests. Thus the information logged shouldn't be significantly different between releases. For general tracing, we might log every value that could be useful for debugging. But for testing, we might want to log only the functions called, the parameters and return values, and a few key computations done on the way.

An option would be to use the TRC_ENTER and TRC_EXIT macros without parameters, for entering and exiting functions, and define a new macro called TRC_TEST, which would be used for tracing those key values that aren't likely to change between releases. TRC_TEST would also report on parameters, global variables used, and return values.

Another option would be to use TRC_ENTER and TRC_EXIT with parameter tracing, and just to use TRC_TEST for reporting the key values that aren't likely to change.

How do you turn tracing on and off?

There are several options. You could turn tracing on by the use of command line parameters, by the use of logicals/environment variables at startup time, by the use of logicals/environment variables that are checked periodically, by sending messages to the software, or by looking for a file that contains information about what to trace. I will describe the file method.

The lines in the file generally consist of lines of paired strings. The left string is the type of the value, and the right string is the value. Lines starting with ! are ignored. The following are keywords:

FUNCTION ''function_name''—Log trace messages if the software is in this function. The software knows because you made a call to TRC_ENTER or trc_vf_enter with the function name as a parameter. There may be many of these lines to allow tracing in multiple functions.

FUNCTION-TREE ''function_name''—Log trace messages if the software is in this function or in a function called by this one. The software knows because you made a call to TRC_ENTER or trc_vf_enter with the function name as a parameter. There may be many of these lines to allow tracing in multiple function trees.

OUTPUT ''filename''—File to log to. The last filename specified wins. Default is stderr.

ERRORS—If this is on, the program doesn't do normal tracing. Instead, it simply logs errors in the matchup between function enters and function exits. Note that we also print errors when we are tracing, but this option allows us to only log the errors. This code doesn't take a paired value.

PARAMETERS—If this is specified, the program reports the parameters passed to the functions on which it is reporting. This allows us to show parameters only if necessary.

TESTING—If this is specified, the software reports special key values that shouldn't change between releases, functions called, and parameters passed.

INPUTS—If this is specified, the software traces any inputs from files, etc. This allows us to trace inputs only, if necessary.

TRACE—If this is specified, the program does normal tracing.

Now here's the function to read the file.

```
FUNCTION int trc_if_read_file (char *capr_name)
{
    char                ca_buff[ORG_LINE_LEN + 1];
    char                ca_type[ORG_LINE_LEN + 1];
    char                ca_value[ORG_LINE_LEN + 1];
    FILE                *Fp_file;
    int                 i_stat;
    struct trc_function *sp_func;

    if (capr_name == NULL)
        return (ORG_NULLPTR);

    /* Set up the various defaults */
    trc_B_function_tracing_on   = FALSE;
    trc_B_show_errors           = FALSE;
    trc_B_show_parameters       = FALSE;
    trc_B_show_inputs           = FALSE;
    trc_B_testing_on            = FALSE;
    trc_B_tracing_on            = FALSE;
    trc_Fp_log_file             = NULL;

    /* If we already have a function list, delete it */
    if (trc_vp_func_list_hdr != NULL)
        (void) dll_if_delete_list (trc_vp_func_list_hdr);

    /* Try to open the file */
    if ((Fp_file = fopen(capr_name, "r")) == NULL)
        return (SYS_NONEXIST);

    /* Loop, reading each line from the file, until all lines are exhausted.
       Replace the trailing \n with a \0. */
    while (org_cpf_fgets(ca_buff, ORG_LINE_LEN, Fp_file) != NULL)
    {
        /* Ignore comment lines. */
        if (ca_buff[0] == '!')
            continue;

        /* If there isn't a type string, ignore the line */
        if (sscanf (ca_buff, "%s", ca_type) != 1)
            continue;

        /* See what type of line this is. */

        if (strcmp(ca_type, "ERRORS") == 0)
            trc_B_show_errors = TRUE;
        else if (strcmp(ca_type, "PARAMETERS") == 0)
            trc_B_show_parameters = TRUE;
        else if (strcmp(ca_type, "INPUTS") == 0)
            trc_B_show_inputs = TRUE;
        else if (strcmp(ca_type, "TESTING") == 0)
        {
            trc_B_testing_on = TRUE;
```

```
                        /*  turn parameter tracing on too  */
                        trc_B_show_parameters  = TRUE;
            }
        else if (strcmp(ca_type, "TRACE") == 0)
            trc_B_tracing_on = TRUE;
        else
        {
            if (sscanf (ca_buff, "%s %s", ca_type, ca_value) != 2)
                continue;
            if (strcmp(ca_type, "OUTPUT") == 0)
            {
                i_stat = trc_if_open_file (ca_value);
                if (i_stat != SYS_SUCCESS)
                    return (i_stat);
            }
            else if (strcmp(ca_type, "FUNCTION") == 0 ||
                    strcmp(ca_type, "FUNCTION-TREE") == 0)
            {
                if (trc_vp_func_list_hdr == NULL)
                {
                    trc_vp_func_list_hdr    = dll_vpf_create_list();
                    trc_B_tracing_on        = TRUE;
                    trc_B_function_tracing_on = TRUE;
                }
                /* Allocate enough memory for the function name, plus a
                   character to denote the type of function.  */
                sp_func = dll_vpf_add(trc_vp_func_list_hdr,
                                    sizeof (struct trc_function));
                if (strcmp(ca_type, "FUNCTION") == 0)
                    sp_func->c_type = 'F';           /*  Normal Function */
                else
                    sp_func->c_type = 'T';           /*  Tree-type Function */
                strcpy(sp_func->ca_function, ca_value);
            }
        }
    }

    if (trc_B_show_errors)
    {   /*  If we are simply listing errors in our tracing setup,
            turn everything else off */
        trc_B_show_parameters  = FALSE;
        trc_B_show_inputs      = FALSE;
        trc_B_testing_on       = FALSE;
        trc_B_tracing_on       = FALSE;
    }
    return (SYS_SUCCESS);
}
```

If you have all the tracing calls compiled in, doesn't it use extra code space and extra execution time?

In a language like C, you have the wonderful option of using macros, which allows you to compile the tracing calls in, or compile them out. In other languages you may be able to use a C preprocessor to process macros, but the variable-list arguments may be beyond the capability of the language.

The basic tracing macro is:

```
TRC((format_string, ....));
```

Note the double parentheses at both ends; these are necessary because of the way that C does macro expansion for parameters. If we knew how many arguments there were, we could have single parentheses, but because we are using variable-list arguments, we have to make the compiler think there is a single argument, which is everything inside the outermost parentheses. This macro is used as if you were using printf, except for the double parentheses.

In this tracing software I've taken advantage of two C features: the ability to deal with a variable list of arguments, and C's macro capability. Other languages won't necessarily provide you with these, so you may have to do some of the tracing software differently. You would use TRC_TEST for the regression testing macro.

```
TRC_TEST((format_string, ....));
```

You'd also need to modify a line in the trc_vf_trace function to not return if trc_B_testing_on is TRUE.

```
if (trc_B_show_errors || (trc_B_tracing_on != TRUE && trc_B_testing_on !=
TRUE)
    return;
```

There are also some other macros:

```
TRC_ENTER(function_name);
```

        or

TRC_ENTER((function_name, format, ...));

TRC_EXIT(function_name);

that keep track of which function the program is in for function-level tracing. They also log the function just entered and the function just existed. Again, note the double parentheses in the second example of TRC_ENTER.

The macros are compiled in by defining the macro TRC_COMPILE. If this is not defined, the macros are compiled out. To save execution time, you may want to avoid compiling in the tracing calls in the released software. If you want tracing compiled in, you need to have a line for each source file as follows:

```
#define TRC_COMPILE
```

If you don't want tracing compiled in, don't define TRC_COMPILE. The easiest way to do this is to have xxx_debug.h as the first #include in each source file. In xxx_debug.h you can define TRC_COMPILE.

In the include file trc.h you would have the following. Note the use of the *do* {...} *while (0)* construct. This is a way to make something into a single statement so that it doesn't mess up any *if-else* constructs. The code between the braces is guaranteed to execute exactly once with a *do-while(0)*.

```
#if defined (TRC_COMPILE)            /* Compile in the function call */

#define TRC(args)        do {                        \
                            if (trc_B_tracing_on)  \
                               trc_vf_trace args ; \
                         } while (0)

#define TRC_TEST(args)   do {                        \
                            if (trc_B_testing_on)  \
                               trc_vf_trace args ; \
                         } while (0)

#define TRC_ENTER(func)  do {                                      \
                            if (trc_B_tracing_on || trc_B_show_errors) \
                               trc_vf_enter(func);                    \
                         } while (0)

#define TRC_EXIT(func)   do {                                      \
                            if (trc_B_tracing_on || trc_B_show_errors) \
                               trc_vf_exit(func);                     \
                         } while (0)

#else                             /* Make them all noops  */

#define TRC(args)
#define TRC_TEST(args)
#define TRC_ENTER(func)
#define TRC_EXIT(func)

#endif
```

If you want to trace parameters in the TRC_ENTER call, you would define the macro as:

```
#define TRC_ENTER(args)  do {                                            \
                            if (trc_B_tracing_on || trc_B_show_errors || \
                               trc_B_show_parameters)                     \
                               trc_vf_enter args;                         \
                         } while (0)
```

If you want to trace inputs to the program separately, you'd define your own macro to take account of the form of the input, and how you want to trace it:

```
#define TRC_PARAMETER(xxxx)   do {                         \
                                 if (trc_B_show_parameters)  \
                                    if_your_func(xxxx);       \
                              } while (0)
```

Notice that, using the macros, we don't actually make the call unless some type of tracing is on. So if we leave the code compiled in, the two costs are: the test of the two values, trc_B_tracing_on and trc_B_show_errors, to see if they are non-zero; and the slight increase in code size. By removing the #define TRC_COMPILE, you remove both those costs completely, but the code is still in the source file waiting to be used again should you define TRC_COMPILE back in.

You could simplify the functions themselves by removing the lines near the top of the functions that return if the appropriate flags aren't set, e.g.,

```
if (trc_B_show_errors || ! trc_B_tracing_on)
    return;
```

These lines are important if you plan to call the functions directly, but if you always use the macros, there's no need for these lines because the macros already check to see if the flags are set.

This can completely clutter the code.

Yes it can, so the question becomes: "is it useful?" If you may need all the information for debugging, sprinkle trace statements before and after all major decisions. If you want simplicity, just using TRC_ENTER and TRC_EXIT with parameters, globals, and return values, will avoid the clutter but still provide useful information for regression testing and debugging.

Give me an example of using all these tracing calls.

```
FUNCTION static int    if_validate_in_time(void)
{
    static char    ca_fname[]="if_validate_in_time";
    int            i_stat;
    int            i_hour;
    int            i_mins;
    int            i_current_day;
    char           ca_msg[ORG_MSG_LEN];
    char           ca_data[ORG_LINE_LEN];

    TRC_ENTER(ca_fname);

    win_vf_get_field (ca_data);
    TRC(("Data = %s\n", ca_data));

    /* Get the index of the current day */
    i_stat = if_get_day_index (&i_current_day);
    TRC(("Status after call to if_get_day_index=%d.  Current day index= %d\n",
        i_stat, i_current_day));
    if (i_stat != SYS_SUCCESS)
    {
        TRC(("Reporting error status = %d\n", i_stat));
        err_vf (i_stat, ca_fname, ERR_L, err_ca_please_inform,
            "Can't figure out index of current day.");
```

```
            i_stat = FALSE;              /* Validation failed */
            goto Exit;
        }
        i_stat = org_if_time_check (ca_data, &i_hour, &i_mins, ca_msg);
        TRC(("After call to %s with data %s. i_stat=%d, i_hour=%d, i_mins=%d\n",
            "org_if_time_check", ca_data, i_stat, i_hour, i_mins));
        if (i_stat == SYS_SUCCESS)
        {
            sa_Times[i_current_day].i_in_mins = 60 * i_hour + i_mins;
            TRC(("sa_Times[%d].i_in_mins=%d\n",sa_Times[i_current_day.i_in_mins]));
            i_stat = TRUE;               /* Validation passed */
        }
        else
        {
            TRC(("Invalid time.  Calling org_if_popup with message:\n  %s\n", ca_msg));
            (void) org_if_popup (ca_msg, "Press any key to continue. ");
            i_stat = FALSE;              /* Validation failed */
            goto Exit;
        }
Exit:
    TRC(("Returning with status.\n", i_stat));
    TRC_EXIT(ca_fname);
    return (i_stat);
}
```

Further Reading

Ward, Robert. 1989. *A Programmer's Introduction to Debugging C.* Lawrence, KS: R&D
  Publications.

Summary

Sometimes it is very useful to be able to log information about what the program is
doing, especially when you are debugging on a system without a good debugger. In
this chapter we looked at ways to track the information, and showed program listings for the different ways. This included:

- Logging the information in a file
- Logging the information in a linked list
- Tracking only specific functions, and the functions they call
- Tracking by levels
- Tracking function parameters only
- Tracking for regression testing

We also discussed ways to turn the tracking on and off, and how to write the
tracking calls as macros that can be compiled in, or compiled out.

27

Technical Reviews

Why have reviews? I thought your focus was on getting things right, rather than finding things that are wrong.

There are many reasons to hold reviews, some of which are:

- To prevent errors
- To catch errors as quickly as possible
- To improve communication
- To provide management with information about the state of the product
- To help people learn better techniques
- To make people adopt techniques and approaches that help quality but aren't as much fun as hacking
- To prevent chaos
- To communicate the lessons that were learned through trial and error
- To help spread knowledge about the software

Let's go through each of these in more depth.

To prevent errors.   Reviews help prevent errors because people often pay more attention to doing things right if they know their work will be reviewed. Reviews also point out errors that people make and make it more likely they will avoid similar errors in the future. It may become apparent that certain types of errors are common and that perhaps training, new procedures, or better tools could prevent those classes of errors.

To catch errors as quickly as possible.   There are two basic ways to increase quality. The first is to prevent errors and the second is to detect them. The former is undeniably the better method, but until an organization has figured out how to prevent errors and put into place the appropriate mechanisms, there will always be a need to detect errors. In fact, it's probably impossible to prevent *all* errors in software—even if there are no coding bugs, there will almost certainly be some things that are incompletely understood or defined—and we need a way to detect those errors. Of the ways to detect errors, reviews are among the best. You may find the same errors when testing, but you find them a lot *sooner* with reviews. Additionally, the total time to find errors when testing is the sum of the times of testing *and* time-consuming debugging, which can be high.

People make mistakes and have blind spots—errors of requirements, design, logic, and omission can often be quickly discovered during a review. A few hours of review can save days of rework. Studies have shown that over 70 percent of errors found during software development can be found in design and code reviews. This is especially significant for real-time systems and for system-level software because errors in this type of software are often timing-dependent and very hard to reproduce and debug.

Remember the diagram in Chapter 1: the higher the quality of output from each component, the higher the quality of input into the next. Reviews help increase that quality.

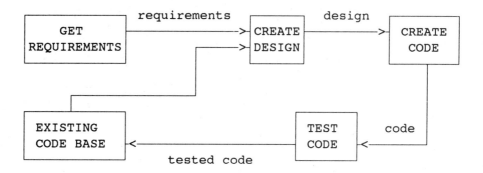

To improve communication.   People obviously communicate during a review, but one of the big benefits of reviews is that you get a lot more communication before reviews. No one likes to have their work criticized during a review, so they often try to learn other people's ideas and opinions beforehand, so they can do things in a way that won't generate criticism during the review.

To provide management with information about the state of the product. You can't expect people to accurately evaluate the quality of their own work. Managers can easily get information on the cost of the project so far, but it's hard to get information about the state of the product. Without this information they can't tell if projects are over budget or over schedule until it's too late. A review provides an independent evaluation of the product and its quality, and this information can help managers understand if the product is on schedule. Of course, managers have to figure out what to do if the reviews tell them the project is in trouble. Reviews are one of the best ways for managers to get control over their development processes.

To help people learn better techniques.   We learn in two ways: from our mistakes, and from seeing things done right. A software engineer who receives no ideas from other, more experienced engineers learns only from mistakes, and learns only enough to avoid errors. Only by talking with others will he learn better ways of doing things and better ways of detecting errors.

As a general rule I believe that three heads are better than one. There are a few supremely gifted people who are so far out in front of everyone else that other people's ideas are of less importance (although even these people can often use others as sounding boards to help them clarify their thoughts). For most of us, the ideas and suggestions of others can almost always help us reach a better solution.

Why do we expect people to design, test, and code well? Have we given them training? Have we ever looked at their techniques? Reviews help to point out people's weaknesses and give them the skills and knowledge to overcome those weaknesses.

To make people adopt techniques and approaches that help quality but aren't as much fun as hacking.   People change when there's a reason for changing. Having products rejected in reviews tends to be a good reason for change, especially when using the appropriate techniques or approaches would have prevented it. Producers who sit in reviews while their work is being reviewed or who review others' work, soon learn that they are better off building quality into their product rather than waiting for a review to show the lack of it.

To prevent chaos.   The universe tends towards chaos; it's only organization that fights that tendency. Every person brings with him a unique combination of ambition, beliefs, care, desires, energy, interests, knowledge, motivation, skills, and thoughtfulness. The work he does and the way he does it is colored by that combination. Left alone, each person will produce a uniquely different output. An organization, however, can't run effectively in that type of environment; some commonality is essential. Accounting would break down if some people treated Accounts Receivable as a debit account and others regarded it as a credit account.

Some level of standards and conventions is necessary, and it's up to the system to make sure that things conform to those standards. In software, you may decide that to aid future comprehension and maintenance, you need standards for variable naming, documentation, and the use of global variables. If you never check for conformance to the standards, you won't get it. Reviews hold back the tendency toward entropy.

To communicate the lessons learned through trial and error.   There is a tremendous body of knowledge learned through trial and error. Why should everyone have to make the same mistakes? Reviews help prevent this.

To help spread knowledge about the software.   Involving other people in reviews helps them learn about the software. People move on, resign, or take on new projects, and others end up maintaining the product and making the next changes. Reviews give others the information they need to make this task easier.

Tell me more about the reviews themselves. What is the difference between reviews, inspections, and walkthroughs?

There's no single answer because different people mean different things. The greatest consensus seems to be that reviews and inspections are basically identical, although inspections normally refer to code inspections, where the code is examined against a checklist of things that must be satisfied. During walkthroughs you walk test cases through a design or a piece of code. They're a way of testing without using a computer.

What should be reviewed?

Everything—conformance of the product to the specs, analysis, requirements, functional spec, design, key algorithms, user guide, test plans and test cases, code, bug fixes. The sooner a problem is found, the less the rework.

How much should be reviewed?

In general, sessions shouldn't take longer than two hours, although sometimes intensive, all-day, off-site sessions can be effective, especially with groups of users. People seem to have an effective concentration limit of about two hours, and even that should probably have a five-to-ten-minute break in the middle. Also, a couple of serious review sessions a week is as much as most people can handle effectively.

What if you have more than can be reviewed in this time?

Split the review into pieces. For code reviews, some organizations have learned from experience that they can review about 250-lines of non-commented source code in a review session, so they break the code into 250 line chunks and schedule enough meetings to cover all the chunks. Optimum rates seem to be in the range of

90 to 150 non-commented source lines per hour. Once you have reviews well established, if you track errors found, you can vary the rate and find the optimal rate for your organization.

If you need to split the product up for reviewing, don't break it into arbitrary pieces because it would then lose all context information. Any product being reviewed should be reviewed in one or more self-contained "modules."

When should you do reviews?

Do you mean at what time of day? Or at what point in the development cycle? If we are talking time of day, 10:00 A.M. and 3:00 P.M. seem to be the best times. Of the two, 10:00 A.M. is probably better because people's energy level is usually higher. Reviews are supposed to discover problems, not to solve them. If the review session ends at lunchtime or at the end of the day, people have an opportunity to continue informally and to solve problems and discuss alternative ways of doing things.

If we are talking points in the development cycle, there are two key points to consider. First, how long do you want to go without knowing the state of the product? The longer you go, the harder it is to get a project back on track if there are problems. Second, you don't want to dictate how people work. Software developers work in a variety of ways. Some people do most of their conceptual work away from the terminal, while others need to type, cut, and paste to refine their ideas. You shouldn't care how people develop—that's a matter of personal style.

To combine the two, I'd suggest that you should review something every two-to-four weeks, closer to two when possible. This gives you something predictable in the schedule, a date that you can track to.

Doesn't this force people into an arbitrary, meaningless way of doing things?

What it does is force people to do and design things in a way that there is something that can be reviewed every two to four weeks. Let's look at the different ways people develop software. (I won't even discuss the less-experienced developer because there's no way I'd want an inexperienced developer going more than four weeks without having his work reviewed.)

For experienced developers, there are two extremes. Some study, think, and make notes for a long time before they start writing code, but when they start to write, the code tends to flow quickly, be generalized, and require few corrections. People who work like this have a reviewable design before they start coding, so it should be easy to have a review every two to four weeks.

The other extreme is developers who start with a design idea and add new functionality in an incremental way until the total functionality is mostly there.

While doing this the developer notices better ways of organizing the code, and similarities between components, and he does a lot of cut and paste to remodularize and generalize the software. So the design evolves while he codes. (This is not the same as just sitting down to code without a design because it requires a substantial commitment to reorganizing the code constantly as things become more apparent, something less-experienced developers rarely have.)

But even working in this mode allows you to have reviewable work in two to four weeks. Even with trial and error, the overall design should be almost nailed down within this time, then the next sub-component in the next two-to-four-week period, then the next, and so on. The main difference is that by the time the detailed design is ready for review, the code probably is too.

So, however people work, it should be possible to break down any task in a way that there is something reviewable every two to four weeks. Of course, if something is not ready at that time, don't force it to be reviewed—there's no point in reviewing something that's not ready. By postponing it, and having the review leader document that, you gain the knowledge that this particular project may be in danger.

What about projects that aren't large enough to wait two weeks between reviews?

Every project should have a series of "gates" that it passes through when the product changes hands or gets embodied in a new form. An example of the gates you might have is:

- Requirements gate
- Solution gate
- User guide gate
- High-level design gate
- Low-level design gate
- Code check-in gate
- Release to QA organization gate
- Release to customer gate

In this example, I've made the arbitrary assumption that you have two levels of design—high level and low level. If you have more, say four levels, there is a gate at the end of each of those four levels of design, because the product is taking on a new form.

A piece of software must pass each gate in the order shown. The requirements for passing through a gate are specified by your organization, but consist mainly of reviewing and accepting one or more documents or prototypes, and satisfying some checklist. For projects in which the gates are less than two weeks apart, dispense with the intermediate reviews and simply require that the software pass through each gate.

Can't I just leave it up to the developer when to have his work reviewed? Won't any tendency to do too much be self-correcting when a developer learns that he has to make substantial changes?

It's certainly an attractive idea, but it does have problems. First, managers no longer have any idea how the project is progressing if the developer can wait months before the product is reviewed. When the review finally happens, there may be serious issues raised which require major rework. There's no longer any predictability, which is something managers desperately need.

Second, if a developer waits a long time before the product is reviewed, people are likely to spend insufficient time reviewing the product because there's so much to review. Third, people may be reluctant to raise issues that should be raised, because it will require rework of huge amounts of already completed work. Even if the issues are raised, there may be tremendous pressure to ignore the issues, with the promise that "things will be fixed for the next release."

The idea of the gates is very important, because it marks the "official" end of a phase and says that the documents are now in good shape for the document customers and for the next phase. However, gates alone are not sufficient for large projects.

What about code reviews? Should you review them before or after testing?

There are several different approaches:

- Before testing—you're trying to avoid having to test, debug, and fix.
- After some initial sanity testing has been done to prevent people wasting time finding obvious defects.
- When less errors are found in an hour of testing than would be discovered during a review. (You'll need to gather data on number of errors found during reviews.)
- After the testing is all done.

There's a good case for reviewing code before testing it—it reduces the time spent debugging, and it avoids having to retest code after making changes required by the review. Also it's psychologically easier for reviewers to get fired up for a review if they know they'll find lots of errors.

On the other hand, it does make some sense to do a small amount of testing to shake out the obvious errors. My preference is to allow a small amount of testing to detect the obvious bugs, but I'd recommend reviewing the code before a complete test is run, especially if the testing is significant. If you spend a lot of time testing, then find that code changes are needed, it means going through the whole test again (of course, because there will probably be changes in the future, the test suite should be complete and easy to run).

If the review is being done on untested or partially tested code, you'll have to make that clear in the review. There will probably be more bugs in untested code and you don't want the developer to feel victimized.

Regardless of which way you review code, you should run it through the appropriate tools first. There's no point in reviewing code that doesn't compile. And if there are tools, such as lint, that will catch certain types of errors, or style analyzers, such as CodeCheck from Abraxas Software, that will check for conformance to organization standards, I'd use them first. Why look for things a tool can find better? Since the layout of a source file has a big impact on readability, you can run the file through a formatter, such as indent on UNIX.

And what about test plan reviews? Should you review them before or after coding?

The temptation is always to start coding before you've thought of how you'll test the software, but it's much better to do the test plans before you code. Once you've written the code, you'll be sorely tempted to just start testing, without giving enough thought to how or what you'll test. Any test plans you write after coding will probably test what the code *does* rather than what it *should do*. If you do the test plans before coding you'll be able to think more clearly about what you are trying to do.

If you write and review the test plans before coding, you'll also be in a better position to change the design if it becomes apparent that it will be difficult to test the software.

How many people should attend a review?

As many people as it takes to cover the material and determine if the product does its job. However, more than seven people (including the leader and recorder) tends to bog down the review, while fewer than three reviewers can lead to secret agendas being pushed through.

Everyone in the review should be able to contribute to the review, so don't have seven people just for the sake of seven people. If you can do a good review with five people, do it with five. If you can't do a good review with three to seven people, split the review into chunks. The number of people should be such that the two rules apply: the purpose of the review is to determine if the product will do the job it's supposed to do, and everyone should be able to contribute.

Should you have the same number of people attending code reviews as attend requirements reviews?

Code is conceptually easier to review than design or requirements, and errors are often much more obvious and concrete. It's usually more cost-effective to do code reviews with fewer people than you'd use in a design review. (This assumes you've done design reviews and are reviewing just the coded implementation of the design.)

The best way to do code reviews is to have three to five people in a code review and give people specialized responsibilities, using a specific checklist. This makes people responsible for aspects of the product quality and helps make sure things don't fall through the cracks. One of the people should be a reader, who leads the review slowly through the code, paraphrasing each line to explain what it is doing.

Experiments have also shown that a very cost-effective way of doing code reviews is to have two programmers (neither one of whom is the producer) independently review the code looking for errors, then get together and pool their results. There is often little overlap in the errors found. This probably works well because both people feel committed, whereas in a larger group people can feel that if they don't find the error, someone else will. Also there's often an aspect of competition to find the most errors.

However, my inclination is to have a reader and two or three reviewers, each of whom has his own checklist to go through. If statistics show that too many errors are getting through, add reviewers.

Who should attend reviews?

The primary goal of the review is to make sure the product does the job it's supposed to do. So invite people who can contribute to that goal. Don't invite people who aren't qualified to contribute (except for education reasons), or for whom the review will be a conflict of interests. Exactly whom you invite will depend on what is being reviewed and on how your organization is structured, but consider the following.

○ A review leader. You need someone to keep people focused on the product, to make sure that concerns are aired, to solicit ideas from each person, and to shut up people who are becoming repetitive.

○ A recorder. Someone should publicly record the errors and issues raised. This prevents repetitive discussions of the same point, helps ensure that there is a consistent understanding of the issues among the reviewers, and allows you to give accurate information back to the producers.

○ People who are good at the type of thing being reviewed. If you are reviewing a design, you might invite people from other groups who are recognized as being good designers. This usually involves a high-level commitment to reviews because you'll be taking these people away from the work they are doing for their group.

- People who are good reviewers. In particular, people who are good at spotting major problems and potential downstream problems.

- People who invite themselves because they are interested in the product being reviewed.

- Someone who understands the existing system. If you are doing maintenance on old, poorly-structured code, you need to make sure that your changes won't affect or be affected by other parts of the system. Thus you need reviewers who are familiar with the system and its intricacies.

- The system architect. This person would focus on whether there is consistency across the whole product or system.

- Someone from the maintenance organization. This person should focus on whether the design or code is maintainable. Some organizations don't accept software unless it has been approved by the maintenance organization. If you try this approach, the maintenance person must be able to state explicitly why a product is not acceptable.

- Someone from the test organization. This person should focus on whether the product is testable. Again, this person must be able to state explicitly why a product is not acceptable.

- Someone from the standards group. (Some organizations have a separate group that defines standards and ensures they are followed.) If you have standards that are supposed to be followed, review for them. People will stop conforming to standards if they are not enforced.

- New or inexperienced users of the document being reviewed. They will have particular insight into the intelligibility of the document.

- Users and marketing people. They should attend reviews at the analysis, requirements, and functional specification stages. If you can't get users to participate, form a team within the software organization to act as devil's advocates, but don't try to cut these people down, intimidate them, or penalize them if they raise objections (having a manager or the senior developer on the devil's advocate team may prevent this).

Some people suggest that the leader invites people to be reviewers, but that they are not obligated to accept the invitation. If you require that people participate in some minimum number of reviews, they will probably choose the sessions based on how well they work with the leader, which provides some competition and incentive for leaders to improve their skills.

The key points in selecting reviewers are that people must be able to contribute and that there be no conflicts of interest. Part of being able to contribute means being prepared, having studied and checked the materials.

Some people are too busy to do prereview checking.

If some people won't or can't check the documents prior to the review, don't invite them. The review should determine if the product will do the job it's supposed to do. If someone hasn't studied the material, you won't get an answer you can trust. If that person is essential to the review, put off the review or alter that person's priorities.

How do you know if people have done their checking?

The classic approach is to go round the room and ask each person for a positive comment about the product and a negative comment—this shows at least some degree of study and checking.

What do you do if people haven't done their checking?

The main reason for review failures is that people don't do their prereview checking adequately. You don't want to be in the situation where a group of six people has "approved" the product, but three of them didn't review it. If people come to the review unprepared, the best thing to do is cancel the review, giving the exact reason for the cancellation on the summary report that goes to management. It shouldn't take too many such reports before people start taking their responsibilities seriously. (One of the better ways to make sure people take prereview checking seriously is to make it a specific item in their performance evaluation. Another way is to use the test results from the test organization in evaluations of developers. However, the results from reviews should *never* be used to evaluate developers.) If it's vital that the review be carried out, do it without those people who are unprepared and document that in the summary report.

I notice you haven't included the person or people whose work is being reviewed.

That's because the producer is a special case and needs to be talked about separately. There are both advantages and disadvantages to having the producer present.

What are the disadvantages?

The producer of the work has a conflict of interest—he has an interest in ensuring the product is judged to be good, so may try to persuade people that the product is better than it is. It may be difficult for the producer to be open and non-defensive because he probably feels an emotional attachment to his work.

Another disadvantage of having the producer at the review is that he may have an incorrect understanding of the product, especially if it's a modification to already heavily modified code. Letting the producer explain his misunderstanding usually gives everyone else the same faulty information. He is likely to explain his assumptions and beliefs as though they were facts.

What are the advantages?

There can be a significant advantage to having the producer available to answer questions and explain things. As a general statement of philosophy, the product shouldn't need someone to defend it—it should be able to speak for itself. If it can't, why isn't there documentation to cover the points of confusion? If some future developer wants to understand the software, or understand the history of the product, he may not have the luxury of being able to ask someone and will have to rely on the written word.

However, in practice, especially when you first start doing reviews, this level of documentation is unlikely to be there, and it will be hard to get through reviews without asking for explanations. So there is a practical advantage to having the producer present.

So what do you recommend?

I'd start with the producer present, but have a rule that he is there only to answer direct questions, and may not enter the discussion. You should require that any answers the producer gives are also put in the documentation. If the producer starts to say "what I'm trying to do here is...," ask why he hasn't said it in the documentation, and make sure it gets added. Over time, developers may begin to produce work that doesn't need them to personally explain it.

Certainly the producer should never be the leader. Since he believes he understands the product, he may rush over things or cause reviewers to overlook problems.

What about including managers?

A manager has two potential conflicts of interest and so you don't want to include him. Schedules for which he is responsible may depend on this work, in which case he may want to accept something that is flawed. And the producer may work for him, in which case he may be evaluating the producer as well as the product.

When managers participate in the reviews, software developers are afraid their abilities are being evaluated. Reviews work best when there is an open give-and-take atmosphere—having a manager present can destroy this atmosphere. Additionally, managers are often not technically competent enough to contribute to the review.

If you have managers who can contribute and who are not directly involved, there's probably no reason to exclude them from reviews. In such a situation a manager might make a good review leader.

But don't managers have a legitimate need to know how well the reviews are being done, and to know the areas where their employees need to improve?

Yes to both, but there are ways of getting this information that don't involve being in reviews where they have a conflict of interest. First, the manager could take the product being reviewed and look for errors or better ways of doing things. He would compare his findings with the recorded results to see if the errors he found were found at the review. Second, employees will naturally improve by having their work reviewed—people will learn from their mistakes because they'd rather have their work accepted than rejected.

What about the use of reviews to train people and disseminate information?

This happens automatically to people who participate in the review. If you want to use reviews to train or inform people who can't contribute to the review, you could include them as observers. Have them sit away from the table to emphasize that status. You might include:

- New software developers. Attending the reviews will help them get a feel for the design and for good and poor practices.

- People from other groups or departments who want to get more knowledge about the software.

Don't people feel they are being attacked in a review?

Not if the producer isn't there. However, if you invite the producer to participate, he may feel this way and react defensively, which is one reason to insist that the producer just answers questions that are asked of him. You must stress that it's an understood part of the job that there will be errors for a variety of reasons: time pressures, lack of experience, oversight, blind spots. Everyone makes mistakes. The purpose of the review is to catch those mistakes as soon as possible to avoid rework. And it's the output that's being reviewed, not the person.

Consistent rules for what gets reviewed also reduce the feeling of personal attack because which pieces of work get reviewed becomes an understood part of the job. Invite people to be reviewers at least once before they have their own work reviewed, so they get a better understanding of how reviews work and appreciate that they are not going to be personally attacked. It may help if the first few reviews go over the work of the more senior people.

The bottom line is that people who don't want to learn what they are doing wrong aren't the sort of people to depend on if you are striving for quality.

What should the procedure be before a review session?

The leader should gather together all the documents that will be required for people to do a good job of reviewing the product, and hand out the package prior to the review. One day's notice is often enough for code reviews, and two or three days is usually plenty. Requirements and high-level design may take a little longer. The leader should also book a room and the necessary equipment.

Reviewers should study the material for about two hours and record any errors they find. This preview study is important for finding the maximum number of errors. Use the time allocated looking for more errors. If you've been through the document at least once before and have found no errors in the last 15 minutes, maybe it's time to stop.

If you are a reviewer, study the previous document then examine the product under review, both to see if it satisfies the previous document and to see if there are errors. For example, in a high-level design review, will the design satisfy the requirements? Are there holes or flaws in the design. Does the design meet organizational goals of maintainability, flexibility, etc? In a code review, does the code implement the design? Are there coding errors? As a general rule, there are four classes of things to look for:

- Does the product do what is specified in the previous document?
- Does it do things not asked for?
- Are there errors in the product?
- Are standards followed?

Make sure you write down every error or concern, or you'll forget them. Mark every occurrence of an error. In fact, when you find an error in a code review, it's a good idea to scan the rest of the code looking for the same error, then come back to where you were.

Should everyone check for the same things?

No. The most effective way to do reviews is to provide one-page checklists for people, with each reviewer checking for something different (of course, they may also find errors outside their specific responsibilities). Doing this makes it less likely things will fall between the cracks, and also makes the review more predictable and repeatable, as different groups of reviewers will be more likely to find the same errors. It also makes it easier for people to participate.

Using the checklist, the reviewer checks that the entire product complies with the items on the list. For the most part, it takes only one person to check things such as internal documentation, source code layout and readability, conformance with programming practices and standards, initialization of variables, exiting from loops, etc. It may take more than one person to cover all of this, but only one person is needed for any one of these aspects.

On the other hand, checking for completeness, conformance to the previous document, maintainability, and flexibility will probably take more than one person.

How do we make sure people can do a good job of reviewing the material?

It's a good idea to define some standard templates for requirements, functional specs, designs, and so on, so that people know where to find things. Having a set of checklists that can be used when reviewing work makes it more likely that errors will be caught (there's a separate chapter on checklists).

What materials should be distributed?

Anything that will be needed for the reviewers to do a good job of checking prior to the review. For code reviews, distribute copies of the design being implemented, the code being reviewed, any include files referenced, etc. For design reviews, distribute copies of the requirements or functional spec that the design is supposed to implement.

If you need to distribute unrelated material just to help people understand the work being reviewed, either the design or the documentation is poor and should be revisited.

What happens in the review session?

1. The leader makes a brief statement of what's being reviewed.
2. The leader introduces people who may not be known to everyone and describes their function in the review.
3. The leader introduces the recorder and the method of recording.
4. The leader goes through the material checklist and makes sure everyone has the full list of materials.
5. The leader describes the rules about finding errors and raising issues rather than solving problems. He describes the rules for raising stylistic and standards issues.
6. The review happens.
7. The recorder summarizes the issues raised, and the reviewers decide whether to accept or reject the product.

What should people talk about in the review?

- *Overall issues.* Start with overall issues before going through the document page by page. If these concerns are serious enough that major rework is needed, why waste time on the details that may be changed during rework.

- *Errors*. Finding errors is the bottom line of the review. People should have already checked through the materials, so the review itself is simply a time when previously discovered errors and issues are described. There should be no discussion of whether a suspected error is really an error. If a reviewer feels something is wrong then it *is* wrong, and needs to be addressed, even if that just means modifying the documentation.

- *Non-conformance to standards,* if there are standards.

- *Understandable, usable documentation.*

- *Maintainability and portability problems.*

- *Inefficiencies*. However, inefficiencies should not be grounds for rejection of the product, unless they cause doubt that the product will meet measurable performance goals.

It seems to me that code reviews are likely to degenerate into discussions about programming style.

Inconsistent style can cause poor understanding, and thus errors. Style may not matter at run time, but if a person can't understand the code, it reduces his confidence in it. So discussions of stylistic issues have value. However, if you don't have stylistic standards, don't review for them; in this case, the leader should shut down discussions of style. If you find that there is a constant tendency for people to bring up stylistic issues but there are no standards, you might consider adopting some.

If we are trying to help people improve, shouldn't we also be discussing solutions and better ways of doing things?

The main purpose of the review is to see if the product will do the job it's supposed to do. All other considerations come second. The danger of providing solutions is that the review will be diverted into time-consuming discussions that don't help in the main purpose. However, there are some other things you can do if you want to discuss solutions.

Some organizations report good results from scheduling three-hour meetings. The first two hours are designated as error-finding time only—no discussion of better ways. The third hour is for a ''better ways'' discussion for anyone who wants to participate. If you schedule your reviews at 10:00 A.M. or 3:00 P.M., the third hour doesn't even cut into company time. Record the key points made and any commitments if possible. (The results from the third hour of discussion might make a good subject for a training session.)

Anyway, someone who feels strongly that there is a better way of doing things is probably prepared to discuss that subject over lunch or after work. If they are not, you have to wonder how strongly they believe in their approach.

Some people recommend that the last half hour of review sessions be devoted to the activities described in Chapter 29, ''Causal Analysis''—brainstorming ways to prevent errors. But whether you do this brainstorming at the end of the review or in a separate session, the activity is distinct from finding errors in the product under review.

How do we handle it if we don't believe the producers will come up with the best solution after the review?

If you find yourself in that situation, you have a problem that goes beyond reviews. You are giving people responsibilities beyond their ability to handle them, and you probably need to pay more attention to task assignments and technical leadership. To solve the immediate problem, you can assign a more senior person or group of people to work with the original developers.

What are the rules for approving requirements, designs, and so on?

The best rule is the Total Consensus rule: a product has to be approved unanimously. This rule is based on several principles:

- If there are doubts about the product, those doubts should be given importance; it shouldn't be possible to outvote the doubters. You may spend a few extra hours addressing the issues, but the other choice is to risk living for years with a poor product.

- The decision should be a decision of the committee, not of some individuals; the personalities should be kept out of it.

- People should not be able to say later: ''I didn't agree with the decision, but was outvoted.'' Product approval must be such that all review members share the blame equally if a poor-quality product is approved.

Total Consensus means that the most conservative opinion is given a lot of weight. The other reviewers are free to try and persuade that person to change his mind, but they can't force him to. Since everyone has to sign his name to the decision, the decision tends to be conservative because no one wants to convince a doubter to put aside his doubts, and later find that the doubts were valid after all. If one person thinks the changes must be rereviewed, the outcome is usually Major Revisions.

In the unlikely event that an agreement can't be reached, report the review as "Incomplete—no consensus," and plan for another review with new people. This also gives the developers a chance to meet the objections that were raised.

Of course, sometimes it's up to the review leader to disallow disagreements if they are irrelevant to the quality of the product. Unless there are stylistic standards, stylistic disagreements should be disallowed, for example. Unless a design won't perform the required task with the required performance, disagreements based on better ways of doing things should be disallowed. The possible outcomes of the product review are:

ACCEPTED
MINOR REVISIONS — No rereview is needed
MAJOR REVISIONS — Must be rereviewed
REDO — Needs to be completely redone. The product is completely inadequate for the job.
INCOMPLETE

Are there other approaches to approval and disapproval?

There are, but none are as effective as Total Consensus. Approaches include:

○ Total Consensus.
○ Total consensus among key individuals, such as managers, system architect, and principal software engineer.
○ Most conservative recommendation.
○ Majority, with key individuals having veto power.
○ Majority among key individuals.
○ Simple majority.
○ Agreement rules depend on what is being reviewed. There are separate rules for analysis, requirements, functional spec, design, user guide, test plans, code, conformance to standards, and bug fixes.
○ Agreement rules depend on the size of the changes.

How do the results of the review get reported?

I've used the approach described by Freedman and Weinberg with good results. The leader produces one to three documents, depending on the decision and the issues. At a minimum he produces a Review Summary Report for management (also distributed to all members of the review and to the producers) which states the conclusions. It lists the product reviewed, the producers, and the material used and contains the names and signatures of all the reviewers.

REVIEW SUMMARY REPORT

Review Number: _____ Starting Time: _____
Date: _____ Ending Time: _____

Work Unit Identification: _____
Description: _____
Producers: _____

Material Used in Review   **Description**

_____   _____
_____   _____
_____   _____
_____   _____
_____   _____

Participants   **Signature**

Leader: _____   _____
Recorder: _____   _____
1. _____   _____
2. _____   _____
3. _____   _____
4. _____   _____
5. _____   _____

Appraisal of Work Unit

ACCEPTED   NOT ACCEPTED (new review required)
_____ As is   _____ Major revisions
_____ With minor revisions   _____ Redo
                                         _____ Review not completed

Other Documents Created   **Description/ID of document**

_____ Issues Report   _____
_____ Related Issues Report   _____
_____ Review not Completed Rpt   _____
_____ Other   _____

If there are issues that were raised and they need to be addressed, the review leader should also produce a Review Issues Report. The Issues Report goes to the producers of the work that was reviewed and describes the issues that were raised so the producers can take care of them. It may include listings or documents with errors marked. It's an issues list, not a proposed solutions list, so avoid the temptation to describe how to solve the problem. That can be left to individual discussions between the reviewers and the producers. Managers probably should not see this report, to overcome fears that it may be used to rate the developers.

REVIEW ISSUES REPORT
Major Revisions

Date: _____

Review Number: _____

Work Unit ID: _____

Review Leader: _____

Review Recorder: _____

REVIEW ISSUES REPORT
Minor Revisions

Date: _____

Review Number: _____

Work Unit ID: _____

Review Leader: _____

Review Recorder: _____

Checker: _____

Date checked: _____

Signature: _____

What if issues were raised that the producers do not control?

That's where the Related Issues Report comes in. This officially brings issues and concerns to the attention of other groups and organizations. If the issue has the backing of the whole review committee, it should probably be written by the review leader; otherwise, by one of the people concerned about it.

REVIEW RELATED ISSUES REPORT

Date: _____

Review Number: _____

Work Unit ID: _____

Review Leader: _____

Review Recorder: _____

Author: _____

How do you make sure something happens if you create a related issues report?

You can't. Once it goes to another organization it's beyond the control of the review committee and becomes a problem for the managers. If the top managers feel it's important to track and resolve these types of issues, they can require that managers who receive a Related Issues Report respond in some fixed time, such as a week. If it's something vital to the product, it will have to be pushed at the management level.

What is the review not completed report?

If the review didn't happen, or was not completed, managers need to know about it. They also need to know why, so that they can address any problems.

REVIEW NOT COMPLETED REPORT

Date: _____

Review Number: _____

Work Unit ID: _____

Review Leader: _____

Reason for non-completion of review

_____ Work unit not ready
_____ Participants late
_____ Participants not prepared
_____ No agreement reached
_____ Other

Details

What happens after the review?

The developer makes the changes required by the review. If the review requires major revisions, he submits the product for rereview. If the review requires minor revisions, he shows the changes to the review leader or the person designated as the checker, who officially signs off on the changes. If only minor revisions are required, there should be a specified time limit for the changes, such as 5 or 10 days. If any documents change, those changes should be distributed to the customers for that document.

How do you make sure that the producers actually do the rework in a minor revisions situation?

Someone is designated as the checker. This is usually the review leader, although it may be someone else if this other person has a strong personal interest in the rework. The review is not complete until the checker has verified that the changes were made and that they didn't cause other errors, and has signed and dated the Issues Report. If the producers haven't done the rework in the required time (usually 5 or 10 days), the review leader should send a memo to managers stating that the review is not yet complete because the rework is not yet done. The leader should continue to send the memo, week after week, until something happens.

What happens if the developer disagrees with the requested changes?

There needs to be a mechanism to address disagreements. Probably the most effective is to allow the producers to talk with the reviewers and try to persuade them that the rework isn't necessary. If the review decision is Minor Revisions, the person who raised the point should officially sign off that he agrees the rework is not necessary.

One on one, the producer might be able to bully the reviewer, which is probably not a big problem with Minor Revisions, but is a potential problem with Major Revision rework. However, when the review meeting reconvenes, the reviewer can again go with his conscience, which prevents a producer with a strong personality from pushing through a poor product.

If this mechanism doesn't work and the producer still refuses to accept the changes, you've got a managerial problem. Probably the best thing is to organize a team of people to address the technical problem, working with the producer. Perhaps he'll convince them his way is best, perhaps not.

If even this doesn't work, you have to consider how much you value the producer. Is he so good you will override the review recommendation? What message will this send to the rest of the organization? And of course, if you force the producer to do something, he may try to make the new approach fail. The best option may be to put him on a different project and let someone else take over this one.

Tell me more about leading. This seems to be a key part of the review process.

The leader is responsible for making sure the review is good—without a good leader reviews can be completely ineffective. The leader should:

1. Collect and distribute all relevant materials.
2. Schedule reviews, rooms, and equipment.
3. Cancel the review if appropriate, and report the reasons to management.
4. Introduce the product and reviewers and specify how decisions will be made.
5. Go round the room asking each reviewer for a positive comment on the product, then go round again asking for a negative comment. This helps determine if people are prepared.
6. Ask if there are any general issues people want to raise before going into the details of the product.
7. Depending on the type of review or inspection the leader can:
   - Lead the reviewers through the document, a section at a time.
   - Go through the checklist an item at a time, asking if anyone found any parts of the product that didn't satisfy the item. Once the checklist is done, lead the reviewers through the document or code asking for

errors.
- Go through the code, line by line, asking for errors on each line.
- Lead the reviewers through the product, playing test cases through.

8. Paraphrase errors to ensure they are understood and to help the recorder keep up.
9. Add errors to the checklist if appropriate.
10. Allow concerns to be aired within the constraints of the discussion. Prevent discussion of issues outside the constraints (if this happens a lot, you might want to move to a "third hour" format).
11. Keep the meeting flowing, so that between one and three errors are noted per minute.
12. Stay out of technical discussions. The leader is supposed to be leading.
13. Ensure that everyone contributes:
    - Neutralize the dominators—"That's a good point. Please make a note of that, recorder. Does anyone else have comments on this section?" Or, go round the room and ask people for issues, starting with their most important issue.
    - Encourage the quiet people—"What are your concerns?"
    In fact, when you use checklists, these problems are reduced.
14. Keep the meeting focused—"That's a good point. Getting back to the material we are reviewing, does anyone have any concerns on page/section/line ##?"
15. Stop people from becoming fixated or repetitive.
16. Ensure the recorder is recording everything—"Did you get all the information?"
17. Cancel the meeting if it gets out of control.
18. Break out material for another review if it becomes apparent that there's too much to review this session.
19. At the end of the meeting, ask the reporter to summarize, then get the consensus opinion.
20. Write and distribute the review reports.
21. Schedule a follow-up review if necessary.

How do we train people to lead reviews well?

The quality of the review depends largely on the quality of the leader, so I commend you for wanting to train the leader. There are courses to which you can send people; and there are consultants who will come in and train your people. There are also videos you can buy, such as the one from the Software Engineering Institute.

One approach is to train the two or three people you think have the most potential as review leaders, use them exclusively for a while until they have mixed their learning with some experience, then have them train new leaders.

If you can't afford the training, have two people work as a team for all your initial reviews, one person leading and the other one observing and making notes on the leader's performance. After the review they can discuss the review and the leader's performance. Alternate who leads and who observes.

Incidentally, it's worth it to put together a short document about reviews for all first-time participants, with one page describing how the review works, and other pages showing the various documents that will be produced.

Tell me more about what the recorder does.

The recorder is responsible for recording information that will be needed for the review reports. There are three types of information: corrections to the document, documentation that needs to be added to explain what the producer had to verbally explain, and issues. Corrections can be made directly on the document.

Issues should be summarized and recorded in a way that ensures people don't bring up the same points repeatedly. That means recording points publicly so that they are in full view. There are several ways to do this:

- Use a flip-chart, and tear off pages and stick them on the walls.

- Use a white board with photographic capabilities, or sufficient standard white boards that things don't have to be erased. Alternatively, use a white board, then take a short break to allow information to be written and possibly photocopied.

- Use a PC or workstation with outlining software, such as Grandview, hooked to a projection unit or an overhead display. Similar software on workstations is even more effective because of the ability to display multiple and larger windows. (In *Shared Minds*, Michael Schrage talks at length about the ability of tools such as these to foster collaboration.)

Recording issues publicly also ensures that the points have been understood. At the end of the review, the recorder should summarize the issues to ensure that everyone was heard and understood, and all the issues recorded correctly.

What if we don't have the facilities to record things publicly?

Then the recorder will have to write things down privately. However, there are several problems with this. You don't know if the recorder has understood the points made, people often feel their points are missed and repeat them in different words, and it makes the leader's job more difficult when the issues begin to repeat but there's nothing in writing to show that.

If it's the only thing you can do, make sure the recorder summarizes at the end of the meeting. It can also help if, before recording the point, the recorder paraphrases it to make sure he's understood the point. Otherwise people have a natural suspicion that their points were ignored or misunderstood.

Can the leader be the recorder, to avoid having too many people?

Yes, but it can be problematic. If there are few issues brought up, it's fairly easy for the leader to both control the review and record the points. However, if a lot of concerns are aired, it's a full-time job to record them and the leader is likely to lose control of the meeting. It's also hard for the leader to record the points publicly.

You could rotate the recorder role between the reviewers, either based on time or on how much individuals have to say about the next section. If there are only one or two other reviewers, the leader could also be the recorder or could contribute as a reviewer.

Tell me more about walkthroughs.

A walkthrough is a session in which people walk through test cases, seeing what would happen. In effect, they pretend they are the computer. The most obvious type of walkthrough is the code walkthrough, in which you take the various test cases and go through the code, line by line, looking at what will happen. Walkthroughs allow you to test small, internal parts of functions that might otherwise be very difficult to test. Similarly, you can test a design by walking through test cases, checking that the design can handle them.

The producer can obviously use a solo walkthrough to test his product, but as with other types of testing, relying solely on the producer means you are at the mercy of his blind spots, his knowledge of how things should work, and his desire that the product have no errors.

What does a developer do in the time between when his work is ready for review and when the review actually happens?

There are any number of things. If requirements are being reviewed, start working on the design or another part of the requirements. If high-level design is being reviewed, start working on the low-level design. If low-level design is being reviewed, there are probably many other parts of the low-level design to complete. If not, start translating the low-level design into code. If code is being reviewed, code another module. Stagger the work so that you are testing the previous module while waiting for the current module to be reviewed.

Doing all these reviews takes so much time. It hardly seems worth it.

Reviews take time, but so does designing, coding, testing, debugging, and reworking.

Initially, an act of faith may be required because the time spent *now* on the review is obvious and seemingly large. The time saved by less debugging and less rework is neither noticed or measurable. So it's easy to think that reviews simply consume time. But studies have shown that over the full project life, reviewing the product does save time and does improve quality.

And there's such a large body of evidence about the effectiveness of reviews that there's no good reason to doubt their value. In *Handbook of Walkthroughs, Inspections, and Technical Reviews*, Freedman and Weinberg quote a tenfold reduction in errors reaching each stage of testing when a system of reviews is in place, with a 50 to 80 percent reduction in testing costs even after the cost of reviews is added in. They also quote a fivefold reduction in maintenance costs for a product that was reviewed during development and during maintenance changes.

If you find that reviews are not effective, it's almost certainly because you are not doing them well. It has been repeatedly shown that the effectiveness of reviews is proportional to the extent that the rules are carefully followed.

If reviews are so good, why should we bother testing?

For two reasons. First, reviewers aren't perfect and some errors will be missed. Second, testing is much better at finding errors related to timing, performance, transaction rates, and system interactions.

If our management still disbelieves in reviews, what can I do to convince them?

Give them copies of books and articles that give hard data about the benefits of reviews. There is plenty of evidence out there. Still, there's a natural tendency among people to think their situations are unique and maybe you'll need your own measurements to convince them. There's more on measuring reviews in Chapter 4, "Metrics."

If we start doing reviews, there will probably be a huge immediate impact on schedules, because I suspect most products will be rejected.

That may well happen. But if products are rejected because they need changes, what does that say about the quality of the product if you hadn't done a review? Either a lot of rework would be needed later on, when it's more time-consuming and expensive, or the product would be shipped with flaws.

As people get better at reviews and better at creating products that will be accepted by the reviewers, things should become more predictable and stable. But you're right, even though reviews save time in the grand scheme, they take time to do. That time must be scheduled. (It's hard to add reviews into an existing schedule, since people are probably already overscheduled.) And there's probably a maximum number of reviews in a given week in which people should participate—two seems to be a reasonable number.

So how much time should we schedule for reviews?

Until you've got some information of your own, schedule 15 percent of the estimated total time for the project specifically for reviews. Now, before you protest that there's no way you can afford a schedule 15 percent longer than your present schedule, which you are already under pressure to reduce, stop.

If you are doing work without reviews, your schedule adherence is probably unpredictable, with most projects taking longer than their schedules. You probably have more errors than you'd like. By allowing time in the schedule for reviews, you make it much more likely that you'll meet your schedules with a higher-quality product. And that's just during the initial creation. The reviews make it easier, cheaper, and quicker to do future maintenance work.

In fact, you should start seeing a fairly immediate benefit because once people understand what will be rejected, they'll pay more attention to standards, to effective modularization, and to good design. People will probably start doing informal reviews with their peers, which is often where the really good ideas happen. If you don't start seeing these benefits, you're probably doing something wrong.

Fifteen percent doesn't seem high enough. If people do two reviews a week, that's more than 15 percent of their time.

A review of about two hours, with two hours of prereview checking, is four hours, or 10 percent. Two reviews is 20 percent, so you might have to schedule 20 percent of certain individuals' time. However, not everyone will be involved with reviews, which pulls the average time down. Certainly, when putting together individual schedules, you should factor in the reviews each person will be doing.

Okay, but I still don't agree that you should review all code—it would take far too long.

If you don't review all the code, how do you know that it's safe not to review it? Start by reviewing it all, then slowly back off when you can get statistics to show that it's more effective not to review certain code. Besides finding errors and giving management more control, code reviews force people to code according to standards and produce sufficient documentation in the code. If you are starting a project in a new language, code reviews help the developers learn the language more quickly. So, for all these reasons it's important to start reviewing all code. (An internal study at Hewlett-Packard's Waltham Division found that 60 percent of all pre-release errors were introduced during the implementation (i.e., coding) phase. A number this high makes a good case for taking code reviews seriously.)

After a while, people will start coding in a way that will satisfy a review committee, and then you may be able to back off and decide not to review everything. There are various ways to choose what code to review. You can review code that meets one or more of the following criteria:

- Greater than a certain size (number of lines, number of non-commented statements).
- Greater than a certain age.
- Greater than a certain complexity (defined as you think necessary: too high a cyclomatic complexity number, too many different things being done, too many levels of indentation, too many gotos, etc.).
- Greater than a specified number of changes already made to it.
- Greater than a specified number of errors reported against it.
- Greater than a specified cost associated with changes or bug fixes (lifetime, per year, per month, etc.).
- A specified percentage of changed modules, chosen randomly.

But remember, you should be able to demonstrate with statistics that it's more effective to review based on one of these subsets.

Tell me more about how reviews can help prevent errors.

By analyzing the errors found during reviews (and testing), you can understand the types of errors created. By understanding errors, their frequency, and their relationship to other factors, you can figure out ways to prevent the errors from happening. Were the errors caused by:

- Lack of knowledge?
- Lack of understanding?
- Lack of communication?
- Lack of specs or holes in specs?
- Too much time pressure?
- Not following a procedure?

There's a lot more about this in Chapter 29, "Causal Analysis."

Should you review the work of experienced programmers and designers?

Experienced doesn't automatically mean good or right! I'll assume you mean "good programmers and designers." I'd start from the default position of reviewing everything unless you can get statistics to prove that it's more effective to drop the reviews. After all, if these people are very good, they are probably doing more significant work. And the more significant the work, the more necessary it is to review it.

Software development is very iterative in nature. How do reviews fit into an iterative process?

Each document should have an identified audience, made up mostly of "customers" for the document: marketing, support organization, QA organization, documentation group, future developers, other development groups, etc. Each customer has a real need for an accurate, high-quality document. So if a developer learns something that will require a change to the document, the document should be updated and the new information passed out to the document customers, plus the people who initially reviewed and accepted the document.

If the document is large, I wouldn't distribute the full document, just an update sheet showing the pages, sections, and changes, especially since there may be several sets of changes before that phase is complete. Any customer wanting a full copy can request one, but most people will wait until the end when they can be fairly sure it won't change any more.

If any of the customers feel that the changes should be reviewed, then the product has to go through another formal review. Now, in many organizations people are swamped with work and won't even read the document properly if it's not going to be formally reviewed. To prevent problems not being discovered because people don't read the document, you can require that all the initial reviewers sign that they accept the document.

A lot of our work is maintenance rather than totally new systems. How do you do reviews in a maintenance environment?

The problem with software in a maintenance environment is that you end up with patches on patches on patches. Problems get solved by adding global variables and by making variables do more than one job. Changes have ripple effects through the whole system. So there are some key things to look for in a review:

- Does the new code do what it's supposed to do?

- Does it break anything or do things it's not supposed to do? The biggest danger in maintenance work is breaking something else. The best way to review for this is to have a checklist of possible side effects, and to examine the code for each one of these. Every time you come across a side-effect error, add that side effect to your checklist. If the code uses global variables, you may have to search other modules for those globals to be sure there are no side effects.

- Does the new code look like a patch? To prevent the code from deteriorating further, no change should look like a patch. In fact there's a good case for requiring that all maintenance changes not only prevent deterioration, but actually improve the code—it makes the software easier to maintain in the future and it's more fun. If you do this, resist the temptation to fix the world, and just improve the code associated with the change you are making.

We have projects ranging in size from simple bug fixes through projects that last a year. How do the reviews differ for large and small projects?

Projects come in different sizes. What is appropriate for a large project is overkill for a bug fix. There are no easy answers, but you might try a scheme such as the following guidelines, that makes some fairly arbitrary decisions about projects of different sizes, then modify the rules as you get feedback on how well it works.

- Greater than one person-month. Separate, full reviews of requirements, functional spec, and design, followed by code reviews.

- One person-week to one person-month. A requirements review by two or three people, then a single full review of functional spec and design, followed by code reviews.

- Up to one person-week. A single requirements, functional spec, and design review by two or three people, followed by code reviews.

- Small bug fixes. A code review by two people and a reader. Allocate a couple of hours for these people, and have them review as many bug fixes as can be fit into this time. If they decide there are too many design issues involved in the bug fix, they can send it back for design review.

What problems are you likely to encounter with reviews?

There are several potential problems:

- Management doesn't believe in reviews. Hire someone to come in and give a one day "Managers' Introduction to Reviews" seminar. Give managers literature about reviews. From the literature, put together a summary of all quantified benefits. Invite managers to audit reviews. Ask why they are against reviews and explain how their concerns are unjustified.

- Management becomes too involved and destroys the open atmosphere. Don't invite managers to the reviews if there will be conflicts of interest or if technical reviewers are uncomfortable having managers present.

- The leader is ineffective in keeping things focused. Train the leader or get a new one.

- Things aren't recorded well. Train the recorder or get a new one. Record things publicly so that it's obvious if a point wasn't understood.

- There's no consistent approach to finding errors. Develop document templates and review checklists to make it easier.

- Too much discussion of matters of style. If you have stylistic standards, enforce them. If you don't have stylistic standards, kill discussions about matters of style.

- People get fixated on certain issues. Ask the recorder to make sure that point is recorded then ask other people if they have points to make.

- People want to solve the problems rather than just point them out. Point out that the purpose of the review is to find problems, not solve them. Change the format to a "third hour" format.

- People are consistently late or unprepared. Cancel the review and report the reason. Don't invite these people to participate in reviews.

- People don't contribute. Try to find out why. Cancel the review if people haven't done their prereview checking, and give details in the summary report. Replace those who don't contribute.

- Tactlessness or personal attacking. "I've never seen anything so stupid." "This is the worst possible way to do it." Stress the positive. We want to find better ways of doing things, not point out the worst. Don't invite persistently aggressive or negative people.

- Too much defensiveness. Explain that it's understood that people will sometimes make errors. Insist that the producer speak only when directly asked questions or don't invite the producer.

- People try to rush through the review too quickly. Postpone it if necessary, or cut the amount of material being reviewed.

- People blame other people or standards for problems. Don't accept it. Cut off this type of excuse.

Problems can all be overcome. The main point is to start doing reviews. Then you can review the review process and refine the way you do reviews. If they aren't working, the problem is not with the reviews, but with the way they are implemented. Enough organizations have reported successes to prove that reviews, when well-done, are useful.

Further Reading

Freedman, Daniel, and Gerald Weinberg. 1990. *Handbook of Walkthroughs, Inspections, and Technical Reviews: Evaluating Programs, Projects, and Products (3rd Edition)*. New York, NY: Dorset House.

Hollacker, Charles. 1990. *Software Reviews and Audits Handbook*. New York, NY: Wiley.

Yourdon, Ed. 1989. *Structured Walkthroughs (4th Edition)*. Englewood Cliffs, NJ: Yourdon Press.

Papers

Ackerman, A.F., L.S. Buchwald, and F.H. Lewski. May 1989. *Software Inspections: An Effective Verification Process*. IEEE Software.

Fagan, M.E. March 1976. *Design and Code Inspections to Reduce Errors in Program Development*. IBM Systems Journal, Volume 15, No. 3.

Fagan, M.E. 1986. *Advances in Software Inspection*. IEEE Transactions on Software Engineering, Volume SE-12, No. 7.

Knight, J.C., and E.A. Meyers, July 1991. *Phased Inspections and Their Implementation*. ACM Software Engineering Notes, Volume 16, No. 3.

Parnas, David, and David Weiss. August 1985. *Active Design Reviews: Principles and Practices*. Proceedings of the Eighth International Conference on Software Engineering. Published by IEEE.

Russell, Glen. January 1991. *Experience with Inspection in Ultralarge-Scale Developments*. IEEE Software, Volume 8, No. 1.

Video

Software Engineering Institute, May 1991. *Scenes of Software Inspections*. CMU/SEI-91-EM-5-0. Costs $50 ($25 for universities and government). Available from: Education Program, Software Engineering Institute, Carnegie Mellon University, Pittsburgh, PA 15213-3890. Internet address: customer-relations@sei.cmu.edu or education-@sei.cmu.edu

Summary

Technical reviews help prevent errors, catch errors quickly, give management information about the state of the product, and spread information about products and techniques. This chapter discussed when to do technical reviews, how to do them, who should attend, the roles of the leader and recorder, and what the rules for acceptance should be. It then showed some sample forms for reporting the results of the review.

28

Review Checklists

Checklists help you remember to look for typical errors or omissions. It's easy to forget things when reviewing a large document or piece of code, and a checklist is a memory aid. A checklist should contain a list of typical errors that your organization tends to make.

When checking prior to a review, each reviewer should be responsible for checking a specific area and should have a checklist that covers that area. The checklist shouldn't be more than one page, or checking for each item becomes too difficult. So for each type of review (requirements, design, code, etc.), there should be several checklists, each covering a different aspect of the product. Each reviewer should be responsible for covering all the items in a checklist.

This document gives you a starting point. Start by selecting the particular things that may useful for you, then, as you get experience with reviews, you can add to or delete from the checklist as you discover the types of errors that people in your organization tend to make. It's a good idea to also review the checklists.

Sample Checklists

Requirements Review Questions

○ Does the requirements document address the following:
  - Cost?
  - Timeframe?
  - Functionality?

- Exception handling?
- Quality aspects, with measurable requirements?
  - Compliance to standards
  - Maintainability
  - Reliability
  - Security
- Space?
  - Memory usage
  - Disk usage
- Performance?
  - Response times
  - Anticipated number of operations per second
  - Anticipated data flow volumes
  - Peak data flow volume
  - Size of typical data transaction
  - Maximum size of data transaction
- Training?
  - Ease of learning
  - Self-paced training
- Ease of use?
  - Help
  - Beginner/Expert modes
  - Consistency of user interface
  - Predictability of results
- Installation?
  - Ease of installation/setup
  - Ease of configuration
- Support?
  - Ease of support
  - Ease of recovery
- Hardware platforms?
  - Vendor
  - Hardware
  - Operating system
  - Terminals/Workstations/PCs
  - Color/Monochrome
- Hardware interfaces?
- Communications interfaces?
- Database requirements?
- Programming languages?
- International capabilities?
  - Translated text and error messages
  - Input/recognition of accented characters, etc.
  - Date/time formats and separators
  - Numeric separators
  - Sorting sequences
- Future requirements that are likely?
  - Are there any inconsistencies or conflicts in the requirements?
  - Are there any unclear or vague areas?
  - Are there any incorrect assumptions?

- Are there any unstated assumptions that should be stated?
- Are all assumptions stated to be assumptions, and justified with evidence?
- Do all critical facts have their sources documented? Have you checked the source?
- Do all estimates have evidence to support them?
- Do all estimates and numeric values have their sources documented?
- Can you trace each requirement back to its reason for existence?
- Are the priorities clearly stated?
- Are the constraints clearly stated?
- Are the cost and timeframe requirements clearly stated?
- Are any of the requirements really solutions?
- For each requirement, is this really a special case of a more-general requirement?
- For each requirement, will it be possible to state explicitly whether or not the requirement has been met?

Design Review Questions

- Clarity
  - Is the documentation clear?
  - Do you understand the reasons for the design?
  - Do you understand the data structures and algorithms?
- Compatibility with existing software
  - Will this design cause side-effects in other software?
  - Does this design rely on side-effects of other software?
  - Does this design rely on other software doing things that are not always done?
- Component-level
  - Are the interfaces well-defined?
  - Are the main data structures defined?
  - Are the main algorithms defined?
  - Is the data/control flow described?
- Data structures and algorithms
  - Are the data structures defined?
  - Are data structures in third normal form?
  - Are the access methods to the data structures defined?
  - Are the algorithms defined?
  - Are the algorithms correct?
  - Do the algorithms and data structures solve the problem?
- Error/exception handling
  - Does the program handle typing errors?
  - Does the software validate user input?
  - Does the software give the user correction hints if the user enters invalid data?
  - Does the software validate other input?
  - Does the software give explicit, non-threatening error messages if a program error occurs?
  - Does the software tell the user what to do when it displays a program error message?
  - Does the program provide error messages to help programmers debug and fix errors?
  - Can the program be restarted from any point?
  - Does the program gracefully handle exception conditions such as access violations and floating point errors?
  - Does the software attempt to continue when possible, perhaps in a restricted mode?
  - Is the error handling consistent?
- Function interfaces
  - Does the number of actual parameters match the number of formal parameters?

- Do the type and size of actual parameters match the type and size of formal parameters?
- Are constants passed as modifiable parameters?
- Does the function rely on module-scope globals?
- Does the function rely on external-scope variables?
- Are global variables defined and used consistently between modules?
- Is all communication documented, i.e., parameters and shared data?
- Are all parameters and global data explicitly stated to be for input, output, or both?

○ Function-level
- Does the function do something very similar to an existing function?
- Is there a library function that will do the same thing?
- Is the function excessively complex?
- Could the function be broken into separate, more logical pieces?
- Is the function of acceptable size?
- Does the function do only one logical thing?
- Does the function rely on function scope static variables?
- Is the function easily maintained?
- Is the function easily tested?
- Are side-effects described?

○ Quality
- Are the goals of the design stated (reliability, flexibility, maintainability, performance, etc.)?
- Does the design meet its stated goals?
- Is there evidence that more than one design option was considered?
- Are several design options discussed and reasons listed for their adoption or rejection?
- Are the design assumptions stated?
- Are the design tradeoffs stated?
- Is the design efficient?
- Is the design maintainable?
- Is the design portable?
- Is the design simple or complicated?
- Will the design handle a variety of changes to the external environment with minimal modification?
- Does the design use fixed size arrays or is memory allocated as needed?
- Does the design get key values externally—from environment variables, files, etc.—or are they hard-coded?

○ Requirements
- Does the design satisfy each requirement?
- Is there traceability between the design and the functional specifications or requirements?
- Can the design meet the development cost requirements?
- Can the design meet the unit cost requirements?
- Can the design be implemented in the required timeframe?
- Does the design provide the required functionality?
- Does the design stay within the required memory constraints?
- Does the design stay within the required disk usage constraints?
- Does the design satisfy the response-time requirements?
- Will the design handle the expected rate of transactions?
- Will the design handle the expected data flow volumes?
- Does the design do more than meet the requirements and any stated future requirements?

○ Reuse
- Does this functionality already exist in another module or library function?
- Is this functionality sufficiently general-purpose that a library function should be created?

○ System-level
- Can this design be implemented on the required hardware platforms and operating systems?
- Can this design be easily ported to other hardware platforms and operating systems?
- Does this design handle the required terminals, workstations, PCs, and printers?
- Will this design handle future terminals, workstations, PCs, and printers?
- Does the program offer output on a variety of printers?
- Will the design allow training to be done easily?
- Will the design allow self-paced training?
- Will this design allow for easy installation and configuration?
- Are you using a database package with 4GL capability?
- Does this design have full international capabilities? Does it handle:
  - Translated text and error messages.
  - Input/recognition of accented characters, etc.
  - Date/time formats and separators
  - Numeric separators
  - Sorting sequences
○ Testing
- Does the design incorporate a built-in mechanism for easy regression testing?
- Does the testing scheme tell you if there is a discrepancy between anticipated and actual results?
- Can the software display all input data if requested?
- Can the software display all function parameters if requested?
- Can the software display intermediate program steps if requested?
○ User interface
- Have you prototyped the user interface in collaboration with users?
- Is the software intuitive, consistent, and predictable?
- Does the software allow users to tailor the system to their needs?
- Does the program offer various modes for beginners through experts?
- Does the program allow the user to define macros for commonly performed actions?
- Can commands be abbreviated?
- Does the program provide sensible defaults to avoid redundant typing?
- Does the software provide full context sensitive help?
- Is there detailed help information available on each command?
- Can the user learn the program without assistance from people or manuals?
- Can users cancel time-consuming operations?
- Can users perform more than one action while in a particular screen or do they have to exit and back up a menu hierarchy?
- Is it easy to back out, wherever the user is in the program?
- Is it obvious what format to enter information? For example, is it obvious that dates must be entered in DD/MM/DD or MM/DD/YY or YYMMDD or DD-MMM-YYYY format?

Code Review Questions

○ Have tools such as lint or CodeCheck been used to check for appropriate items in the code?
○ Checking
- Is input data checked?
- Are parameters checked?
- Are subscript indexes checked before being used?
- Are subscript indexes out of range?
- Does the program check for division by zero before doing divisions?
- Do switch/case blocks contain default conditions?

- Do if-else if blocks have an else condition to trap all other situations?
- Is the code self-checking?
- Are all error messages descriptive and understandable?
- Do all error messages tell the user what to do?
- Do all calls to functions check the status return and have the appropriate error-handling code?
- Do all functions return an error status? Even if they don't need it, it's useful to return a status that the calling code can check; then, if the function changes in the future to need a status return, callers can already handle it.
- Does the software use the standard error reporting routines?

○ Control flow
- Is there a single entry point to the module?
- Is there a single exit point?
- Are there gotos that go back from the current location?
- Are there gotos that go to places other than the end of the module?
- Is all the code reachable?
- Can the program terminate in one place only?

○ Design
- Does the code do exactly what the design says it should do—no more and no less?
- Is the programming style consistent?
- Is the code simple and clear? If not, is there a good reason for it, well-documented in the code?
- Are modules broken down into an excessive number of functions that more logically belong in a single place?
- Are library routines used for common operations?
- Is there any code that could/should be generalized and made into a shareable routine or a library routine?
- Does each module perform one unique function?
- Does the code actually do what it's supposed to do? Does it implement the design?

○ Documentation and comments
- Does function documentation follow conventions?
- Does function documentation cover:
  - Function overview
  - Caller obligations
  - Function obligations
  - Parameters—input
  - Parameters—output
  - Acceptable/unacceptable values
  - Global variables read
  - Global variables modified
  - Return values
  - Error reporting done (displayed, added to linked list, etc.)
  - Danger points and potential problems
  - Limitations
  - Assumptions
  - Dependencies
  - Impact of changes on other modules
  - Called from (if only a few fixed places)
  - Functions called
- Are there comments describing each block of code?
- Is there any obscure, uncommented code?
- Are all comments meaningful and unambiguous?

- Do comments describe "why" as much as "what"?
- Are parentheses used to ensure people can understand what complex evaluations are doing?
- Are all unusual program termination conditions described?

○ Efficiency
- Do the data structures lend themselves to efficient algorithms?
- Is integer arithmetic used rather than floating-point where possible?
- Are mixed data types avoided in arithmetic and logical operations where possible to avoid data conversions.
- Are files blocked efficiently?
- Is the most efficient data type used for subscripts?
- Is as much initialization as possible done at compile-time rather than run-time?
- In an if-then-else if-else if-else type of construct, are the conditions listed in order of probability?

○ Indentation and formatting
- Is code properly indented?
- Are there no more than ### levels of indentation?
- Are there no more than ### levels of if statements?
- Is there, at most, one instruction per line?

○ Language
- Is there any obscure or trick code?
- Are there any non-standard language features used?
- Does the program pass lint or other code-checking tools?

○ Loops
- Is the loop control variable the only variable used to index inside the loop?
- Does the loop control variable have a meaningful name?
- Does the loop contain code that should not be done every time, i.e., that should be outside the loop?
- Are all loops guaranteed to terminate?
- If the loop is counting things, and if the count is being done by the loop counter, is this correct? Some languages/compilers adjust the counter before evaluation of the continue condition, while others adjust it after evaluation.
- Are there any off-by-one situations with the loop boundary conditions?

○ Names
- Are there any unnecessary labels?
- Are there any labels other than Exit labels?
- Are all variable and function names meaningful?
- Do all variable and function names follow naming conventions?
- Do you use variables such as i, j, etc., in any context, other than as loop control variables for small, tight loops?

○ Portability
- Does the code have any knowledge of the operating system?
- Does the code have any knowledge of the terminal type?
- Does the code have any knowledge of the printer type?
- Does the code have any knowledge of the file storage?
- Does the code have any other knowledge of hardware or I/O specific things?
- Does the program use machine/operating system extensions of the standard programming language?
- If the language is C, does the code use short and long explicitly, rather than depending on the machine size of int; i.e., does the code care whether an int is two or four bytes?
- Does the code depend on the bit representation of alphanumeric characters?

- Does the code depend on the bit representation of floating point numbers?
  o Values and variables
    - Are there any unused variables or labels?
    - Are values such as maximum counts or table sizes:
      - Hard coded?
      - Defined in #defines or the equivalent?
      - Read from a file or an environment variable?
      - Enlarged when the program realizes that it's reached the bound?
    - Are there any external-scope globals that could be eliminated or made into parameters?
    - Are there any module-scope globals that could be eliminated or made into parameters?
    - Are all fields in the structure logically related?
    - Are there any off by one conditions with array indexes?
    - Are any variables used for more than one purpose?
    - Have new global variables been added to solve this problem?
    - Are all variables initialized prior to use?
    - Are flags correctly initialized and reset?
    - If pointers are incremented, are you sure the new value is valid?
    - Is precision being lost on assignments (e.g. short = long)? If so, why?
    - Are you assigning signed variables to unsigned, or vice versa (e.g., iu_count = i_count)? If so, why?

Test Plan Review Questions

  o Is the scope of the test defined, i.e., is it obvious what is being tested?
  o Are the equivalence groups defined?
  o Is there data from each equivalence group?
  o Is there data from each side of every group boundary?
  o Are troublesome values, such as 0 and 1, being used?
  o Are you testing with data that the software is supposed to reject?
  o Are you testing with data that the software is supposed to accept?
  o Are values being used that will cause pointers to be incremented invalidly?
  o Is data being used that will test each condition in the code effectively? (If this is impossible, perhaps the design is inadequate.)
  o Are the expected results shown?
  o Is error handling tested?
  o Have all program branches been tested?
  o Is performance being tested?
  o Is there a described relationship between the test plan and a requirement?
  o Are all requirements being tested?

Further Reading

Freedman, Daniel, and Gerald Weinberg. 1990. *Handbook of Walkthroughs, Inspections, and Technical Reviews: Evaluating Programs, Projects, and Products (3rd Edition)*. New York: Dorset House.

Kernighan, Brian, and P.J. Plaugher. 1978. *The Elements of Programming Style (2nd Edition)*. New York: McGraw-Hill.

29

Causal Analysis

What is causal analysis?

Causal Analysis, also known as Root Cause Analysis, is a way of preventing errors by looking at the errors you find, analyzing their causes, and figuring out what actions you can take to prevent those types of errors. Its value is that if you prevent errors, you can use the time you would have spent tracking down and fixing errors to do more productive work.

It sounds like learning from experience.

It's true that we do learn from experience, but we often forget the lessons, and, as George Santayana said, ''Those who cannot remember the past are condemned to repeat it.'' Causal analysis gives a specific focus on errors, causes, and preventive actions, and this tends to give us better lessons, a better memory of the lessons, and elimination of various types of error. The end result should be three types of action:

- *Actions to prevent similar errors from happening in the future.* The greatest value of causal analysis is to translate the knowledge obtained from understanding the cause of the error into actions that will prevent future errors. Things to consider include: training, procedures, document templates, tools such as lint, and regular discussions between people.

- *Actions to help find the error sooner.* If you can't prevent errors, you want to at least find them as soon as possible. Things to consider include checklists and reviews.

○ *Actions to find and remove similar errors from the product.* Are there things you can look for in your documents or source code that are likely to be causing similar problems?

What information should you gather to come up with preventive actions?

The goal is to understand enough about the errors and their causes that you can find actions that will eliminate classes of errors. Useful information includes:

○ *What was done wrong?* Bad parameters not being detected? Return values not checked? Variables not initialized? Incorrect algorithm? Incorrect use of variable addresses? Pointers being incremented incorrectly? Error conditions not being trapped? Incorrect use of the programming language? Code being commented out by mistake? Incomplete requirements?

○ *What caused the error to occur?* Lack of knowledge about the programming language? Lack of knowledge of what had to be done? Not using tools such as lint? Code too complex to understand? Design that didn't consider all the possible conditions? Lack of understanding of requirements? False assumptions? Not following a procedure?

○ *In what part of the process did it originate?* Was the error purely a coding error, i.e., miscoding something that was correctly understood? Was it an algorithmic error? Was it caused by a design error? A requirements error?

○ *How was the error found?* Was it detected by a test case? By a technical review? By a customer?

○ *Why wasn't the error found sooner?* Why wasn't it found in the appropriate review: code review, design review, requirements review? If the error was found after the testing phase, why wasn't it detected during the test phase? Why did the test plan review not detect the lack of a test to cover this error?

What about information about who made the error?

I'd ignore this initially. If developers think causal analysis will be used to evaluate them, they will resist causal analysis. Focus on ways to prevent errors, and ignore the individual human side for the time being, otherwise you won't get causal analysis started. Unfortunately, in the final analysis, many of the causes of errors are purely human, and some people are more prone to causing errors than others. After all the process changes, new tools, and new procedures, there may still remain the issue of human fallibility. Ultimately you may have to address the ability of individuals, but leave it till later. Even then, you should focus on trying to help the individual succeed, rather than penalizing him.

How do you figure out the cause? It seems you can go several levels deep.

True, each cause can be seen as the result of a deeper cause. How deep should you go? As deep as you need to go in order to come up with useful actions.

There is a diagram that can help you figure out the causes, and causes of causes—the Ishikawa, or Fishbone diagram. Here's an example of a modified Fishbone diagram analyzing a bug in which a pointer was incremented out of range, causing the program to crash with an access violation. You'll notice that, after brainstorming about the causes, we've ended up with several different paths to follow:

- How could we have prevented the error from being introduced?
- How could we have checked for this condition in our code?
- How could we have found this error by testing?
- How could we have prevented the invalid pointer from crashing the program?

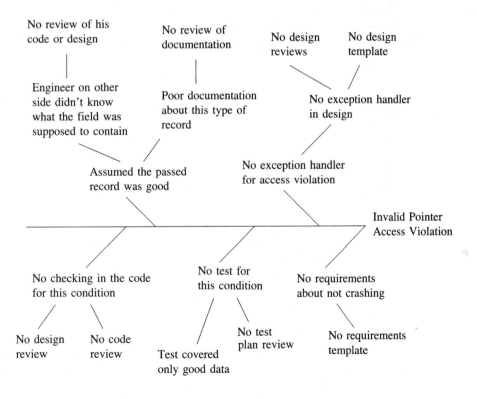

But remember, the purpose of the exercise is to prevent errors, not to analyze them to death. Don't let this become simply an intellectual exercise.

What's the best way to do causal analysis as an individual?

Record the errors you make on three-by-five cards, analyze them using Fishbone diagrams, and brainstorm about how you might be able to avoid them in the future. As you analyze and record each error you should learn something; then, when you have enough bugs recorded, look for patterns. As you accumulate errors and actions, you'll probably see some common actions. Some will be actions you can take alone, while others will involve outside work. Once you've built a sufficient list of errors, causes, and actions, you should be able to talk with your manager about implementing some of the actions that you can't take as an individual. With the detailed documentation you should be quite persuasive, especially if you've also recorded the time it took to detect, find, and fix the errors.

If you want to improve your causal analysis, and don't mind admitting your errors to others, arrange lunchtime meetings to analyze errors and brainstorm solutions. Start by asking for other people's help in figuring out how you can avoid making errors—people will probably be very happy to help analyze your errors and tell you how to prevent them. Don't ask about errors they make—that may be too threatening. If they see value in what you are doing and realize that it's not crushing to the ego to admit errors, they will probably want to discuss their own errors.

(This is one of the better ways to start a causal analysis/defect prevention program—by the developers themselves starting it, finding it useful, and extending it. If you are a manager and want to start a program like this, the easiest way is to find a good developer who people respect and who is receptive to new ideas, and ask him to try doing this. Wait for the program to develop before formalizing it. You'd like it to live past either you or the individual who started it, and once it's established and working no one will have a problem with formalizing it.)

Who should you include in this type of informal meeting?

If you want it to continue, invite people who work well together, who trust each other, and who are interested in this approach. Of this group, people who make few errors are natural candidates because, presumably, they are already doing something that prevents errors.

When should you have a meeting to analyze the errors and figure out preventions?

When you have enough errors to make a meeting worthwhile, but before you've forgotten why they happened, and before you have too many errors to deal with. If there's just been a technical review of your work where errors were discovered, that might be an appropriate time. Or you could start when you've accumulated 10 to 20 errors, and just see how it goes.

Is it so important to write things down?

Definitely. Write down the error, the cause, and all suggestions for preventing it. After a while you'll probably find that suggestions start becoming repetitive, and that a few actions will help solve multiple problems.

Even if you don't discover preventive actions you can implement, the list of errors and causes you accumulate is a valuable document that you and others can use. Refresh yourself with it whenever you start a new phase of a project (requirements, design, code, etc.), to mentally note the typical errors (and their causes) that you make in this phase. Reading the list should make you a little less likely to make these errors again.

If you are implementing a causal analysis program across a project or group, what is the best way to do it?

Start by gathering strong management support; unsupported programs rarely last long. Then find a manager and a technical person, who are respected and have credibility, to drive the program. (Most new programs are best implemented by a combination of respected management and technical people.) Once you have support for the program, make a presentation to the developers, describing how causal analysis works, its costs, and its benefits.

Introduce causal analysis as a pilot program, with the focus on the causal analysis rather than on the schedules. Developers who feel under pressure to meet schedules are likely to resist anything that takes time away from them. When people have become familiar and comfortable with causal analysis, you can introduce it into more critical projects. Try to get some quick successes to establish the credibility of the program. Implement and publicize some preventive actions.

As to the causal analysis itself, there are four main components to consider:

- Formal causal analysis meetings
- A database and tools to track errors, causes, and actions
- An action team
- Stage kickoff meetings

Tell me about the meetings.

For about the first hour and a half, the leader should go through the errors, and everyone should try to analyze why each error happened, and suggest ways that it could have been prevented (i.e., actions that will prevent similar errors from happening in the future). Keep the meeting moving, and don't get bogged down in the exact cause if it's not easy to discover. The preventive actions are much more important than a detailed analysis of the cause. To keep the meeting focused, use a whiteboard and record:

- The error number.
- A brief description of the error.
- The cause category (communication, education, oversight, transcription).
- A brief description of the cause.
- The stage in which the error was introduced (requirements, architecture, high-level design, low-level design, coding, etc.).
- The stage in which the error should have been caught.
- Preventive actions.
- Actions that would have caught the error earlier.

For the last part of the meeting, the leader should lead the team to take a wider view of the defects and consider any trends or patterns in the errors. Are there any other lessons to be learned? What has been going well? What has been going badly? Is there any way to save time, or help another team save time? Are there any other ideas on how to improve error detection?

As with most meetings, don't go on longer than two hours. People stop thinking effectively after that.

How often should you hold causal analysis meetings?

Hold a causal analysis meeting at the end of each stage (requirements, high-level design, etc.), or more frequently if there are lots of errors, after the errors have been corrected. The meeting shouldn't last more than about two hours, so hold a meeting after you've accumulated enough errors to make the meeting last two hours. Start with 20 unique errors, and see how that goes.

It's important to hold causal analysis meetings regularly and consistently, otherwise the meetings will slowly fade away. Incidentally, once causal analysis is well-established, you'll probably find that people begin to make suggestions outside of the meetings.

What if there are too many errors to analyze?

Start by consolidating all duplicate errors, then choose a representative sample of errors. Try to include errors from all the developers so that some people don't feel they are being singled out. Make a note of the number of duplicate errors to give you a feel for which errors are most common.

Should you include the developers who created the errors?

Definitely. They are the best people to identify the causes. They also receive direct feedback about their errors.

Tell me more about the error categories.

Some organizations like to classify errors in many different categories, then do lots of analysis of patterns and trends. However, it's not been shown that breaking down errors into more categories does anything to help discover preventive actions. If anything, the focus on classification may take away from the work of preventing the errors. Classifying errors into one of the following four categories seems to be all that is really needed, because the key part is to describe the specific cause, then brainstorm for specific preventive actions.

Communications failure. This includes incorrect information, information not communicated, or information not given to the right people. To come up with the specific cause, ask: "What information wasn't communicated, from whom to whom?" These errors can often be prevented by assigning communication responsibility to particular individuals, automatic notification when things change, and checklists.

Education. Errors in this category generally occur because the developer didn't understand some part of the product or process. To get the specific cause, ask: "Exactly what was not understood?" These errors can often be prevented by product-related classes, software development classes, presentations on new-release functionality, and new-hire education checklists.

Oversight. This category covers errors where the developer didn't consider all cases and conditions. Ask "What was not thoroughly considered? What was overlooked?" These errors can often be prevented by templates, checklists, common error lists, tools to check things, on-line documentation, stage kickoff meetings, discussing work with team members, and reducing schedule pressure.

Transcription error. This category covers errors that occurred because the developer understood what to do, but simply made a mistake when creating the product. Ask: "What procedure was being followed that allowed this error to happen?" These errors can often be prevented by using the appropriate tools.

Some errors make it past the test group and out to the field. How do you involve the test group?

Errors that are missed by the test group should: (a) have not been created, (b) have been caught by the developer, and (c) have been caught in test. The development organization should be doing causal analysis to prevent errors of this type being introduced, and to catch them before they leave development.

However, the test group should also be doing causal analysis of it's own with respect to errors that made it to the field. Why weren't they caught? What can be done to prevent such errors escaping in the future?

What does the action team do?

It implements the preventive actions. Many of the preventive measures will be ones that can't be implemented by individual developers because their scopes are more universal. Some actions may require changes to processes, some may involve purchasing or writing tools, and some may mean that formal technical reviews need to be established. Such actions can be taken only by people with the correct authority or by people who have been given the time.

Being on the action team is not usually a full-time job, but it must have the support of the team member's manager, otherwise the team member will be ineffective. Teams should be about 3 to 4 people for an organization of 20 to 50 people, or as many as 8 to 10 people for much larger organizations. Assign specific responsibilities to people because the pressures of other activities often cause things to fall through the cracks if there's no defined responsibility. Each member should have a specific area of expertise: tools, education, process, cross-organization negotiation, etc.

It's important that the team implement preventive actions, otherwise people lose faith in the process and stop paying attention to causal analysis. The action team should also provide feedback to the developers who made the suggestions, even if the suggestion couldn't be implemented; people like feedback, and no one wants to think his ideas got lost in the void.

What about tracking the actions.

It's important to track all this information, otherwise it gets lost. Store:

- The ID of the action
- A description of the action
- The projected completion date
- The name of the person responsible for the action
- The name of the person who suggested the action
- Priority
- Status
- Projected cost
- Final cost

Should managers participate in causal analysis meetings?

A manager should be on the action team to provide management focus and to be the person who communicates and negotiates with other groups. Apart from that, I'd recommend not. Managers have a potential conflict of interest—on the one hand they want to help prevent errors, but on the other hand they may be rating the person whose errors are being discussed. Management presence can also inhibit free and open discussion. Apart from a manager on the action team, management participation should be limited to full support and encouragement of causal analysis, provision of resources for the action team, and support for the recommended actions.

Should managers do causal analysis on their projects?

Managers can and should learn things from projects that they are working on, things that will help improve the next project. However, things that go well with a project or go badly with a project aren't usually tracked as bugs, so the way the analysis is done will be a little different.

The temptation is to wait until the project is complete, then to go back and analyze it (sometimes known as a "post mortem"). This approach is obviously better than nothing, but it has problems. It's easy to put off, with the pressures and excitement of the new project that is starting; recommendations are often lost in the subsequent reorganization for the next project; much, if not most of the information will have been forgotten, as will the reasons that things happened; there is rarely a formal mechanism to make sure recommendations are implemented; and it becomes an intellectual exercise rather than a problem-solving exercise.

It's better to record and understand things when they happen, while the facts are fresh in people's minds, and causes of the facts can be more easily discovered. The manager might talk with the developers after individual tasks are completed or after particularly serious failures, or once each month. Again, the outcome should be practical suggestions to help improve the next project or task.

At a minimum, the manager and the developers should answer the following questions. The answers should become part of the project notebook (for the project manager to use when planning the next project) and part of the developers' notebook (for helping developers to become more effective at scheduling and resisting schedule pressure, foreseeing obstacles, and making contingency plans).

- What did the schedule say?
- How long did the task/project actually take?
- What went badly; what difficulties did we encounter?
- How can we avoid those things in the next project?
- What activities improved the way things were done?
- How can we make those activities permanent?

What are the stage kickoff meetings you mentioned earlier?

These are meetings that are held at the start of each stage (requirements, high-level design, coding, etc.). They are led by the chief programmer or technical lead on the project, who goes through the team assignments, the schedule, how things will be done during the stage, what input is expected, what output is expected at the end of the stage, what inspections or reviews will be done, and the common error list. The common error list is a list of errors that are commonly made during this phase of the work, perhaps with examples. Going through the list should make it more likely that developers will avoid these errors, or at least catch them early.

For a lot of development organizations, there is no clear-cut start or end to a phase. Some people in a team will be working in one phase, while others will be working in another. Some organizations don't really even organize as teams. And in a very iterative development environment, you might even ask what the start of a phase really means. It's still worth having kickoff meetings, if only to reinforce how things are done, and to go over the common error list. Involve the people who are starting the next phase, who will be starting soon, and who have just started. In the iterative environment, consider a phase to be when most of a person's work will be in the area of requirements, design, coding, etc.

What about bugs that developers find while writing and debugging their code?

There's always a trade-off. When developers are developing their code and are in the cycle of testing and debugging, they will rarely want to record the bug in a bug-tracking system, then fix it, then record the fix. Record what's easy to record, and don't record what's difficult. If individual developers want to extend causal analysis to include the bugs they find during their testing and debugging, make that possible, but don't require it.

If you are doing technical reviews, and the reviews happen before significant testing is done, you should find a lot of errors before testing and you'll be able to record and analyze those bugs.

Should you be selective about what you address?

You'll get better management support if you provide cheap solutions to expensive problems. One way to determine which actions to take is to calculate the relative payback value of the actions. IBM reports that process changes tend to be 30-to-70 percent effective in preventing errors, while tool and product changes are 70-to-100 percent effective. Gather statistics over time and look for the effectiveness in your organization.

Multiply the estimated effectiveness (E) of the action by the number of errors it will prevent (N), then divide by the number of person days it will take to implement the action (D) and you get a relative payback figure (P).

$$P = E * N / D$$

If you have the data, you can also factor in the average cost to fix this type of error in person days (C)—the more expensive it is to fix, the more appropriate it is to prevent it.

$$P = E * N * C / D$$

Some actions won't happen because they are too expensive, or the relative payback is too low. If you decide not to implement an action, document the reason, and tell the person who made the suggestion. If suggestions disappear into black holes, people stop making suggestions.

Tell me about the different types of preventive actions.

Obviously you can dream up many different categories of actions, but here are some that are effective. When you brainstorm for preventive actions, brainstorm first without regard to category. Then go through each category of preventive action and try to brainstorm further. What tools could help? What process improvement could prevent these errors? And so on.

Communications improvement.   Many errors happen because of poor communication among people or departments. Improvements might include automatic notification of changes, regular group or team meetings, regular meetings between designated people from different groups, and better documentation.

Education.   Many errors happen because people don't know how things could be done better, or they don't know how something works. Education can be accomplished through formal classes, a lunchtime seminar series, or documents that are distributed.

Process improvement.   Some error-prevention actions may require documenting existing procedures, enforcing existing procedures, formalizing informal processes, developing new procedures, or reorganizing the ways things are done.

Product improvement.   Some errors happen because the product is poorly designed, poorly implemented, poorly documented, uses unobvious variable names, or has non-intuitive function parameter sequences. Some errors may be prevented by improving or rewriting parts of the product.

Tools. New tools and enhancements to tools may help find errors more quickly, or may support new or better procedures. Examples are revision control tools, make, and source code checkers such as lint.

IBM has found that tools and product improvements tend to be the most effective approaches in preventing future errors.

You mentioned earlier that some organizations classify errors in much greater detail. Can you give me an example?

The reason for greater detail is so you can do more complete analysis of patterns and trends. Here are some classifications you might use, although you might want to modify them for your own situation.

- Origin: where was the error introduced?
  - Requirements
  - Architecture
  - High-level design
  - Low-level design
  - Code
  - Fix on a fix
- Where was the error detected?
  - Requirements review
  - Architecture review
  - High-level design review
  - Low-level design review
  - Code review/inspection
  - Unit test
  - Integration test
  - System test
  - Beta test
  - Field use
- Where should the error have been detected?
  - Requirements review
  - Architecture review
  - High-level design review
  - Low-level design review
  - Code review/inspection
  - Unit test
  - Integration test
  - System test
  - Beta test
- Category of error (depends on the origin)
  - Requirements
  - Functionality
  - User interface
  - Interprocess communication
  - Data definition

- Module design
- Error handling
- Logic
- Computation
- Data initialization
- Data handling
- Performance
- Timing
- Module interface implementation
- Documentation
- Comments
- Standards
  ○ Type of error
    - Missing
    - Unclear
    - Wrong
    - Changed
    - Other
  ○ Why was the error introduced? What was the cause?
    - Inadequate communication or documentation
    - Poor workmanship or oversight
    - Lack of education or training
    - Inadequate methodology or procedures
    - Lack of resources or poor planning
  ○ Why was the error not detected in the correct phase?
    - Oversight
    - Lack of education or training
    - Inadequate methodology or procedures
    - Lack of resources or poor planning
    - Lack of preparation

The causes (why was the error introduced, why was it not detected in the correct phase), can be broken down into more detailed causes. What type of oversight, what methodology is inadequate, what type of preparation was lacking? These detailed causes should be based on what makes sense in your organization.

However, while classifying errors in this way will help you analyze patterns and trends, it doesn't do much to help prevent errors. For that you have to closely examine each error, figure out why it was caused, and try to think of things that could have prevented it. Errors must be treated as individuals, each with their own unique personality, rather than as representatives of their classification.

Are there other ways of doing causal analysis?

Some people suggest that the last 30 minutes of technical review sessions should be devoted to causal analysis activities and suggest that the review team also be the action team. I haven't tried this approach, but it sounds promising for two reasons: it's easier to get started than formal causal analysis meetings, and it may be a good approach in smaller organizations because it's a less-formal approach and because it's easier in small organizations to implement actions across multiple projects. A key point is that the focus should be on ideas that the review team can actually implement, as opposed to ideas that take considerable coordination and commitment from others.

Why don't more organizations practice causal analysis?

Two reasons. First, as with so many good practices, there's a visible cost associated with it, but the benefit is not necessarily measurable. If an organization doesn't track how much it costs to fix errors, it won't know how much it's saving by not making errors. The second reason is psychological—in the end, many errors come down to human error, and so you may have to say "this person's skills are inadequate." A lot of people prefer not to deal with this issue.

But causal analysis can save considerable time and money. Unfortunately, most American business is not geared towards quality for quality's sake, so you'll usually have to show that a particular action or process change will save time and money (time often being the more critical). You'll need to accumulate enough data on your own to show this.

Get information about other people's experiences with causal analysis (from books, magazines, and Usenet), and use this information to justify a proposal. Or you can track your own bugs over a period of time, showing how identifying the causes has helped you prevent similar bugs. However, if you manage to reduce or eliminate categories of bugs, you'll be able to write more code, which may introduce other bugs. For an accurate picture of how causal analysis has affected the bugs you create, you should show bug trends as a percentage of non-commented lines of source code.

Further Reading

Mays, Jones, Holloway, Studinski. 1990. *Experiences with Defect Prevention.* IBM Systems Journal, Volume 29, Number 1. The address is IBM Systems Journal, Armonk, NY 10504.

Summary

The goal of causal analysis is to prevent errors. You brainstorm the causes of individual errors, then brainstorm ways to prevent those errors. Then you implement the preventive actions. A good tool for discovering causes is the Ishikawa, or Fishbone, diagram.

If you are doing causal analysis by yourself, use three-by-five cards to record the errors, causes, and preventive actions. Involve others, over lunch, to help you brainstorm. If the preventive actions are ones that you can't implement by yourself, record the costs of the errors and make a case to your manager that the actions should be implemented.

If you are implementing causal analysis across a group or department, you should think about implementing the following:

- Formal causal analysis meetings
- A database and tools to track errors, causes, and actions
- An action team
- Stage kickoff meetings

Suggested Reading

Algorithms and Data Structures

Esakov, Jeffrey, and Tom Weiss. 1989. *Data Structures: An Advanced Approach Using C*. Englewood Cliffs, NJ: Prentice Hall.

Horowitz, Ellis, and Sartaj Sahni. 1976. *Fundamentals of Data Structures*. Woodland Hills, CA: Computer Science Press.

Karsh, James, and Leonard Garrett. 1988. *Data Structures, Algorithms, and Programming Style Using C*. WS-KENT.

Knuth, Donald. 1973, 1981, 1973. *The Art of Computer Programming—Volume 1: Fundamental Algorithms (2nd Edition); Volume 2: Semi-Numerical Algorithms (2nd Edition); Volume 3: Sorting and Searching*. Reading, MA: Addison-Wesley. The definitive algorithm books. These three books are available from a planned series of five.

Sedgewick, Robert. 1988. *Algorithms (2nd Edition)*. Reading, MA: Addison-Wesley.

Sedgewick, Robert. 1990. *Algorithms in C*. Reading, MA: Addison-Wesley.

Sengupta, Saumyendra, and Paul Edwards. 1991. *Data Structures in ANSI C*. Orlando, FL: Academic Press.

Tremblay, Jean-Paul, and Paul Sorenson. 1984. *An Introduction to Data Structures with Applications*. New York: McGraw-Hill.

Analysis and Design

DeMarco, Tom. 1979. *Structured Analysis and System Specification*. Englewood Cliffs, NJ: Yourdon Press. The classic on Structured Analysis.

Freeman, Peter, and Anthony Wasserman. 1983. *Software Design Techniques (4th Edition)*. Washington, DC: IEEE Computer Society Press.

Gause, Donald, and Gerald Weinberg. 1990. *Are Your Lights On? How to Figure Out What the Problem Really Is*. Dorset House. A book about general problem solving.

Hansen, Kirk. 1984. *Data Structured Program Design*. Ken Orr and Associates.

Martin, James, and Carma McClure. 1985. *Diagramming Techniques for Analysts and Programmers*. Englewood Cliffs, NJ: Prentice Hall. A comprehensive survey of diagramming notations for analysis and design.

Martin, James. 1987. *Recommended Diagramming Standards for Analysts and Programmers*. Englewood Cliffs, NJ: Prentice Hall.

Martin, James, and Carma McClure. 1988. *Structured Techniques for Computing: The Basis for CASE*. Englewood Cliffs, NJ: Prentice Hall. A very complete book that describes many of the techniques of structured analysis and design, and analyzes and compares their various strengths and weaknesses.

McMenamin, Stephen, and John Palmer. 1984. *Essential Systems Analysis*. Englewood Cliffs, NJ: Yourdon Press.

Modell, Martin. 1988. *A Professional Guide to Systems Analysis*. New York: McGraw-Hill.

Myers, Glenford. 1978. *Composite/Structured Design*. New York: Van Nostrand Reinhold.

Orr, Ken. 1977. *Structured Systems Development*. Englewood Cliffs, NJ: Yourdon Press. The basic reference on Warnier-Orr diagrams, filled with examples.

Page-Jones, Meilir. 1988. *The Practical Guide to Structured System Design (2nd Edition)*. Englewood Cliffs, NJ: Yourdon Press. An excellent guide to structured system design, written in a very readable style. It describes in detail what makes a good module, with numerous, easy to follow examples.

Ward, Paul, and Stephen Mellor. 1985, 1986. *Structured Development for Real-Time Systems—Vol. 1: Introduction and Tools; Vol. 2: Essential Modeling Techniques; Vol. 3: Implementation Modeling Techniques*. Englewood Cliffs, NJ: Yourdon Press. Uses extensions to DeMarco structured analysis to aid specification of real-time systems.

Weinberg, Gerald. 1975. *An Introduction to General Systems Thinking*. New York: Wiley.

Weinberg, Gerald. 1988. *Rethinking Systems Analysis and Design*. Dorset House. An excellent, well written book on problem analysis.

Weinberg, Victor. 1980. *Structured Analysis*. Englewood Cliffs, NJ: Yourdon Press.

Wood, Jane, and Denise Silver. 1989. *Joint Application Design*. New York: Wiley.

Yourdon, Ed. 1989. *Managing the Structured Techniques (4th Edition)*. Englewood Cliffs, NJ: Yourdon Press.

Yourdon, Ed. 1989. *Modern Structured Analysis*. Englewood Cliffs, NJ: Yourdon Press. An excellent book, incorporating many of the best ideas of Yourdon and the consultants who have worked at Yourdon, Inc., over the years. Gives two complete examples, one real-time and one MIS application.

Yourdon, Ed, and Larry Constantine. 1979. *Structured Design*. Englewood Cliffs, NJ: Yourdon Press. The original book on structured design.

Book Sources

Books in Print
Your library should have copies of the Books in Print volumes. There is a *Subject Guide*, with plenty of books listed under Software Engineering, Data Structures, etc. The *Titles* volumes will give you ideas about books as many book titles start with similar words. In the *Authors* volumes you can look up authors whose books you like, to see what else they have written.

Single Source
Software Quality Engineering
3000-2 Hartley Road
Jacksonville, FL 32257
1-800-423-8378
Single Source maintains an up-to-date offering of what they consider to be the best books about software engineering, management, and testing. Their catalog gives a brief synopsis for each book.

Technical Book Buyer's Guide
United Techbook Company (UTC)
P.O. Box 1658
Longmont, CO 80502
(303)-530-5151
1-800-247-4808
FAX: (303)-651-3405
The Technical Book Buyer's Guide is a 340-page book that lists and describes every book carried by UTC. It comes with a diskette that lets you search for books using key words, author, title, and ISBN.

CASE (See Tools and CASE)

Change

Bouldin, Barbara. 1989. *Agents of Change: Managing the Introduction of Automated Tools*. Englewood Cliffs, NJ: Yourdon Press.

Buckley, Fletcher. 1989. *Implementing Software Engineering*. New York: Wiley.

Carnegie, Dale. 1983. *How to Win Friends and Influence People*. New York: Simon and Schuster.

Humphrey, Watts. 1990. *Managing the Software Process*. Reading, MA: Addison-Wesley.

Pressman, Roger. 1988. *Making Software Engineering Happen. A Guide for Instituting the Technology*. Englewood Cliffs, NJ: Prentice Hall.

Weinberg, Gerald. 1985. *The Secrets of Consulting: A Guide to Giving and Getting Advice Successfully*. New York: Dorset House.

Debugging

Smith, Truck. 1984. *Secrets of Software Debugging*. Blue Ridge Summit, PA: Tab Books.

Ward, Robert. 1989. *A Programmer's Introduction to Debugging C*. Lawrence, KS: R&D Publications. A useful book about debugging C programs. C is different than other high level languages because the compiler lets you do all sorts of things you didn't intend to do. C can be a difficult language in which to ensure quality, and this book will help.

Magazines

C User's Journal
2601 Iowa, Lawrence, KS 66046
913-841-1631

CASE Outlook
CASE Consulting Group, 11830 Kerr Parkway, Suite 315, Lake Oswego, OR 97035
$395 per year. Published monthly.

CASE Trends
P.O. Box 294-MO, Shrewsbury, MA 01545-0294
$49 per year. Published bi-monthly.

Computer Language
Miller Freeman Publications, 500 Howard Street, San Francisco, CA 94105
415-397-1881
$35 per year. Published monthly.

Dr. Dobb's Journal: Software Tools for the Professional Programmer
M&T Publishing, 501 Galveston Drive, Redwood City, CA 94063
415-366-3600
$30 per year. Published monthly.

IEEE Design and Test	$22 per year. Published quarterly.
IEEE Software	$25 per year. Published bi-monthly.
IEEE Transactions on Software Engineering	$22 per year. Published monthly.

IEEE Computer Society, 10662 Los Vaqueros Circle, PO Box 3014, Los Alamitos, CA 90720-1264. Available to members of IEEE Computer Society (other magazines are also available). Membership is $54 annually.

IEEE Software Standards
   IEEE Computer Society Press, Customer Service Center, 10662 Los Vaqueros Circle, PO
   Box 3014, Los Alamitos, CA 90720-1264. Tel: 1-800-CS-BOOKS. Catalog number
   1001 covers all the IEEE software standards.

Software Maintenance News
   7331 Hayden Avenue
   Sebastopol, CA 95472
   $50 per year. Published monthly.

Software Quality World
   ProQual Inc.
   P.O. Box 337
   Medfield, MA 02052-0003
   $25 per year. Published eight times a year.

The Software Practitioner
   P.O. Box 213, State College, PA 16804
   $40 per year. Published monthly.

Maintenance

Higgins, David. 1986. *Data Structured Software Maintenance: The Warnier/Orr Approach.*
   New York: Dorset House.

Martin, James, and Carma McClure. 1983. *Software Maintenance: The Problem and Its
   Solution.* Englewood Cliffs, NJ: Prentice Hall.

McClure, Carma. 1981. *Managing Software Development and Maintenance.* New York:
   Van Nostrand Reinhold.

Parikh, Girish (editor). 1988. *Techniques of Program and System Maintenance (2nd Edition).* Wellesley, MA: QED Information Science. A compendium of articles and reprints
   from other books about software maintenance.

Parikh, Girish, and Nicholas Zvegintov. 1983. *Tutorial on Software Maintenance.* Washington, DC: IEEE Computer Society Press.

Metrics

Arthur, Jay. 1985. *Measuring Programmer Productivity and Software Quality.* New York:
   Wiley.

Card, David, with Robert Glass. 1990. *Measuring Software Design Quality.* Englewood
   Cliffs, NJ: Prentice Hall.

Conte, Samuel, Dunsmore, and Shen. 1986. *Software Engineering Metrics and Models.*
   Redwood City, CA: Benjamin-Cummings.

Ejiogu, Lem. 1991. *Software Engineering with Software Metrics*. Wellesley, MA: QED Information Sciences.

Fenton, N.E. (editor). 1991. *Software Metrics: A Rigorous Approach*. New York: Van Nostrand Reinhold.

Grady, Robert, and Debra Caswell. 1987. *Software Metrics: Establishing a Company-Wide Program*. Englewood Cliffs, NJ: Prentice Hall.

Jones, Capers. 1991. *Applied Software Measurement - Assuring Productivity and Quality*. New York: McGraw-Hill.

Shepperd, M. 1991. *Software Engineering Metrics*. New York: McGraw-Hill.

Zuse, Horst. 1990. *Software Complexity: Measures and Methods*. Hawthorne, NY: de Gruyter.

Object-Oriented Program Development

In his classic article "No Silver Bullet" (IEEE Computer, April 1987), Fred Brooks writes "Many students of the art hold out more hope for object-oriented programming than for any of the other technical fads of the day. I am among them." While object-oriented projects are still far in the minority, C^{++} and ADA seem likely to increase their share of software projects.

Booch, Grady. 1991. *Object Oriented Design with Applications*. Redwood City, CA: Benjamin-Cummings. Currently *the* book on object-oriented design.

Ege, Raimund. 1992. *Programming in an Object Oriented Environment*. San Diego, CA: Academic Press.

Khoshafian, Setrag, and Razmik Abnous. 1990. *Object Orientation. Concepts, Languages, Databases, User Interfaces*. New York: Wiley. An excellent introduction to the concepts of object orientation, with chapters on C^{++} and ADA.

Meyer, Bertrand. 1988. *Object-oriented Software Construction*. Englewood Cliffs, NJ: Prentice Hall. Although the book deals with the language Eiffel, the first four chapters are one of the best introductions to object-oriented software development.

Rumbaugh, Blaha, Premerlani, Eddy, and Lorensen. 1991. *Object Oriented Modeling and Design*. Englewood Cliffs, NJ: Prentice Hall.

Shlaer, Sally, and Stephen Mellor. 1988. *Object Oriented Systems Analysis: Modeling the World in Data*. Englewood Cliffs, NJ: Yourdon Press. A good way to think about the problem domain, even if you don't write in an object-oriented language.

Wirfs-Brock, Rebecca, Brian Wilkerson, and Lauren Wiener. 1990. *Designing Object-Oriented Software*. Englewood Cliffs, NJ: Prentice Hall. An excellent book that describes the responsibility-driven approach to objects.

People

DeMarco, Tom, and Timothy Lister. 1987. *Peopleware: Productive Projects and Teams.* New York: Dorset House. A wonderful book about the importance of teams and the environment in software development.

Weinberg, Gerald. 1985. *Becoming a Technical Leader.* New York: Dorset House.

Weinberg, Gerald. 1971. *The Psychology of Computer Programming.* New York: Van Nostrand Reinhold. A classic.

Weinberg, Gerald. 1988. *Understanding the Professional Programmer.* New York: Dorset House.

Productivity

Jones, Capers. 1986. *Programming Productivity.* New York: McGraw-Hill.

Mills, Harlan. 1988. *Software Productivity.* New York: Dorset House.

Programming

Bentley, Jon. 1986. *Programming Pearls.* Reading, MA: Addison-Wesley.

Bentley, Jon. 1988. *More Programming Pearls.* Reading, MA: Addison-Wesley.

Bentley, Jon. 1982. *Writing Efficient Programs.* Englewood Cliffs, NJ: Prentice Hall.

Kernighan, Brian, and P.J. Plaugher. 1978. *The Elements of Programming Style (2nd Edition).* New York: McGraw-Hill. How to write clear, well-structured programs.

Straker, David. 1992. *C Style, Standards, and Guidelines.* Englewood Cliffs, NJ: Prentice Hall.

Yourdon, Ed. 1976. *Techniques of Program Structure and Design.* Englewood Cliffs, NJ: Yourdon Press.

Programming Language Hints

Holub, Allen. 1987. *The C Companion.* Englewood Cliffs, NJ: Prentice Hall.

Koenig, Andrew. 1988. *C Traps and Pitfalls.* Reading, MA: Addison-Wesley.

Project Management

Abdel-Hamid, Tarek, and Stuart Madnick. 1991. *Software Project Dynamics: An Integrated Approach.* Englewood Cliffs, NJ: Prentice Hall.

Block, Robert. 1987. *The Politics of Projects.* Englewood Cliffs, NJ: Yourdon Press.

Boddie, John. 1987. *Crunch Mode: Building Effective Systems on a Tight Budget.* Englewood Cliffs, NJ: Yourdon Press.

Boehm, Barry. 1981. *Software Engineering Economics.* Englewood Cliffs, NJ: Prentice Hall. The definitive book on analyzing and estimating software project costs. Provides data from many completed software projects.

DeMarco, Tom. 1982. *Controlling Software Projects: Management, Measurement, and Estimation.* Englewood Cliffs, NJ: Yourdon Press.

Gilb, Tom. 1988. *Principles of Software Engineering Management.* Reading, MA: Addison-Wesley. An excellent book, covering evolutionary delivery, requirements, and inspections.

Glass, Robert. 1983. *Computing Catastrophes.* State College, PA: Computing Trends. Real stories about the failures of some mainframe companies.

Glass, Robert. 1977. *The Universal Elixir, and Other Computing Projects Which Failed.* State College, PA: Computing Trends. Fictionalized stories about real projects which failed. Read it before starting the next project.

Humphrey, Watts. 1990. *Managing the Software Process.* Reading, MA: Addison-Wesley.

King, David. 1992. *Project Management Made Simple.* Englewood Cliffs, NJ: Yourdon Press.

Metzger, Philip. 1981. *Managing a Programming Project (2nd Edition).* Englewood Cliffs, NJ: Prentice Hall.

Thayer, Richard (editor). 1988. *Software Engineering Project Management.* Washington, DC: IEEE Computer Society Press. A set of papers on aspects of software project management.

Thomsett, Rob. 1980. *People and Project Management.* Englewood Cliffs, NJ: Yourdon Press.

Whitten, Neal. 1990. *Managing Software Development Projects.* New York: Wiley.

Prototyping

Martin, James. 1991. *Rapid Application Development.* New York: Macmillan.

Smith, M.F. 1991. *Software Prototyping.* New York: McGraw-Hill.

Quality

Card, David, with Robert Glass. 1990. *Measuring Software Design Quality.* Englewood Cliffs, NJ: Prentice Hall.

Cho, Chin-Kuei. 1987. *Quality Programming: Developing and Testing Software with Statistical Quality Control.* New York: Wiley.

Crosby, Philip. 1979. *Quality Is Free.* New York: Mentor.

Deming, W. Edwards. 1986. *Out of the Crisis*. Massachusetts Institute of Technology. The classic book on quality through continual improvement by the man most responsible for helping Japan develop from when ''Made in Japan'' was synonymous with shoddy goods, to where ''Made in Japan'' is synonymous with the highest quality anywhere.

Dunn, Robert. 1984. *Software Defect Removal*. New York: McGraw-Hill. A survey of all the major forms of defect removal.

Dyer, Michael. 1992. *The Cleanroom Approach to Quality Software Development*. New York: Wiley.

Glass, Robert. 1992. *Building Quality Software*. Englewood Cliffs, NJ: Prentice Hall.

Myers, Glenford. 1976. *Software Reliability*. New York: Wiley.

Schulmeyer, Gordon. 1990. *Zero Defect Software*. New York: McGraw-Hill.

Weinberg, Gerald. 1991. *Quality Software Management—Volume 1: Systems Thinking*. New York: Dorset House.

Quality Assurance (see Testing and Quality Assurance)

Requirements

Davis, Alan. 1990. *Software Requirements: Analysis and Specification*. Englewood Cliffs, NJ: Prentice Hall. Includes a survey of the various methodologies and uses them with three different types of problem. Has a very large bibliography (almost 600 references), mainly of papers in journals.

Dorfman, Merlin, and Richard Thayer (editors). 1990. *Standards, Guidelines, and Examples on System and Software Requirements Engineering*. Washington, DC: IEEE Computer Society Press. Details many of the international and military requirements standards, with some examples.

Gause, Donald, and Gerald Weinberg. 1990. *Exploring Requirements: Quality before Design*. New York: Dorset House. Discussion on how to discover the customer's true requirements, with a set of tools for changing a wish list to a set of requirements.

Gilb, Tom. 1988. *Principles of Software Engineering Management*. Reading, MA: Addison-Wesley. An excellent book, covering evolutionary delivery, requirements, and inspections.

IEEE Guide for Software Requirements Specifications. Institute of Electrical and Electronics Engineers, 1984. IEEE/ANSI Standard 830-1984.

Orr, Ken. 1981. *Structured Requirements Definition*. Topeka, KS: Ken Orr and Associates. Describes a specific methodology, Structured Requirements Definition, using mainly entity diagrams and functional flow diagrams.

Thayer, Richard, and Merlin Dorfman (editors). 1990. *System and Software Requirements Engineering*. Washington, DC: IEEE Computer Society Press.

Reviews and Walkthroughs

Freedman, Daniel, and Gerald Weinberg. 1990. *Handbook of Walkthroughs, Inspections, and Technical Reviews: Evaluating Programs, Projects, and Products (3rd Edition).* New York: Dorset House. An excellent book.

Hollacker, Charles. 1990. *Software Reviews and Audits Handbook.* New York: Wiley. Contains sample forms and checklists.

Yourdon, Ed. 1989. *Structured Walkthroughs (4th Edition).* Englewood Cliffs, NJ: Yourdon Press.

Seminars

Technology Transfer Institute
741 Tenth Street
Santa Monica, CA 90402-2899
(213) 394-8305
Currently offering seminars by some of the big names in software, such as:
    Controlling Software Projects—Tom DeMarco and Tim Lister
    Software Inspection—Tom Gilb
    Software Quality Management—Gerald Weinberg

Software Engineering

Agresti, William (editor). 1986. *New Paradigms for Software Development.* Washington, DC: IEEE Computer Society Press.

Boehm, Barry (editor). 1989. *Software Risk Management.* Washington, DC: IEEE Computer Society Press.

Brooks, Frederick. 1982. *The Mythical Man-Month.* Reading, MA: Addison-Wesley. A classic. Essays on Software Engineering by the project manager for the IBM 360 operating system.

Cusumano, Michael. 1991. *Japan's Software Factories.* New York: Oxford University Press.

DeGrace, Peter, and Leslie Hulet Stahl. 1990. *Wicked Problems, Righteous Solutions.* Englewood Cliffs, NJ: Yourdon Press.

DeMarco, Tom. 1979. *Concise Notes on Software Engineering.* Englewood Cliffs, NJ: Yourdon Press.

Department of Defense. 1988. *Military Standard: Defense System Software Development.* DOD-STD-2167A. The official standard for all defense software development.

Dyer, Michael. 1992. *The Cleanroom Approach to Quality Software Development.* New York: Wiley.

Evans, Michael. 1987. *The Software Factory: Concepts and the Environment*. New York: Wiley.

Frakes, William, Christopher Fox, and Brian Nejmeh. 1991. *Software Engineering in the UNIX/C Environment*. Englewood Cliffs, NJ: Prentice Hall.

General Electric Company. 1986. *Software Engineering Handbook*. New York: McGraw-Hill.

Glass, Robert. 1982. *Modern Programming Practices: A Report from Industry*. Englewood Cliffs, NJ: Prentice Hall.

Glass, Robert. 1981. *Software Soliloquies*. State College, PA: Computing Trends. Essays that contradict conventional computing wisdom.

King, David. 1984. *Current Practices in Software Development: A Guide to Successful Systems*. Englewood Cliffs, NJ: Yourdon Press.

Marco, Allen. 1990. *Software Engineering: Concepts and Management*. Englewood Cliffs, NJ: Prentice Hall.

Ng, Peter, and Raymond Yeh. 1990. *Modern Software Engineering*. New York: Van Nostrand Reinhold.

Oman, Paul, and Ted Lewis (editors). 1990. *Milestones in Software Evolution*. Washington, DC: IEEE Computer Society Press. A collection of papers that changed the course of software development.

Pfleeger, Shari. 1991. *Software Engineering: The Production of Quality Software (2nd Edition)*. New York: Macmillan.

Pressman, Roger. 1988. *Making Software Engineering Happen. A Guide for Instituting the Technology*. Englewood Cliffs, NJ: Prentice Hall.

Pressman, Roger. 1992. *Software Engineering: A Practitioner's Approach (3rd Edition)*. New York: McGraw-Hill.

Sommerville, Ian. 1992. *Software Engineering (4th Edition)*. Reading, MA: Addison-Wesley.

Yourdon, Ed (editor). 1982. *Writing of the Revolution: Selected Readings on Software Engineering*. Englewood Cliffs, NJ: Yourdon Press. This book consists of writings by some of the most prominent people in software engineering: people such as Dijkstra and Knuth. These are the writings that introduced some of the revolutions in software—ideas such as Structured Programming.

Software Reusability

Biggerstaff, Ted. 1989. *Software Reusability—Volume 1: Concepts and Models; Volume 2: Applications and Experience*. New York: ACM Press.

Freeman, Peter (editor). 1987. *Software Reusability*. Washington, DC: IEEE Computer Society Press.

Tracz, Will (editor). 1988. *Software Reuse—Emerging Technology*. Washington, DC: IEEE Computer Society Press.

Teams

DeMarco, Tom, and Timothy Lister. 1987. *Peopleware: Productive Projects and Teams*. New York: Dorset House. A wonderful book about the importance of teams and the environment in software development.

Schrage, Michael. 1990. *Shared Minds: The New Technologies of Collaboration*. New York: Random House. A discussion about collaboration, its role in creative advances, and techniques and technologies for collaboration.

Testing and Quality Assurance

Beizer, Boris. 1983. *Software System Testing and Quality Assurance*. New York: Van Nostrand Reinhold. Integration testing, test plans, test teams, and software quality management.

Beizer, Boris. 1990. *Software Testing Techiques (2nd Edition)*. New York: Van Nostrand Reinhold. Testing techniques aimed at testing individual routines.

Chow, T.S. (editor). 1985. *Software Quality Assurance: A Practical Approach*. Washington, DC: IEEE Computer Society Press. A set of papers about aspects of software quality assurance.

Dunn, Robert, and Richard Ullman. 1982. *Quality Assurance for Computer Software*. New York: McGraw-Hill.

Hetzel, Bill. 1988. *The Complete Guide to Software Testing*. Wellesley, MA: QED Information Sciences.

Meyers, Glenford. 1979. *The Art of Software Testing*. New York: Wiley. A classic.

Perry, William. 1991. *Quality Assurance for Information Systems*. Wellesley, MA: QED Technical Publishing Group.

Schulmeyer, Gordon, and James McManus (editors). 1987. *Handbook of Software Quality Assurance*. New York: Van Nostrand Reinhold.

Time Management

Bliss, Edwin C. 1984. *Doing It Now*. New York: Bantam Books. Useful ideas on how to overcome procrastination.

Bliss, Edwin C. 1984. *Getting Things Done*. New York: Bantam Books. Full of suggestions on how to get things done more effectively.

Oncken, William. 1984. *Managing Management Time*. Englewood Cliffs, NJ: Prentice Hall. A wonderful book that will help any manager make the most of his or her time. It introduces the concept of the Monkey on the Back.

Tools and CASE

Darwin, Ian. 1991. *Checking C Programs with lint.* Sebastopol, CA: O'Reilly & Associates.

Fisher, Alan. 1991. *CASE: Using Software Development Tools, Second Edition.* New York: Wiley. An excellent introduction to analysis and design methodologies, with a look at how several commercially available CASE tools implement these methodologies.

Kernighan, Brian, and P.J. Plaugher. 1976. *Software Tools.* Reading, MA: Addison-Wesley. A hands-on book about writing your own simple tools.

Lewis, T.G. 1991. *CASE: Computer Aided Software Engineering.* New York: Van Nostrand Reinhold.

McClure, Carma. 1989. *CASE Is Software Automation.* Englewood Cliffs, NJ: Prentice Hall.

Schindler, Max. 1990. *Computer Aided Software Design.* New York: Wiley.

Steve Talbott. 1991. *Managing Projects with make.* Sebastapol, CA: O'Reilly & Associates.

Usenet News

If you have access to Usenet (most UNIX development sites do), you can read the news. In general, type:

    rn   - Read News

then you can look at all the newsgroups your site subscribes to by pressing:

    L   - List

To look at the articles in a specific group, type:

    g <group name>   - Go to named group

For example:

    g comp.software-eng   Software engineering discussions
    g comp.lang.c   C language discussions
    g comp.lang.fortran   Fortran discussions

User Interface

Shneiderman, Ben. 1987. *Designing the User Interface: Strategies for Effective Human-Computer Interaction.* Reading, MA: Addison-Wesley. An excellent introduction by one of the gurus of user interface design.

INDEX

INDEX

Failure, of projects, 110
Feasibility study, 119
Fishbone diagram, 349
Flowcharts, 129
Functions
    flow, 205-208
    how much code in, 212
    relationship to files, 214-216
    tracing, 291, 294
Functionality
    attributes of, 75
    describing, 75
Functional requirements, 112
Functional Specification, 70, 166,
    177

Gates, 311
Global variables, 127, 136-139,
    218
Goals
    communication of, 99
    goals/questions/measurements,
        29, 41
    project, 99
    setting, 39
Golden Road, 3
Goto rule, 208
Growing software, 94-95

Halstead Effort metric, 32
Help system, 123
Hiring, 40
Hungarian notation, 190
Improvement
    continual, 7-11
    the human way, 9

Include files, 217, 220
Indentation, 226

Influencing people, 37
Information hiding, 126
Inspections, see Reviews
Integrated development
    environments, 55
Interfaces, well-defined, 127
Intuition, 279
Involvement 40
Ishikawa diagram, 349
Issues Report, 325
Iterative development, 79, 175,
    335

Job security, 21, 47

Kick-off meeting, 24, 356
Knowledge, 14

Leader, 328
Library, 24
Lint, 56
Learning, 20, 255, 286, 308
Leverage, 47, 48
Logic, 279

Maintenance, 81-89
    costs of, 81
    ease of, 87
    human side of, 86
    lessons from, 87
    reasons for, 81
    stigma of, 89
Make, 56
Marketing Requirements, 70
McCabe Cyclomatic Complexity,
    32
Measurements, see Metrics
Mentor, 22
Methodologies, 151-154